EDUCATIONAL IDEALS
in the
ANCIENT WORLD

EDUCATIONAL IDEALS
in the
ANCIENT WORLD

William Barclay

BAKER BOOK HOUSE
Grand Rapids, Michigan

Reprinted 1974 by Baker Book House
with the permission of Westminster Press

Formerly published in the U.S. under the
title, *Train Up a Child*
Formerly published in England under the
title, *Educational Ideals in the Ancient World*
Library of Congress Catalog Card No. 60-6188
ISBN: 0-8010-0635-5

PHOTOLITHOPRINTED BY CUSHING - MALLOY, INC.
ANN ARBOR, MICHIGAN, UNITED STATES OF AMERICA
1974

To K. B. B.

CONTENTS

FOREWORD

THIS BOOK contains the substance of the Kerr Lectures, delivered in Trinity College, Glasgow, in the spring of 1957. I should be sadly lacking in courtesy, if I did not begin by expressing my very deep gratitude to the trustees of the Kerr Lectureship for appointing me to deliver these lectures, and to my colleagues on the staff of Trinity College for arranging time in which they might be delivered.

In *Greek Byways*, in his essay on "The Boy and the Theorist," T. R. Glover caustically remarked: "Probably most human beings would by now regard it as a truism, or even an axiom, that to be tedious it is only necessary to discuss education." None the less it is ancient education which forms the subject of these lectures. The importance of such a study for the correct understanding of the New Testament is certain beyond argument. Before we can understand the reaction of the Jewish and the Graeco-Roman world to that which Christianity brought to it, we must first understand what it brought to Christianity. So in these lectures there are discussed the Jewish, the Spartan, the Athenian and the Roman ideals and methods of education. The very expansion of Christianity compelled the Church to come into constant contact with the pagan world and its culture, and so we go on to discuss the attitude of the Church to secular learning and education. And finally we discuss the place which the Church gave to the education of the child. In these lectures we are mainly concerned with the education of the child; to discuss higher education and university education in the ancient world would require another volume.

The debts of this book are obvious. I have not tried to make the bibliography complete, but have included in it only such books as I have used and consulted in detail. Anyone who tries to cover so wide a field must constantly be in debt to the results of the labours of others.

It is my hope that these lectures may do something to shed some light on one aspect—and that a most important aspect—of the life and thought of that world into which Christianity first came.

WILLIAM BARCLAY

Trinity College, Glasgow
August 1957

I. Education Among the Jews

THE TRAINING OF THE INDIVIDUAL IN THE SERVICE OF GOD

No nation has ever set the child in the midst more deliberately than the Jews did. It would not be wrong to say that for the Jew the child was the most important person in the community. It was Rabbi Judah the Holy who uttered the famous saying: " The world exists only by the breath of school children." Another Rabbi thought of God as saying: " Dearer to me is the breath of school children than the savour of sacrifice." One of the loveliest things of all is the Midrash on *Exodus* 25. 34. In that passage there is the description of the seven-branched golden candlestick in the Temple; every item on it is allegorised and given a homiletic expansion. The verse runs: " And in the candlestick shall be four bowls made like unto almonds, with their knops and their flowers." Then comes the interpretation—" the flowers—these are the children who learn in school." [1] The Jew was sure that of all people the child was dearest to God.

With such an ideal it is obvious that education will stand very high in the list of Jewish priorities. In *I Chronicles* 16. 22 we read: " Touch not mine anointed, and do my prophets no harm "; and, " touch not mine anointed " was referred to school children; and " do my prophets no harm " to their teachers. The writer of the Prologue to *Ecclesiasticus* claims that " we must give Israel praise for *instruction* (*paideia*) and *wisdom* (*sophia*)." " So long as there are children in the schools," says the Talmud, " Israel's enemies cannot prevail against her." [2] " Get thyself a teacher," said Rabbi Joshua ben Perachiah.[3] Of such importance was education regarded

[1] Pes. R. 29 b. quoted in *A Rabbinic Anthology*, selected by C. G. Montefiore and H. Loewe.

[2] *Ber. Rab.* 65. [3] *Sayings of the Fathers* 1. 6.

that it was held that even the building of the Temple could be interrupted, before education was interrupted. "Perish the sanctuary, but let the children go to school." [4] Josephus writes: "Our ground is good, and we work it to the utmost, but our chief ambition is for the education of our children." [5] In the same passage he goes on: "We take most pains of all with the instruction of children, and esteem the observation of the laws, and the piety corresponding with them, the most important affair of our whole life."

In one sense, this education could not begin too early. "If we do not keep our children to religion, when they are young," says the Talmud, "we shall certainly not be able to do so in later years."[6] Josephus writes: "If anyone should question one of us concerning the laws, he would more easily repeat them all than his own name; since we learn them from our first consciousness, we have them, as it were, engraven on our souls." [7] Philo writes: "Since Jews esteem their laws as divine revelations, and are instructed in the knowledge of them from their earliest youth, they bear the image of the Law in their souls. . . . They are taught, so to speak, from their swaddling-clothes by their parents, by their teachers, and by those who bring them up, even before instruction in the sacred laws and the unwritten customs, to believe in God, the One Father and Creator of the World." [8] It is easy to see what a place schools would have in an atmosphere like that. It is told of one of the great Rabbis that he would not break his fast in the morning, until he had taken his child to school.[9]

Schechter says that the school was the equivalent of Mount Sinai, and the day of entry into it as the Feast of the Revelation of the Law.[10] Schechter gives a full account of the ceremonies which were carried out on the first day on which a boy went to school. These ceremonies are no doubt later than New Testament times, but they are both relevant and worth citing, as showing the Jewish ideal of education at any time. On the day when he was to go to school for the first time, the boy was wakened early, before dawn, and when

[4] *Babyl. Shabbat* 119 b. [5] Josephus: *Against Apion* 1. 12.
[6] *Yoma* 82a. [7] Josephus: *Against Apion* 2. 18.
[8] Philo: *Leg. ad Caium* 31. [9] *Kid.* 30a.
[10] S. Schechter: *Studies in Judaism, First Series*, p. 302.

it was still dark. He was bathed, and then dressed in a gown "with fringes." As soon as dawn came, he was taken to the Synagogue, by his father, or by a wise friend of the family, if his father was not available. He was put on the reading-desk with the roll open in front of him at *Exodus* 20. 2–26, the passage which tells of God's revelation of the Law to Moses. That passage was then read aloud as the passage for the day. He was then taken to the house of the teacher, who welcomed him by enfolding him in his arms. He was shown a slate, with the alphabet written on it in various combinations, and with two of the basic texts of the Law—"Moses commanded us a law, *even* the inheritance of the congregation of Jacob,"[11] and, "And the Lord called unto Moses, and spake unto him out of the tabernacle of the congregation."[12] In addition to that there was one further sentence: "The Law will be my calling." These things the teacher read to the lad, and the lad repeated them after the teacher. The slate was then smeared with honey, and the lad was bidden to lick it off. This was in memory of Ezekiel's experience when he ate the roll: "And it was in my mouth as honey for sweetness."[13] Then he was given sweet cakes to eat, with passages from the Law in praise of the Law written on them. Finally there was a prayer to the angels to open the boy's heart and to strengthen his memory and school had begun for another Jewish boy.[14] It can easily be seen that this was a ceremony which would remain printed on the boy's mind for ever. Such then was the place which the school held in the Jewish ideal. But there are two essential facts still to be added to this general Jewish idea of education.

It has always to be remembered that Jewish education was entirely religious education. There was no text-book except the Scriptures; all primary education was preparation for reading the Law; and all higher education was the reading and the study of it. "The foundation was the text of Scripture, and its highest aim was to train up its disciples in the way of God, which is based on a detailed knowledge of the Law."[15] Josephus says of Moses: "He commanded to instruct children in the elements of knowledge

[11] *Deuteronomy* 33. 4. [12] *Leviticus* 1. 1. [13] *Ezekiel* 3. 1–3.

[14] S. Schechter: *Studies in Judaism, First Series*, pp. 302, 303.

[15] G. H. Box in *E.B.* 2. 1201.

(*grammata*), to teach them to walk according to the laws, and to know the deeds of their forefathers." [16] Shammai said: "Make the study of the Law thy special business." [17] Hillel said: "an ignorant man (that is, a man ignorant of the Law) cannot be truly pious." He said: "The more teaching of the Law, the more life; the more school, the more wisdom; the more counsel, the more reasonable action." [18] The Jew never pretended that this was easy. Such knowledge was only to be won at the cost of toil. A man cannot inherit his father's knowledge, as he might his fortune. That knowledge is there, but each generation has to win it, and enter into it for itself. Rabbi Joses the Priest said: "Give thyself trouble to learn the Law, for it is not obtained by inheritance." [19] Welhausen said: "The sacred writings became the spelling-book, the community a school, religion an affair of teaching and learning. . . . Piety and education became inseparable; whoever could not read was no true Jew." [20] So wide-spread and far-reaching was this education in New Testament times, that A. C. Bouquet says that it was an "age of the widest literacy for eighteen hundred years to come." [21]

But the second great fact to be added to this pattern is the most important fact of all. It is the fact which is the centre of the whole situation. However high the Jewish ideal of the school, the fact remains that to the Jew the real centre of education is the home. To the Jew education is not education in any kind of academic or technical knowledge; it is education in holiness. Speaking of the early days of Israel, Morris Joseph writes: "Of secular education there is scarcely a trace. All the ordinances dealing with education deal with it in its larger aspects as a preparation for the moral and religious life, as a means of developing character." [22] If that be the function of education, then clearly the home is the centre of it. In the pre-exilic days of Jewish history there is no trace of schools at all. "The home was the only school, and parents the only

[16] Josephus: *Against Apion* 1. 12. [17] *Sayings of the Fathers* 2. 5.
[18] *Sayings of the Fathers* 2. 5; 2. 7. [19] *Sayings of the Fathers* 2. 12.
[20] Quoted by G. H. Box: *E.B.* 2. 1191.
[21] A. C. Bouquet: *Everyday Life in New Testament Times*, p. 156.
[22] Morris Joseph in *E.R.E.* 5. 194.

teachers."[23] The only definite exception to that is that royal children may have had special tutors. *II Kings* 10. 1, 5 refers to "them that brought up Ahab's children," and to "the bringers up of the children." A. R. S. Kennedy says that *II Samuel* 12. 25 may very probably mean that the child Solomon was entrusted to the care of the prophet Nathan.[24] However it may have been in royal palaces, certainly in the homes of the ordinary people the parents were the only teachers. Morris Joseph sees in two passages slight hints of professional teachers. In *Psalm* 119. 99 the Psalmist says: "I have more understanding than all my teachers." And in *Proverbs* 5. 13 the appeal is for attention to wisdom, lest the day come, when the careless will say with regret: "I have not obeyed the voice of my teachers, nor inclined mine ear to them that instructed me." But in any event these passages refer to times much later than pre-exilic days.

So then the home is the centre of the education of the child. Isidore Epstein writes: "The home must be the nursery of all Jewish virtues. . . . In no other religion has the duty of the parents to instruct their children been more stressed than in Judaism." As he sees it, however high the function of the school, the school in essence remains "an auxiliary home."[25]

The writer of *Proverbs* knew the joy which comes to the parents of a well-trained child, and the grief which comes to those whose child had not accepted home training and home discipline. "A wise son maketh a glad father, but a foolish son is the heaviness of his mother." "The father of the righteous shall greatly rejoice: and he that begetteth a wise child shall have joy of him." "A foolish son is a grief to his father, and bitterness to her that bare him."[26] So then the responsibility for educating the child is laid fairly and squarely on the parents, and that was true in the days when there were schools, just as much as in the days before schools came into being.

[23] G. H. Box: *E.B.* 2. 1190. Cp. A. R. S. Kennedy in *D.B.* 1. 646: "In the whole range of pre-exilic literature there is no trace of any provision by public authority for either elementary or higher education."

[24] A. R. S. Kennedy: *D.B.* 1. 647.

[25] Isidore Epstein: *The Jewish Way of Life*, 196, 197, 199.

[26] *Proverbs* 10. 1; 23. 24; 17. 25.

A father had a duty to teach his son a trade, for, as the Talmud has it: "Whosoever does not teach his son a trade, teaches him to steal." [27] The threefold duty of the father is "to instruct his son in the Law, to bring him into wedlock, and to teach him a handicraft." [28] Repeatedly this parental duty is implied or laid down. "My son, hear the instruction of thy father, and forsake not the law of thy mother." "Hear ye children the instruction of a father, and attend to know understanding." "My son, keep thy father's commandment, and forsake not the law of thy mother." "A wise son heareth his father's instruction." [29] The injunction to parental instruction runs like a chorus through *Deuteronomy*. "Only take heed to thyself, and keep thy soul diligently, lest thou forget the things which thine eyes have seen, and lest they depart from thy heart all the days of thy life: but teach them to thy sons, and thy sons' sons; specially the day that thou stoodest before the Lord thy God in Horeb." "And thou shalt teach them (these words) diligently unto thy children, and shalt talk of them, when thou sittest in the house, and when thou walkest by the way, and when thou liest down, and when thou risest up." The parent must be ready to give an answer, when "thy son asketh thee, in time to come, saying: 'What mean the testimonies, and the statutes, and the judgments, which the Lord our God hath commanded you?'" "Set your hearts unto all the words which I testify among you this day, which ye shall command your children to observe to do, all the words of this Law." [30] The parent must always be able and ready and willing to rehearse to the child the great things that God has done for His people Israel. "Remember the days of old, consider the years of many generations; ask thy father and he will show thee; the elders, and they will tell thee." "We will not hide them from their children, showing to the generation to come, the praises of the Lord, and His strength, and His wonderful works that he hath done." [31]

Again and again the Rabbis stress the father's duty. "A father," said Rabbi Salomo, "might as well bury his child as neglect his

[27] *Erubin* 29a. [28] *Kiddushin* 30b.

[29] *Proverbs* 1. 8; 4. 1–4; 6. 20; 13. 1.

[30] *Deuteronomy* 4. 9–10; 6. 7; 6. 20–5; 11. 19; 32. 46.

[31] *Deuteronomy* 32. 7; *Psalm* 78. 4.

instruction." [32] As soon as a child can speak (that is, after his third year) he is to be instructed in the Law by his father.[33] It is often said that the Jews objected to the education of women, and it is true that technical education completely neglected them, but it is relevant to note the place of the mother in this parental education. She is mentioned again and again; and King Lemuel, the sage, passes on the prophecy " that his mother taught him." [34] In the Jewish home father and mother shared responsibility for the education of the child. In any examination of Jewish education it is essential to remember two things—first, that Jewish education was almost exclusively religious education; and second, that, at all periods of it, the centre is the home, and the responsibility of teaching the child is something that the parent cannot evade, if he is to satisfy the Law of God.

So, then, having seen the place that education held in the scale of Jewish values, we now turn to examine the actual processes of Jewish education. For this purpose Jewish education falls broadly into two sections—before Ezra, and after Ezra; that is, before and after the people became so very definitely a people of the Law. We have already seen that in pre-exilic times there was no such thing as a school or public education among the Jews. How then in those days was education given?

In the very earliest days Israel was primarily an agricultural people; and agriculture is essentially a religious sphere. Nowhere is it possible to see God more clearly than in the processes of birth and growth, which pervade the activities of the agricultural life. It is true to say that he who lives near the soil also lives near God, if he has eyes to see it. It is of very great interest to study the biblical references to the agricultural needs and processes, and to see the religious principles and convictions which lie behind them in biblical thought.[35] From these references certain basic beliefs emerge.

The tasks of the soil were laid upon men by God. When man was banished from Eden, he was sent out " to till the ground from

[32] Quoted by Wetstein on 2 *Timothy* 3. 15. [33] *Sukkah* 42a.

[34] *Proverbs* 1.8; 6. 20; 31. 1–9; 2 *Timothy* 1. 5.

[35] Cp. the article on Agriculture in *E.B.* I, columns 77–87, by H. W. Hogg, especially column 87.

whence he was taken." [36] The man who worked on the soil was doing the work which God had laid on him to do, even if that work could be regarded as a punishment.

The knowledge which man has of that work is given him by God. In a very real sense, the knowledge of the processes of agriculture is also a revelation from God. Isaiah says: " Doth the plowman plow all day to sow? Doth he open and break the clods of his ground? When he hath made plain the face thereof, doth he not cast abroad the fitches, and scatter the cummin, and cast in the principal wheat, and the appointed barley and the rye in their place? For his God doth instruct him to discretion, and doth teach him." [37] Isaiah is in effect saying that the man working on the land would not know what to do, unless the requisite knowledge had been revealed to him by God. The farmer, as the prophet, is taught by God.

The success or failure of the harvest is due to conditions which only God can create. Jeremiah speaks of " the Lord our God, that giveth the rain, both the former and the latter, in his season." He demands if there are any of " the vanities of the Gentiles " who can give rain.[38] It is God alone who controls the universe in such a way that the harvest comes.

Further, the Jew believed that the universe was morally controlled; that the natural order is morally conditioned; that in the natural order the moral law is working itself out. God not only gives the rain, but also, if His people sin, He withholds the rain. Amos hears God say: " I have withholden the rain from you, when there were yet three months to the harvest." [39] In *Deuteronomy* it becomes a principle that God uses the natural universe to enforce His holy law: " And it shall come to pass, if ye shall hearken diligently unto my commandments which I command you this day, to love the Lord your God, and to serve him with all your heart, and with all your soul, that I will give *you* the rain of your land in his due season, the first rain and the latter rain, that thou

[36] *Genesis* 3. 23.

[37] *Isaiah* 28. 24–9. The passage finishes with the words: " This also cometh forth from the Lord of hosts, who is wonderful in counsel and excellent in working."

[38] *Jeremiah*, 5. 24; 14. 22. [39] *Amos* 4. 7.

mayest gather in thy corn, and thy wine, and thine oil. And I will send grass in thy fields for thy cattle, that thou mayest eat and be full. Take heed to yourselves, that your heart be not deceived, and ye turn aside, and serve other gods, and worship them; and *then* the Lord's wrath be kindled against you, and he shut up the heaven, that there be no rain, and that the land yield not her fruit; and *lest* ye perish quickly from off the good land which the Lord giveth you."[40] The Jew saw God acting continuously in the natural processes on which life depends.

Finally, as the Jew saw it, the land which he inhabited belonged to God. It was God's land, and he was only a tenant in it. "The land shall not be sold for ever; for the land is mine; for ye are strangers and sojourners with me."[41] The Jew saw himself as nothing more than the tenant of God.

All these things were built into the Jewish view of agriculture and the land. The Jew might forget them, but there was always a prophetic voice to recall him to them, or there were natural happenings which drove him back to the conviction of his dependence upon God. Long before there was any formal education lads and young men must have been trained in the simple processes on which food and life depend; and in that training they could not help, perhaps half-unconsciously, perhaps by a process of soaking them in rather than of learning them, acquiring these beliefs in their hearts. For the Jew to work on the land must have been to be educated continuously in the ways of God.

There was another integral part of Jewish communal life which must have provided a very real vehicle of instruction. Such a vehicle must have been found in the three great national feasts and festivals—The Passover, Pentecost, and the Festival of Tabernacles. Jewish law laid it down that a father must explain the great festivals to his son. When a son asked the meaning of "the testimonies, the statutes and the judgments" his father must be ready with an explanation.[42] Now, what is not sufficiently realised is that these great festivals had not only a *historical* significance; they had also an *agricultural* significance. They did not only commemorate events in history; they also marked out the cycle of the agricultural year;

[40] *Deuteronomy* 11. 13–17. [41] *Leviticus* 25. 23.

[42] *Exodus* 13. 8; *Deuteronomy* 4. 9; 6. 20.

and it may well be true that their agricultural significance was more primitive than the historical significance which was attached to them. Their historical significance was as follows. The Passover commemorated the deliverance of the Jewish people from slavery and bondage in Egypt; Pentecost commemorated the giving of the Law on Mount Sinai; The Festival of Tabernacles, with its living in booths made from branches, commemorated the journey through the wilderness to the promised land. In *Exodus* there is the list of the three great feasts, when " all thy males shall appear before the Lord God." The Passover is described in historical terms. It is to be observed in the time of the appointed month Abib, " for in it thou camest out from Egypt." But Pentecost is actually described as the *Feast of the Harvest*, and Tabernacles is actually described as *The Feast of Ingathering*.[43] That is to say, in the case of the latter two festivals it was the agricultural significance which at that time was paramount. And in *Leviticus* the Passover also is given an agricultural significance.[44]

Now let us see what the agricultural significance and ritual was in the case of each of the festivals.

The Passover, in the month of April, marked the beginning of the barley harvest. A sheaf of the first fruits of the harvest had to be taken by the priest and waved before the Lord (*Leviticus* 23. 9–11). Connected with this there were certain picturesque ceremonies. On 14th Nisan, men appointed for the task went out into a field of barley. It could be any field, and in that field they chose certain of the best of the sheaves, and bound them and left them standing in the ground. The only condition was that the barley must have grown in an ordinary field, not in a garden, or an orchard, or in any piece of ground specially treated and prepared. It was barley from an ordinary crop. On the next day, at evening time, three men went out, each with a sickle and a basket, to reap the sheaves which had been marked out. This was a very popular ceremony and was attended by great crowds. The men turned to the crowd and asked certain specified questions. " Has the sun gone down ? " " With this sickle ? " " Into this basket ? " " On this day ? " " Shall I reap ? " When the questions had been answered in the affirmative, they began to reap. They cut the barley and brought

[43] *Exodus* 23. 14–17. [44] *Leviticus* 23. 10–12.

it to the Temple court. There it was threshed with soft canes so as not to bruise it. It was then parched over the fire in a perforated pan, so that each grain might be touched by the fire. It was then exposed to the wind so that the chaff might be blown away. It was ground in a barley mill. Two handfuls of it, mixed with oil and incense, were flung on to the altar of the incense. Of the remainder about five pints were offered as an offering, while the rest was the perquisite of the priests, and might be used for any clean purpose. And it was not until then that the new barley could be sold and bought in the shops, and that bread made from new barley flour could be eaten. No doubt that is a description of the fully developed form of the ritual; but it can be seen at once with what interest a child would watch all this going on; how he would ask why it was done and what it meant; and what a door to teaching was offered by his questions.

Pentecost came seven weeks later, at the beginning of June. It commemorated the ingathering of the wheat harvest; and part of the ritual was the offering of two loaves of fine flour to the Lord.[45] In later times there were detailed instructions for the making and baking of these loaves. The flour had to be sieved twelve times; they were kneaded and rolled outside the Temple Court, but baked inside; they were seven handbreadths long and four wide; at the corners they had little horns, like the horns of the altar, four finger-breadths high; of all Temple offerings they were the only ones which were leavened, in order to show that they stood for ordinary, everyday bread.[46] Here again the very sight of the loaves was bound to awaken questions; and again an opportunity to teach was offered, and no doubt accepted.

The Festival of Tabernacles came at the end of September. It was the most joyous of all the feasts and came at the end of the grape harvest, when all the harvests had been gathered in. It was in fact close to being a harvest-thanksgiving festival. The characteristic of the Feast of Tabernacles was the carrying of the *Lulab*. The instruction was: " Ye shall take the boughs of goodly trees, the branches of palm-trees, the boughs of thick trees, and the willows of the brook." [47] The *boughs of thick trees* were held to be the *myrtle boughs*. So the worshippers made and carried a kind of bundle

[45] *Leviticus* 23. 16, 17. [46] *Men.* 6. 7; 11. 2, 4. [47] *Leviticus* 23. 40.

with a palm branch in the middle, and a myrtle and willow branch on either side. This was the *lulab*. (The word literally means a palm branch.) This was carried and waved in the hand. The fruit of goodly trees was held to be the *citron*, which was carried in the other hand.[48] Everything in this ritual stood for some thing in the various stages and experiences of the Israelites as they journeyed across the desert and came to the promised land. The *palm* stood for the valleys and the plains, where the palm-trees grew; the *myrtle* stood for the willows and the bushes on the mountains and the hillsides; the *willow* stood for the brooks at which they had drunk; and the *citron* stood for the good fruits of the promised land. Undoubtedly any child would ask what the *lulab* and the *citron* meant; and the explanation would be a doorway to the explanation of history and of the bounty of God.

In one case the instruction was obligatory, and was actually part of the ritual—in the case of the Passover. It was laid down: "Thou shalt show thy son in that day, saying, This is done because of that which the Lord did unto me, when I came forth out of the land of Egypt." [49] In the full Passover celebration this was integrated into the ritual. After the mixing of the second cup, the son is bidden to ask his father (and if the son has not enough understanding his father instructs him how to ask): "Why is this night different from other nights? For on other nights we eat seasoned food once, but on this night twice. On other nights we eat leavened or unleavened bread, but this night all is unleavened; on other nights we eat flesh roasted, stewed or cooked, but on this night all is roasted." Then, according to the understanding of his son, the father instructs him. "He begins with the disgrace and ends with the glory. And he expounds, 'A wandering Aramean was my father' (*Deuteronomy* 26. 5 ff.) until he finishes the whole section." [50] At the Passover the instruction of the child was nothing less than obligatory, and was an essential part of the feast.

It can easily be seen that the Jewish Feasts and Festivals were in themselves unparalleled opportunities for instruction in history and in the generosity of God. Before there was ever a school to teach him, a son would learn from his father the history of his country,

[48] The regulations regarding the *lulab* and the *citron* are in *Sukkah* 3. 1–9.

[49] *Exodus* 13. 8. [50] *Pes.* 10. 4.

the holy righteousness of God, and the bounty of God in the world of nature. In a Jewish home the father was bound to accept the duty of the religious education of his son.

We have been dealing so far with Jewish education as it took place within the home; and it is late in Jewish history before schools in the public sense of the term emerge at all. But now we must note two events which made the ultimate coming of schools certain in the end. The first was the publication of *Deuteronomy* in 621 B.C. Here we have the introduction of a written code, which actually enjoins that its precepts and statutes and commandments should be taught to children.[51] Here there was a definite written corpus of teaching material. But even more important was the work of Ezra. Ezra " had prepared his heart to seek the law of the Lord, and to do it, and to teach in Israel statutes and judgments." [52] In *Nehemiah* we read how the people were called together, how the Law was read to them, and how they pledged themselves to obey it, and to live by it.[53] No doubt that chapter is a highly dramatised version of what happened. We need not regard it as being literally true in every detail; but it is certainly symbolically true. On their return from exile the Jews became " the people of the book." Under the leadership of Ezra, the *Torah*, in its written form, was accepted as " the regulating norm in every relation of life." [54]

At the same time we must be careful to understand what this means. The Jews were not " the people of the book " in the sense that every Jew possessed the book, and read, and studied it. Few indeed possessed the book, and instruction was oral. G. H. Box writes: " A knowledge of books is not now, and never has been essential to culture in the East." And he quotes Robertson Smith as saying: " The ideal of instruction is oral teaching, and the worthiest shrine of truths that must not die is the memory and heart of the faithful disciple." [55] The Jews were " the people of

[51] *Deuteronomy* 4. 9: Teach them thy sons, and thy son's sons; 6. 7, 20: Thou shalt teach them diligently unto thy children; 11. 19: And ye shall teach them your children.

[52] *Ezra* 7. 10. [53] *Nehemiah* 8. [54] A. R. S. Kennedy in *D.B.* 1. 647.

[55] G. H. Box: *E.B.* 2. 1190; Robertson Smith: *The Old Testament in the Jewish Church* (second edition), p. 299.

the book " not because each individual one of them possessed the book, but because the book was the container of the law of life, which was inserted into their minds, and graven upon their hearts, by oral teaching.

If, then, the book was all-important, and all-inclusive of truth, the book had to be interpreted, explained and expounded. Where then did that dissemination of the truth within the book take place? The answer is that it took place within the Synagogue. There can be little doubt that the Synagogue grew out of the conditions of the exile. During the exile sacrifice was impossible, for sacrifice could only be offered in the Temple. But even when sacrifice was rendered impossible, prayer and the study of God's word were still possible, and these are the essentials of the Synagogue. It was the tendency of the Jews to carry the origin of everything as far back as possible. Both Josephus and Philo carry the Synagogue back to Moses.[56] And the Targums characteristically carry it back to patriarchal times. But the truth most probably is that the habit of meeting on the Sabbath for study and prayer developed during the exile, remained in Jewish life on the return, and was the moving cause of the beginning of the Synagogue.

It was certainly in the Synagogue that this teaching was mainly carried out. It is necessary clearly to remember that the Synagogue was very much more a place of teaching than the modern Church is. The object of the Synagogue Sabbath services was not public worship in the narrower sense of the term; it was not devotion; it was religious instruction. Philo calls the Synagogues " houses of instruction." [57] The characteristic word in connection with the Synagogue in the New Testament is *didaskein*, to teach.[58] Guignebert calls the Synagogue " a meeting place of the pious," " a centre

[56] Josephus: *Against Apion*: 2. 17, 18; Philo: *Life of Moses* 3. 27. The Talmud and the Targums and the writings of the Midrashes—which A. R. S. Kennedy characterises as "those store-houses of magnificent anachronisms " (*D.B.* 1. 646)—carry the origin of the Synagogue and the Rabbinic Colleges back to patriarchal times. The Targum of Onkelos (*Genesis* 25. 27) says that Jacob served in a house of instruction. The Jerusalem Targum (*Genesis* 33. 17) says that Jacob built a house of teaching. The same Targum (*Exodus* 18. 20) says that the father-in-law of Moses urged him to teach the people the prayer they were to use in their Synagogue.

[57] Philo: *Life of Moses* 3. 27. [58] Cp. *Matthew* 4. 23; *Mark* 1. 21; *Luke* 4. 15.

of religious instruction," and says that it is not too much to call it "the popular religious university" of its day.[59] The Synagogue was the centre in which the Law was explained, expounded and applied. In that sense the Synagogue was the centre of public Jewish education. It is here that the Scribe enters the scene. If the Law had to be taught, and explained, and appointed, there must be men who dedicated themselves to that task, men whose life work it was to know and to interpret the Law, and to state its claims authoritatively; and the Scribes were these men.

Into this pattern there enter still another body of men, before we reach what we know as schools. In a sense these men are the same as the Scribes, but their approach was different. These men are the men whom we might well call the Sages, and who taught wisdom. We find their teaching especially in *Proverbs*, which A. R. S. Kennedy called "the oldest handbook of education,"[60] in *Ecclesiasticus, The Wisdom of Jesus, the Son of Sirach*, and in *The Wisdom of Solomon*. There can have been no greater influence on Jewish life and morals than these Sages who taught wisdom. Let us briefly examine this conception of wisdom, and let us see of what it consisted and what it taught.

It was not primarily speculative wisdom and knowledge; it was not primarily intellectual or academic. Oesterley says of it: "In its essence it connoted originally the faculty of distinguishing between what is good and what is evil, or, perhaps more accurately, between what is beneficent and what is harmful."[61] For that very reason it was essentially religious. The most characteristic of all sayings about this wisdom is that sentence which might well be taken as the text on which the Sages continually preached: "The fear of the Lord is the beginning—or, the principal part—of wisdom."[62] *Ecclesiasticus* has variations on this theme—"To fear the Lord is the fullness of wisdom"; "the fear of the Lord is the crown of wisdom"; "the fear of the Lord is the root of wisdom."[63] This wisdom is given by God, and comes from keeping the commandments of God. "She (wisdom) is with all flesh according to

[59] C. Guignebert: *The Jewish World in the Time of Jesus*, p. 75.

[60] A. R. S. Kennedy: *D.B.* I. 648.

[61] W. O. E. Oesterley: *Ecclesiasticus*, p. xlvii.

[62] *Proverbs* I. 7; *Ecclesiasticus* I. 14. [63] *Ecclesiasticus* I. 16, 18, 20.

His gift, and He gave her freely to them that love Him." "If thou desire wisdom, keep her commandments, and the Lord will give her unto thee freely."[64] She is not easily to be had, and yields herself only to those who follow her in a single-hearted pursuit. "At the first she will walk with him in crooked ways, and will bring fear and dread upon him, and torment him with her discipline, until she may trust his soul, and try him by her judgments." "Bring thy feet into her fetters, and thy neck into her chain; put thy shoulder under her, and bear her; and be not grieved with her bonds."[65] For that very reason she never becomes the possession of many. "Wisdom is according to her name; and she is not manifest unto many."[66] The fool cannot contain this wisdom. "The inward parts of a fool are like a broken vessel; and he will hold no knowledge."[67] She can only be retained in righteousness, and may be lost. "If he go astray, she will forsake him, and give him over to his fall."[68] By the grace of God wisdom was the peculiar possession of the people of Israel. "In whose inheritance shall I lodge? Then the Creator of all things gave me a commandment, and He that created me made my tabernacle to rest, and said, Let thy tabernacle be in Jacob and thine inheritance in Israel. . . . And so was I established in Sion. In the beloved city likewise He gave me rest, and in Jerusalem was my authority, and I took root in a people that was glorified, even in the portion of the Lord's own inheritance."[69] All the effort to get her and to retain her is worth while abundantly. "He that giveth heed unto her shall dwell securely."[70] She makes "the lowly to sit in the midst of great men."[71] In material prosperity her reward is great. "She satiateth men with her fruits; she shall fill all her house with desirable things, and her garners with her produce."[72] In the end the chains and the fetters of effort and discipline will be all forgotten. "At last thou shalt find her rest; and she shall be turned for thee into gladness; and her fetters shall be to thee for a covering of strength, and her chains for a robe of glory."[73]

Even from this brief summary one thing will have become clear.

[64] *Ecclesiasticus*, 1. 10; 1. 26. [65] *Ecclesiasticus* 4. 17; 6. 24, 25.
[66] *Ecclesiasticus* 6. 22. [67] *Ecclesiasticus* 21. 13, 14. [68] *Ecclesiasticus* 4. 19.
[69] *Ecclesiasticus* 24. 7–12. [70] *Ecclesiasticus* 4. 15. [71] *Ecclesiasticus* 11. 1.
[72] *Ecclesiasticus* 1. 16, 17. [73] *Ecclesiasticus* 6. 28–31.

This wisdom is wisdom of God and from God; it is essentially religious; but equally it is essentially practical. Its aim was not only to enable a man theoretically to know God, but also practically to make a success of living in this world. J. A. Bewer writes: "Wisdom meant that sagacity and commonsense which enables man to live a happy and prosperous life."[74] John Paterson says of the Sages that they "were the spiritual middlemen who mediated the exalted doctrines of the prophets and interpreted them in terms of common life and experience." He picturesquely puts it that "the task of the schools then, as now, was not so much to work out of human nature 'the ape and the tiger' as to expel the donkey."[75]

The nature of this wisdom may well be seen in one of the favourite words of the book of *Proverbs*, the word *musar*; it occurs in *Proverbs* about thirty times; it means *discipline*, and is most commonly translated *instruction*. This wisdom is training for success in life. A. R. S. Kennedy[76] gives a summary of the things which *Proverbs* inculcates and on which it lays stress; and they show the scope of this wisdom. It teaches prudent forethought; temperance; chastity; diligence; truthfulness; consideration for the poor; a most unusual and truly noble charity to enemies; the value of true friendship; and the dignity of good womanhood.[77]

In its later manifestation, without losing its essentially religious character, and without retreating from the paramount place it gives to the Law, this wisdom comes to embrace much of what we would call culture. In the *Wisdom of Solomon* the Sage claims a wide sphere for his knowledge:

> But to me may God give to speak with judgment,
> And to conceive thoughts worthy of what has been given to me;
> Because Himself is one that guideth even wisdom and that correcteth the wise.

[74] J. A. Bewer: *Literature of the Old Testament*, p. 310.

[75] John Paterson: *The Book that is Alive, Studies in Old Testament Life and Thought as Set Forth by Hebrew Sages*, pp. 66 and 53.

[76] A. R. S. Kennedy: *D.B.* I. 648.

[77] *Proverbs* 24. 27; 21. 17; 23. 20, 21, 29–35; 7. 6ff; 29.3; 6. 6–11; 17. 7; 14. 21; 19. 17; 22. 9; 25. 21, 22; 17. 17; 18. 24; 27. 10; 31. 10–31.

For in His hand are both we and our words;
All understanding, and all acquaintance with divers crafts.
For Himself gave me an unerring knowledge of the things that are,
To know the constitution of the world, and the operation of the elements;
The beginning and end and middle of times,
The alternation of the solstices and the changes of the seasons,
The circuits of the years, and the positions of the stars;
The natures of living creatures and the ragings of wild beasts,
The violence of winds and the thoughts of men,
The diversities of plants, and the virtues of roots:
All things that are either secret or manifest I learned,
For she that is the artificer of all things taught me, even wisdom.
For there is in her a spirit quick of understanding, holy.[78]

There wisdom has opened to a man the knowledge of astronomy, biology, psychology, botany, and every kind of lore.

Ben Sirach's description of the Sage is the description of a much-cultured, much-travelled man, able to move in any society in which he may find himself:

He will seek out the wisdom of the ancients,
And will be occupied in prophecies.
He will keep the discourse of the men of renown,
And will enter in amidst the subtilities of parables.
He will seek out the hidden meanings of proverbs,
And be conversant in the dark sayings of parables.
He will serve among great men,
And appear before him that ruleth;
He will travel through the land of strange nations;
For he hath tried good things and evil among men.
He will apply his heart to resort early to the Lord that made him,
And will make supplication before the Most High,
And will open his mouth in prayer,
And will make supplication for his sins.[79]

Here is the picture of a man who is a scholar, interpreter, traveller, courtier, and man of devotion. It is well to remember this side of

[78] *The Wisdom of Solomon* 7. 15–22. [79] *Ecclesiasticus* 39. 2–5.

the picture when we are stressing the comparative narrowness of the field of Jewish education.

It is little wonder in view of these pictures that the Sage felt that, in order to become a Sage, he must be rid of the work and the activities of the world. It was not that he despised those who did the work of the world; far from it, on them in one sense the world is founded; but for the Sage the life of scholarly leisure is an essential. There is a magnificent passage in *Ecclesiasticus* which sets out this point of view:

> The wisdom of the Scribe cometh by opportunity of leisure;
> And he that hath little business shall become wise.
> How shall he become wise that holdeth the plough,
> That glorieth in the shaft of the goad,
> That driveth oxen, and is occupied in their labours,
> And whose discourse is of the stock of bulls?
> He will set his heart upon turning his furrows;
> And his wakefulness is to give his heifers their fodder.
> So is every artificer and workmaster,
> That passeth his time by night as by day;
> They that cut gravings of signets,
> And his diligence is to make great variety;
> He will set his heart to preserve likeness in his portraiture,
> And will be wakeful to finish his work.
> So is the smith sitting by the anvil,
> And considering the unwrought iron:
> The vapour of the fire will waste his flesh;
> And in the heat of the furnace will he wrestle with his work;
> The noise of the hammer will be ever in his ear,
> And his eyes are upon the pattern of the vessel;
> He will set his heart upon perfecting his works,
> And he will be wakeful to adorn them perfectly.
> So is the potter sitting at his work,
> And turning the wheel about with his feet,
> Who is always anxiously set at his work,
> And all his handiwork is by number;
> He will fashion the clay with his arm,
> And will bend its strength in front of his feet;

He will apply his heart to finish the glazing;
And he will be wakeful to make clean the furnace.

All these put their trust in their hands;
And each becometh wise in his own work.
Without these shall not a city be inhabited,
And men shall not sojourn nor walk up and down therein.
They shall not be sought for in the council of the people,
And in the assembly they shall not mount on high;
They shall not sit in the seat of the judge,
And they shall not understand the covenant of judgment:
Neither shall they declare instruction and judgment;
And where parables are they shall not be found.
But they maintain the fabric of the world;
And in the handiwork of their craft is their prayer.[80]

It is not that in any sense the Sage despises the man who works with his hands. On him the world rests; and with his hands he can pray. Truly for him *laborare est orare.* But none the less, if the Sage is to be a Sage, all common things must be laid aside, in order that he may concentrate on the supreme wisdom.

One of the features of the methods of the Sages was their stress on the need of physical discipline and correction. It is true that "a reproof entereth more into a wise man than an hundred stripes into a fool."[81] But it also remains true that the rod is the sovereign corrective. "He that spareth his rod hateth his son; and he that loveth him chasteneth him betimes." "Foolishness is bound in the heart of a child; but the rod of correction shall drive it from him." "The rod and reproof give wisdom; but a child left to himself bringeth his mother to shame. . . . Correct thy son and he shall give thee rest; yea, he shall give delight unto thy soul."[82] Ben Sirach is even more insistent on discipline and correction.

Hast thou children? correct them,
And bow down their neck from their youth.
Hast thou daughters? give heed to their body,
And make not thy face cheerful to them.[83]

[80] *Ecclesiasticus* 38. 24–34. [81] *Proverbs* 17. 10.
[82] *Proverbs* 13. 24; 22. 15; 29. 15, 17.
[83] *Ecclesiasticus* 7. 23, 24.

And again:

He that loveth his son will continue to lay stripes upon him,
That he may have joy of him in the end.
He that chastiseth his son shall have profit of him,
And shall glory of him among his acquaintance.
. . . .
He that maketh too much of his son shall bind up his wounds;
And his heart will be troubled at every cry.
An unbroken horse becometh stubborn;
And a son left at large becometh headstrong.
Cocker thy child, and he shall make thee afraid:
Play with him, and he will grieve thee.
Laugh not with him, lest thou have sorrow with him;
And thou shalt gnash thy teeth in the end.
Give him no liberty in his youth,
And wink not at his follies.
Bow down his neck in his youth,
And beat him on the sides while he is still a child,
Lest he wax stubborn and be disobedient unto thee;
And there shall be sorrow to thy soul.
Chastise thy son and take pains with him,
Lest his shameless behaviour be an offence unto thee.[84]

So then the Sages taught wisdom, the wisdom which comes from God, and which accepts and obeys the commandments of God, the wisdom which enables a man to bring honour to himself and joy to those who love him, the wisdom which can only be bought through toil, and must be wrought out, if need be, with the rod of chastening and correction.

We have now reached a curious position in regard to Jewish education. We have the paradox that there is abundant evidence for Jewish education; but there is not the slightest mention of the elementary school. There is in fact no mention of the word "school" until the New Testament, and in the New Testament it is only used once, and that once is not in connection with a school for children, but with the school of Tyrannus, in which Paul

[84] *Ecclesiasticus* 30. 1–13.

lectured in Ephesus.[85] This is the more strange in view of the immense importance that later Judaism attached to schools for children. The Talmud repeatedly stresses the essential character of schools. A scholar should never stay in a town where there is no elementary school.[86] A town in which there are no children attending school is to be destroyed, or put under the ban; and Jerusalem itself was destroyed because school children had ceased to be there, and teachers were not respected.[87] It was said that in Jerusalem there were four hundred and eighty Synagogues and that each of them had a school.[88] An ordinance of Ezra was said to enact that as many schoolmasters as chose might settle in any place, and that the schoolmasters already there might not interfere with them, for competition made for good education.[89] It could well be argued that that reference is thinking in terms of competing private schools rather than of public education. Teachers' salaries were, so the Talmud says, to be paid by the community; taxes were levied for the purpose, but only on those who had children; and those who failed to pay could be distrained upon.[90] Somehow or other we have to get from a time when there is no mention of schools to a time when schools are one of the prime essentials of any well-ordered community. According to Josephus the origin of schools goes back to Moses. He ordered that " boys should learn the most important laws, because this is the best knowledge, and the cause of prosperity." [91] " He commanded to instruct the children in the elements of knowledge, to teach them to walk according to the laws, and to know the deeds of their forefathers. The latter, that they might imitate them; the former, that, growing up with the laws, they might not transgress them, nor have the excuse of ignorance." [92] But that is simply a characteristic attempt to carry back origins into antiquity.

There are two great names which are indissolubly connected with Jewish elementary education. The first is that of Simon ben-Shetach. He was the brother of Queen Alexandra, who reigned from 78 to 69 B.C. The Jerusalem Talmud declares that he

[85] *Acts* 19. 9. [86] *Sanh.* 18b. [87] *Shabbath* 119b.

[88] *Jes. Meg*, 73b. [89] *Baba Bathra* 21b. [90] *Pesikta* 178, a, b.

[91] Josephus: *Antiquities of the Jews* 4. 8. 12.

[92] Josephus: *Against Apion* 2. 25.

enacted that " the children shall attend the elementary school." This Simon is a shadowy figure. Morris Joseph simply reports the story, with an " it is said." [93] Schürer, without argument, dismisses the tradition as valueless, and characterises Simon as " quite a meeting point for all kinds of myths." [94] Both G. H. Box and A. R. S. Kennedy are willing to accept the substantial accuracy of the story.[95] On the whole we will probably be justified in accepting the Simon tradition. It is to be noted that it is not said that Simon instituted elementary schools; he is said to have enacted that children should attend them. There must have been some kind of education for children. The very fact that the Jews were " the people of the book " makes that almost essential. We know that at the Sabbath Synagogue service seven members of the congregation were called up to read the scripture lesson,[96] and therefore the ability to read must have been quite general. Simon lived in days when the tide of Hellenism was threatening Judaism, and when the Pharisees were strongly resisting it; and the likelihood is that Simon urged the Jews to a careful observance of the educational facilities which were already there. He enjoined them to accept the obligations of education for their children in the Jewish way. We need not hold that Simon initiated elementary education.

The second great name in Jewish elementary education is that of Joshua ben-Gamala who was High Priest about A.D. 63–65. The Talmud praises him most highly for his part in the universalising of elementary education. It is said of him: " Verily let it be remembered to that man for good, Rabbi Joshua ben-Gamala is his name, for had he not been, the Law would have been forgotten in Israel. At first everyone that had a father alive received from him instruction in the Law, but he that had no father alive learned not the Law. . . . Thereafter teachers for the children were appointed in Jerusalem. . . . But even this measure sufficed not, for he that had a father was brought by him to school, and was taught there, but he that had no father was not brought to be taught there. In consequence of this it was ordained that teachers should be appointed in

[93] Morris Joseph: *E.R.E.* 5. 195.

[94] E. Schürer: *The Jewish People in Time of Jesus Christ*, 2. 2. 49.

[95] G. H. Box in *E.B.* 2. 1195; A. R. S. Kennedy in *D.B.* 1. 649.

[96] E. Schürer: *The Jewish People in the Time of Jesus Christ* 2. 2. 80.

every district. To these the children were sent when they were sixteen or seventeen years of age. When a teacher became angry with a scholar, the latter stamped his feet and ran away. In this condition education remained until the time of Joshua ben-Gamala, who ordained that in every province and in every town there should be teachers appointed, to whom the children should be brought at the age of six or seven years."[97] From this we learn that there was some kind of educational organisation in Palestine before this Joshua, but that he reformed it, and made it much more effective, and universalised it over the whole country. As to when elementary education first began as an organised public service, we are still in doubt. Although ideally it was the duty of the father to give it, in practice the necessity for public education must go far back. What we can say for certain is that it received a new impetus from Simon ben-Shetach, and it received a new and more efficient shape from Joshua ben-Gamala.

The age for beginning school was from five to seven years old. There is a late addendum to the fifth book of the *Sayings of the Fathers*, which sets out the ages of man:

> At five years old, Scripture; at ten years, Mishnah; at thirteen, the Commandments; at fifteen, Talmud; at eighteen, marriage; at twenty, the pursuits of business; at thirty, strength; at forty, discernment; at fifty, counsel; at sixty, age; at seventy, gray old age; at eighty, power; at ninety, decrepitude; at a hundred, as though he were dead, and gone, and had ceased from the world.[98]

[97] *Baba Bathra* 21a. The version of the Talmud passage quoted above is that given by A. R. S. Kennedy *D.B.* 1. 650. The passage is also given by G. H. Box in *E.B.* 2. 1196, and by A. Edersheim in *Sketches of Jewish Social Life in the Days of Christ*, p. 134.

[98] C. Taylor: *Sayings of the Jewish Fathers*, p. 97. In his note Taylor quotes the seven *vanities*, corresponding to the seven ages, as given in the Midrash on *Ecclesiastes* 1. 2: "The child of a year is like a *king*, adored by all; at two or three, he is like a *swine*, dabbling in filth; at ten, he bounds like a *kid*; at twenty, he is like a *horse*, neighing and spirited, and desires a wife; when he has married a wife, behold he is like an *ass*; when children are born to him, he is as shameless as a *dog* in procuring the means of sustenance; when he has grown old, he is like an *ape*, if he has not known and kept the Law, but if he is a son of the Law, like David, he is a *king*, though old (I *Kings* 1. 1.)."

Seven was in fact the usual age for sending a boy to school, for the Rabbis did not believe in beginning technical education too young, although they believed that it was never too soon to begin to impress the mind of the child with the things of God. Rabbi Abujah said: "He who learns as a lad, to what is he like? To ink written on fresh paper. And he who learns when he is old, to what is he like? To ink written on paper that has already been used." [99] How soon then was the child supposed to begin learning about his God and his faith at home? Schechter quotes a Midrash on *Leviticus* 19. 23, 24. That passage lays it down that when a tree is planted, the fruit of it must not be taken for the first three years, and in the fourth year all the fruit is holy to the Lord. That is taken as a parable of the training of the child. For the first three years the child cannot speak, and is therefore exempt from every religious duty. From the fourth year it is the duty of the father to begin to initiate him into the great truths, for life and religion begin when the child can speak distinctly.[100]

But there are certain teachings which the child could and did receive in pre-school days, when he was very young. The *Mishnah* speaks about the law of the *Mezuzah* being binding even on a child.[101] *Deuteronomy* says of the divine laws: "Thou shalt write them upon the posts of thy house and on thy gates." [102] In obedience to that commandment the *Mezuzah* is fixed to the door post of the house, and to the door post of every clean room within the house. It is a little cylindrical box, made preferably of olive wood. In it there is a little scroll of parchment with the two passages *Deuteronomy* 6. 4–9 and 11. 13–21 written on it, in exactly twenty-two lines. In these lines the name of God occurs no fewer than ten times. There is a little circular opening in the centre of the cylinder, and the parchment is so arranged that the word *Shaddai*, the Almighty, appears through the little circle. In going out and coming in everyone touches the opening of the *Mezuzah*, kisses his finger, and says a benediction. It is closely connected in

[99] *Sayings of the Fathers* 4. 27. Taylor, in his note, adds a parallel saying that learning in youth is likened to graving upon stone, but learning in old age is likened to tracing characters on the sand.

[100] S. Schechter: *Studies in Judaism, First Series*, p. 300.

[101] *Berakoth* 3. 3. [102] *Deuteronomy* 6. 9.

Jewish thought with the words: "The Lord shall preserve thy going out and thy coming in from this time forth, even for evermore."[103] It is clear how the youngest child would notice the *Mezuzah*, and would ask what it meant.

It was suggested that, when the child was three, his father should begin to take him to the Synagogue. There were Rabbis who resented the noise the not very well behaved child could make; and there were some who commended the custom of the Sephardim in later days, who segregated the boys in the Synagogue, and set beside them a special overseer with a whip, as a very practical and effective aid to devotion.[104]

The child was not liable to the laws of Sabbath observance, but on the other hand the adult was responsible for seeing that the child did keep the Sabbath,[105] and therefore week by week the child would learn more and more of what these laws were. When the Day of Atonement came round, the child was not bound to fast, but it was recommended that for two or three years before he became liable to keep the fast, he should be encouraged to fast at least a little.[106] We have already seen how it was the duty of the father to explain to the child the reason of the Passover and all that was done in it.[107] When he was still very young, the child was supposed to attend the great festivals in Jerusalem. Shammai said that the child must come, when he could ride upon his father's shoulders. Hillel said that he must come when he could hold his father's hand, and go up on his own two feet.[108] Especially a lad must come to the Festival of Tabernacles. It was laid down that a child "who no longer needs his mother" must come to the Festival of Tabernacles; and that a boy who is "capable of shaking a *lulab*" must keep it.[109] As for actual instruction, as soon as he could speak the child was taught to memorise and to say the two texts: "Hear, O Israel; the Lord our God is one Lord," and, "Moses commanded us a law, even the inheritance of the congregation of Jacob."[110] At the first signs of puberty, that is, when

[103] *Psalm* 121. 8.

[104] S. Schechter: *Studies in Judaism, First Series*, p. 301.

[105] *Shabbath* 16. 6. [106] *Yoma* 8. 4. [107] Cp. *Exodus* 12. 26 f.

[108] *Hagigah* 1. 1. [109] *Sukkah* 2. 8; 3. 15.

[110] *Deuteronomy* 6. 4; 33. 4.

two hairs appeared upon his body, the boy became liable to keep the Law.[111] Finally, there is a regulation, which must have been to a very large extent ideal, that the child must be brought to the Temple, when the Law was read through there on the Sabbatic year.[112] It is clear that long before he went to school the child was daily learning what it meant to be a Jew—and that was what education was designed to teach him.

We now go on to see the actual ways and methods of the schools. But before we begin we must enter one *caveat*. Many of the regulations which we shall describe, and many of the sayings which we shall cite, are obviously descriptions of the ideal rather than of the real; they describe what the school should have been rather than what it was; but they are none the less useful for that, because it is the ideal that we are mainly concerned to see.

Sometime between the ages of five and seven the boy went to school.[113] The school might be a special building; it might be in the teacher's house; but most likely it would be attached to the Synagogue itself. It was laid down that a school, for health's sake, must not be built in a densely crowded and populated area.[114] It was also laid down that if a town was large there must be two schools, especially if the town was divided by a river, for bridges were dangerous things to cross.[115] School did not meet between 10 a.m. and 3 p.m., for these were the hot hours; and there was a regulation that from 17th Thamuz to 14th Ab—that is, roughly July and August—school hours must not exceed four. Ideally the size of classes was strictly regulated. In any area where there were twenty-five boys a schoolmaster must be appointed. If there were forty boys, the master must be given an assistant; and if there were fifty boys, two masters must be appointed.

When the scholar entered school, he sat on the ground at the teacher's feet. Paul speaks of himself as being brought up at the feet of Gamaliel.[116] Rabbi Joses said: "Let thy house be a meeting-

[111] *Nidah* 6. 11. [112] *Deuteronomy* 31. 10–12.

[113] As we have seen the Ages of Man passage sets the age to study the Scripture at five. A later Rabbi gave the advice: "Do not receive a boy into school before his sixth year" (*Kethuboth* 50a).

[114] *Pesahim* 112a. [115] *Baba Bathra* 21a. [116] *Acts* 22. 3.

place for the wise; and powder thyself in the dust of their feet."[117] To sit at the master's feet was a sign of the scholar's humility, and of his eagerness to learn.

There was only one text-book and that was the scriptures. The very name of the school was *Beth Ha-Sepher*, The House of the Book. And of the sacred writings the Law, the Pentateuch was all-important, and the rest of the writings were only commentary on it. One Rabbi said of the Law: "Turn it, and again turn it; for the all is therein, and thy all is therein; and swerve not therefrom, for thou canst have no greater excellency than this."[118] The Law was the sole object of study; the wider culture of the world was as nothing to the Jew. The Mishnah actually contains a statement that during the war of Titus "they forbade that a man should teach his son Greek."[119] In the Talmud there is a story of a progressive young Rabbi who wished to study Greek on the grounds that he had mastered the Law. An older Rabbi reminded him of the words of Joshua: "This book of the Law shall not depart out of thy mouth; but thou shalt meditate therein day and night."[120] "Go then and consider," he said, "which is the hour which is neither of the day or of the night, and in it thou mayest study Greek wisdom."[121] So then Jewish education was exclusively religious education. It was study of the Scriptures for in them is the Law,

[117] *Sayings of the Fathers* I. 4. It was not till later that benches were used. Rabbi Jochanan made the interesting observation that "Easy things are learned standing, and hard things sitting."

[118] *Sayings of the Fathers* 5. 32. Taylor, in his note on this passage, cites further tributes to the all-inclusiveness of the Law. "In it without doubt are history and tale; proverb and enigma; correction and wisdom; knowledge and discretion; poetry and word-play; conviction and counsel; dirge, entreaty, prayer, praise, and every kind of supplication; and all this in a divine way, superior to all the prolix benedictions in human books; to say nothing of it containing in its depths the names of the Holy One, blessed is He, and secrets of being without end (*Leb Aboth*)." The diligent student of the Torah does not need works on science and philosophy, because the Torah contains both "all things necessary to salvation," and "all the wisdom of the world." Study the Torah "and thou wilt not need the books of the philosophers of the nations and their investigations." The Torah is worth more than the whole world, for the world was created in six days, but the Torah was only given in forty days (*Shemoth Rabbah* 47).

[119] *Sotah* 9. 14. [120] *Joshua* I. 8. [121] *Men.* 99b.

and nothing else is necessary. It was just here that the Jews claimed for their system superiority over all other systems of education. The very fact that their study was the study of the Law meant that it was necessarily double-sided. At one and the same time it included both theory and practice, knowledge and action, for the Law had first to be *studied*, and then to be *done*. A. R. S. Kennedy said: " It combines instruction in the positive truth of the ancestral faith with preparation for the practical duties of life." [122] This is a claim which Josephus made long ago. He writes: " There are two ways of coming at any sort of learning, and a moral conduct of life: the one is by instruction in words, the other by practical exercises. Now, other law-givers (that is, other than Moses) have separated these two ways in their opinions, and choosing one of those ways of instruction, or that which best pleased every one of them, neglected the other. Thus did the Lacedaimonians and the Cretans teach by practical exercises, but not by words; while the Athenians, and almost all the other Grecians, made laws about what was to be done, or left undone, but had no regard to the exercising thereto in practice." [123]

Two basic facts must always be borne in mind about Jewish teaching. First, it was based entirely on *oral teaching*; and therefore it was conducted entirely by repetition. The word *mishnah* itself means both *repetition* and *instruction*, for they were one and the same thing. This is typical of eastern education. G. H. Box cites a passage from the Babylonian Epic of Creation, which underlines this:

> Let them stand forth—let the elder enlighten;
> Let the wise, the learned meditate together;
> Let the father *rehearse*, make the son apprehend;
> Open be the ears of the Shepherd and the Flock-master (i.e. the King).[124]

Even Ben Sirach writes:

[122] A. R. S. Kennedy: *D.B.* 1. 646.

[123] Josephus: *Against Apion* 2. 17.

[124] G. H. Box: *E.B.* 2. 1191; Babylonian Epic of Creation, final tablet, reverse, 1. 22 f.

For by speech wisdom shall be known;
And instruction by word of the tongue.[125]

Except for the teacher himself, it may be said that the book hardly existed as an educational tool. All was by word of mouth, and by patient repetition and receptive hearing.

The second basic fact is the direct consequence of this. Education was to a very large extent memorising. Since the material could not be read, it had to be committed to the memory, and therefore the first essential of a good scholar was a trained and retentive memory. One of the most famous of all the Rabbis was Rabbi Eliezer. There are no fewer than three hundred and thirty of his sayings in the Mishnah. His master Rabbi Jochanan said of him that he was like "a plastered cistern that loseth not a drop." [126] Rabbi Dosithai said: "When a scholar of the wise sits and studies, and has forgotten a word of his Mishnah, they account it to him as if he were 'guilty of death.'" [127] In the Talmud it is told of a certain Rabbi Meir that he went to Asya to regulate the Calendar. He found that there was no book of *Esther* there, and he straightway wrote it all out from memory, and read it during the Feast.[128] G. H. Box quotes Jerome as saying that Jewish children can recite the alphabet forwards and backwards; that in childhood they acquire the complete vocabulary of their language, and learn to recite all the generations from Adam to Zerubbabel with "as much accuracy and facility as if they were simply giving their own names." [129] Gfrörer, the Jewish historian, claimed that, if all the copies of the Talmud were destroyed—and the Talmud runs to scores of volumes—any twelve learned rabbis could restore it verbatim from memory.[130] The whole of Jewish education was based on patient repetition and diligent memorising. Rabbi Akiba said: "The teacher should strive to make the lesson agreeable to the pupils by clear reasons, as well as by frequent repetitions, until they

[125] *Ecclesiasticus* 4. 24. [126] *Sayings of the Fathers* 2. 10.

[127] *Sayings of the Fathers* 3. 12. [128] *Megillah* 18b.

[129] G. H. Box: *E.B.* 2. 1200. In the same passage Box quotes Jerome as saying of the Pharisees that "they repeated but never reflected."

[130] Gfrörer: *Jahr. d. Heils.* 1. 170.

thoroughly understand the matter, and are able to recite it with great fluency." [131]

This had one curious effect. The Jews, as did all ancient peoples, read aloud, or at least, as they read, they formed the syllables with their lips. Philip *heard* the Ethiopian eunuch reading the prophet Esaias as he rode in his chariot.[132] So learning a lesson always meant repeating it aloud. The Talmud tells of a pupil who learned his tasks without repeating the words aloud, and who therefore had within three years forgotten all that he had learned.[133] The *Sayings of the Fathers* lists the forty-eight things which are necessary for learning the Torah, and the list begins: "By learning, by a listening ear, *by ordered speech.*" [134] *Repetitio mater studiorum*, repetition is the mother of studies, might well have been the motto of Jewish education. In the *Letters of Benammi* certain sayings about this concentrated repetition and memorising are given. "If you have garnered much, you have really garnered nothing." "Repetition is the mother of knowledge." "Whoso learns the Torah without repetition is like one who sows but does not reap." "Study not only with the eyes, but with the eyes and the mouth." [135]

[131] *Erubin* 54a. [132] *Acts* 8. 30. [133] *Erubin* 54a.

[134] *Sayings of the Fathers* 6. 6. As a matter of interest—and, it may be, of some use to those who learn—we give the whole list: "The Torah is acquired by forty and eight things. And these are they, by learning, by a listening ear, by ordered speech, by discernment of heart, by dread, by fear, by meekness, by cheerfulness, by pureness, by attendance upon the wise, by discussion with associates, by the argumentation of disciples, by sedateness; by Scripture, by Mishnah; by little traffic, by little intercourse, by little luxury, by little sleep, by little converse, by little merriment; by long-suffering, by a good heart, by faith in the wise, by acceptance of chastisements; he that knows his place, and that rejoices in his portion, and that makes a fence to his words, and does not claim merit to himself; he is loved, loves God, loves mankind, loves righteousness, loves uprightness, loves reproofs; and retires from honour, and puffs not up his heart with his learning, and is not forward in decision; bears the yoke with his associate, and inclines him to the scale of merit, and grounds him upon the truth, and grounds him upon peace; and settles his heart to his study; asks and answers, hears and adds thereto; he that learns in order to teach, and learns in order to practise; that makes his master wiser, and that considers what he has heard, and that tells a thing in the name of him that said it."

[135] *Essays on Jewish Life and Thought, The Letters of Benammi, Second Series,* p. 54.

So then Jewish instruction was largely oral instruction; and Jewish learning was largely learning by heart; and in that learning by heart repeating with the mouth played at least as big a part as seeing with the eye.

In the elementary school all Jewish boys learned to read, for, as we have seen, any adult male Jew might be given the privilege and task of reading the lesson in the Synagogue. They learned the essentials of arithmetic; and many, but not all, learned to write.

There was a bare minimum which every child, however simple, was expected to master. At least in later times, as soon as the child could read, he was given little parchment rolls with certain essential passages on them.[136] Even before the rolls were given these passages were regarded as basic. They were as follows:

i. The *Shema*.[137] *Shema* is the imperative of the Hebrew verb which means "to hear." It is the first word of that great verse *Deuteronomy* 6. 4, which is the foundation of the Jewish creed, and the sentence with which every morning service in the Synagogue still begins. It must be recited by every devout Jew, morning and evening, every day.

ii. The *Hallel*.[138] *Hallel* means Praise God!; and this is the series of great praising psalms which were recited at all new moons and festivals, and which had a special place in the Passover ritual.

iii. The Story of Creation.[139]

iv. The essence of the Levitical Law.[140]

In addition to this the child had to find and learn a *personal text*. A personal text was a text which began with the first letter of his name and ended with the last letter of his name. Keith instances as an illustration that a boy called *Abner* could have as his personal text:

[136] Khodadad E. Keith: *The Social Life of a Jew in the Time of Christ*, p. 46.
[137] The full *Shema* is *Deuteronomy* 6. 4–9; 11. 13–21; *Numbers* 15. 37–41.
[138] *Psalms* 113–18. [139] *Genesis* 1–5. [140] *Leviticus* 1–8.

> *A* soft answer turneth away wrath:
> But grievous words stir up anger.[141]

When a boy was able to read and to study the Law in a little more detail, his instruction began with *Leviticus*. That may seem to us a strange choice; but it was necessary that a Jew should have a full knowledge of the laws of purity and of the Temple sacrifices. But even after the destruction of the Temple, when sacrifice had been rendered impossible, *Leviticus* remained the beginning of detailed education, for, as a Midrash beautifully has it: "Sacrifices are pure; and children are pure; let the pure be occupied with that which is pure." [142]

In a community like that of which we have been thinking the teacher is obviously a man of paramount importance. The Law was everything, and therefore the expounder of the Law was the greatest man in the community. And even the place of the elementary school-teacher, who laid the foundations on which the Rabbi might work, was very high.

The teacher must be a man of the highest aims, and of the highest moral qualifications. Edersheim collects from the Talmud a series of sayings on the aim and the quality of the teacher. His aim must be to keep children from all intercourse with that which is vicious; to suppress all feelings of bitterness, even bitterness at wrong done to the child's own parents; to punish all real wrong-doing; never to prefer one child to another. He must rather show sin in its essential repulsiveness than try to threaten a child out of it by speaking of its consequences in this world, or in the world to come. He must never discourage the child. He must never promise and not perform, lest the child's mind become familiar with falsehood and the broken word. He must never lose patience, but, if the child does not understand, he must patiently explain the matter over and over again, in order to make it plain. He must treat the child like a young heifer, whose burden is daily increased. In every case he must first try kindness, and only when kindness fails must

[141] *Proverbs* 15. 1. cp. A. C. Bouquet: *Everyday Life in New Testament Times*, p. 156; Khodadad E. Keith: *The Social Life of a Jew in the Time of Christ*, p. 47.

[142] Midrash Rabba.

he physically punish. Such punishment must never be over-severe; and a teacher could be dismissed for too much severity; when punishment was given, it must be given with the strap, and not the rod.[143] We may add to this list several more significant sayings. It was laid down that "an idle man shall not keep a school for children."[144] And the same passage lays it down that an unmarried man may not teach, and that no woman is eligible to teach. The teacher must be of even temper, for a passionate man cannot teach. The teacher must not compromise his dignity, and he should never jest or eat or drink in the presence of the children.[145] The most interesting and the most significant thing about all this is the salient fact that the Jews were much more concerned about the moral character of the teacher than they were about his academic qualifications. Their first question would not have been: "What kind of a technical scholar is he?" but, "What kind of a person is he?" It was character which the Jews were seeking to produce, and they were well aware that only character can beget character.

In theory the teacher was supposed to teach without any payment at all. It was as if God said: "Just as I gave you the Torah freely, so you must pass it on without asking for payment for it."[146] Rabbi Zadok said: "Make not the words of the Torah a crown in which to glory, or an axe by which to live." And the great Hillel laid it down: "Lo, whosoever makes profit from the words of Torah removes his life from the world."[147] The ideal was that a teacher should have a trade, and that by it he should satisfy his material needs, and so be in a position to teach for nothing. In any event every boy was taught a trade, for "he who does not teach his son a trade teaches him to steal."[148] "Love work," said

[143] A. Edersheim: *Sketches of Jewish Social Life in the Days of Christ*, pp. 135, 136.

[144] *Kiddushin* 4. 13.

[145] *Sayings of the Fathers* 2. 6. Cp. the insistence of the *Pastoral Epistles* that the *episkopos*, the bishop, must be *didaktikos*, apt to teach, and that he must not be *orgilos*, an angry man (*I Timothy* 3. 2; *II Timothy* 2. 24; *Titus* 1. 7); *Yore Deah* 145. 11.

[146] Quoted in *Essays in Jewish Literature, the Letters of Benammi, Second Series*, p. 55.

[147] *Sayings of the Fathers* 4. 9. [148] *Kiddushin* 29a.

Shemaiah.[149] The Rabbis saw that there was a certain danger in what might be called the purely academic life. Rabbi Gamaliel, son of Jehuda ha-Nasi, said: " Excellent is Torah study together with worldly business, for the practice of both of them puts iniquity out of remembrance; all Torah without work must at length fail, and occasion iniquity." [150] There were some very few voices on the other side. We have seen that Ben Sirach did not think that the man who held the plough could become wise.[151] And Rabbi Meir once said: " Have little business, and be busy with Torah." [152] And Hillel once said: " No one that has much traffic is wise." [153] But the balance was very much the other way. We read of Rabbis who followed the trade of miller, shoemaker, tailor, baker, perfumer, clerk, sandal-maker, smith, potter, carpenter.[154] But this custom of free teaching must have been the custom of the Rabbis in their judicial function rather than that of the elementary schoolteacher, who must of necessity have been paid. But even then there were attempts to evade the fact that he was being paid for teaching. He was paid because he had the trouble of teaching the children the mechanical work of reading; because he looked after the children while at school; for his loss of time.[155] The idea behind it all is that it was one of life's greatest privileges to be a teacher, because, as was beautifully said, it was as great a privilege to teach a child the Law, as it was to have received it on Mount Sinai from the hands of God.

It will not surprise us to find in light of all this that the teacher was held in the very highest honour. The honour in which a great Rabbi must be held surpassed even the honour that must be given to parents. " Respect to a teacher should exceed respect for a father, for both father and son owe respect to a teacher." [156] " If a man's father and teacher have lost anything, the teacher's loss has the precedence; for his father only brought him into this world;

[149] *Sayings of the Fathers* 1. 11. [150] *Sayings of the Fathers* 2. 2.

[151] *Ecclesiasticus* 38. 25. [152] *Sayings of the Fathers* 4. 14.

[153] *Sayings of the Fathers* 2. 6.

[154] Cp. David Smith: *Life and Letters of St. Paul*, p. 25; Delitsch: *Jewish Artisan Life*, chapter 5.

[155] *Essays in Jewish Life and Thought, the Letters of Benammi, Second Series*, p. 55.

[156] *Kerithoth* 6. 9.

his teacher, who taught him wisdom, brings him into the life of the world to come." [157] That most exalted of honours was expected only by the greatest of the Rabbis; but even the elementary school teacher was held in great respect. "Let the fear of thy teacher," it was said, "be to thee as the fear of heaven." [158] The teachers were compared to the prophets through whom God had communicated the truth to Israel.[159] It was said that he who learns from his fellow a single chapter, a single law, a single verse, or even a single letter, ought to pay him honour.[160] There is a Midrash on *Numbers* 24. 6, where "gardens by the riverside" are spoken of. "These are the teachers of the little children in Israel, who bring forth from their hearts wisdom, understanding and discernment, and teach them to do the will of their Father who is in heaven." [161] Maybe the greatest tribute of all to teachers was paid by Rabbi Juḍah the Prince. He visited a certain city and asked to see the watchmen of the city. They brought the city officers and the town guard. "Not these," he said, "but school-teachers are the city's watchmen." [162] In Palestine the elementary school-teacher was no half-despised drudge with a thankless task; he was the servant of God and of the community, held in honour because he was doing the greatest work that a man can do. That is precisely why the Jews not only honoured their teachers so highly, but also asked so much from them, for "only when a teacher is like an angel from heaven will the Torah be sought from his mouth." [163]

It would be easy from one point of view to criticise Jewish education. It would be easy to charge it with narrowness. It would be easy to make much of its neglect of the larger culture, and to find fault with it precisely because it was exclusively religious education. It would be easy to make much of the fact that the

[157] *Baba Metzia* 2. 11.

[158] *Sayings of the Fathers* 4. 15.

[159] *Shabbath* 119b.

[160] *Essays in Jewish Life and Thought, the Letters of Benammi, Second Series*, p. 56.

[161] Quoted in *A Rabbinic Anthology*, selected by C. G. Montefiore and H. Loewe.

[162] *Jer. Hagig.* 1. 7.

[163] *Quoted in Essays in Jewish Life and Thought, the Letters of Benammi, Second Series*, p. 56.

higher it went, and the more developed it became, the more it went lost in the minutiæ of the Law, until it issued in that terrible legalism which crucified Jesus Christ. But for all that at the back of Jewish education there lie two great ideals, which have been picked out by two Jewish writers.

Leo Baeck has pointed out that the very basis of Judaism is to be found in the conception of holiness. "Ye shall be holy for I the Lord your God am holy." "Sanctify yourselves therefore and be ye holy; for I am the Lord your God." "And ye shall be holy unto me: for I the Lord am holy, and have severed you from other people, that ye should be mine."[164] That is to say, *it was the destiny of the Jewish people to be different.* Holiness means difference. And their whole educational system was directed to that end. It has been precisely that educational system which has kept the Jewish race in existence. The Jew is no longer a racial type; he is a person who follows a certain way of life, and who belongs to a certain faith. If Jewish religion had faltered, or altered, the Jews would have ceased to exist. As Leo Baeck put it—the Jew had to be "the great non-conformist," "the great dissenter." First and foremost, the Jewish ideal of education is the ideal of holiness, of difference, of separation from all other peoples in order to belong to God. Their educational system was nothing less than the instrument by which their existence as a nation, and their fulfilment of their destiny, was ensured.[165]

Another Jewish writer, Isidore Epstein, has seized on the other essential Jewish educational ideal. In *Jeremiah* 15. 19 the duty of the servant of God is "to take forth the precious from the vile." So, then, Epstein declares that the ideal of Jewish education is *transformation*, the transformation of the precious into the vile. He writes: "Pedagogy, as Judaism understands it, is a faculty of the righteous man to radiate a warmth of piety and love, capable of melting the crust of ice which surrounds the hearts of egoists, of the aggressive, of transforming them into co-operative, considerate, righteous fellow-beings."[166] Here is the complement of the first ideal. Difference in itself need not be ethical difference; holiness

[164] *Leviticus* 19. 2; 20. 7, 26.

[165] Leo Baeck: *The Essence of Judaism*, pp. 267–8.

[166] Isidore Epstein: *The Jewish Way of Life*, pp. 200, 201.

can simply be ritual and ceremonial difference and separation; but the Jewish ideal is difference wrought out in character, and holiness ethically expressed. The Jewish educational ideal has left its mark deeply upon the world, because in the last analysis it aims to educate the child in order to fit him to be a servant of God; it is education of children for God.

II. *Education in Sparta*

THE OBLITERATION OF THE INDIVIDUAL IN THE SERVICE OF THE STATE

IN NO country in the world was education ever so deliberately planned, controlled, and designed by the state as in Sparta, until the rise of the modern totalitarian state. It was precisely this deliberate design and control of education in Sparta that impressed the ancient thinkers. Aristotle said:

> Sparta appears to be the only, or almost the only, state, in which the law-giver has paid attention to the education and discipline of the citizens; in most states such matters have been entirely neglected, and every man lives as he likes, in Cyclops fashion, "laying down the law for himself and his spouse." [1]

Education in Sparta was deliberately planned, designed and controlled for a definite purpose. Therefore, before we examine the details of that educational system, we must first see what its deliberate purpose was.

Spartan education stems back to a definite and far-reaching change in military technique.[2] In the Homeric days the unit of warfare had always been the great individual hero. The presence or the absence of an Achilles meant the difference between victory and defeat. But military technique had radically altered; and the basis of a battle came no longer to lie in the contest between two individual heroes, but in the encounter of two masses of infantry made up of hoplites. It was therefore no longer the outstanding

[1] Aristotle: *Nicomachean Ethics* 10. 9, 13 (the Cyclops quotation is from Homer: *Odyssey* 9. 114 f.). Cp. Aristotle: *Politics* 8. 1, 3: " One might praise the Spartans in respect of this, for they pay the greatest attention to the training of their children, and conduct it on a public system."

[2] H. I. Marrou: *A History of Education in Antiquity*, pp. 15, 16.

individual who won battles, but the solid mass of ordinary men. It was not now the knight who was all-important; it was the ordinary citizen, fighting not as an individual but as one of a solid mass. So then battles were no longer won by the glamorous and romantic exploits of knightly individuals, but by the corporate courage and endurance of the mass of common men, who were willing to stand and to resist, and if need be to die. As Tyrtaeus has it:

> I should not consider a man worthy to be remembered, nor think highly of him, merely because he was a good runner or wrestler—even though he was as big and strong as the Cyclops, swifter than Boreus the Thracian, more handsome than Titho, richer than Midas or Cinyras, stronger than King Pelops, son of Tantalus, though his speech were softer than Adrastus, and he enjoyed every kind of fame—unless he was also valorous in arms, and could stand fast in battle. . . . That is the true valour, the highest reward that a man can obtain from his fellows. It is a good common to all, a service to the city and the people as a whole, when every man can stand firm on his two feet in the front line, and rid his heart of all idea of flight.[3]

It is no longer the individual glory, but the service of the whole which is the thing that matters. It was on that principle that Spartan education was founded. Plutarch describes the Spartan ideal:

> No man was allowed to live as he pleased, but in their city, as in a military encampment, they always had a prescribed regimen and employment in public service, considering that they belonged entirely to their country, and not to themselves.[4]

He sums up the aim and the achievement of the Spartan curriculum which Lycurgus had worked out:

> In a word, he trained his fellow-citizens to have neither the wish nor the ability to live for themselves; but like bees they were

[3] Tyrtaeus: *Fr.* 12. 1–10; 13–18. [4] Plutarch: *Lycurgus* 24. 1.

to make themselves always integral parts of the whole community, clustering together about their leader, almost beside themselves with enthusiasm and noble ambition to belong wholly to their country.[5]

As we shall see, this was a design which produced a number of results which were anything but lovely; but in itself it was a noble thing, and produced splendid things. At its best it cleansed individual Spartans of all unworthy ambition for personal prestige. Plutarch tells of a certain Pandæretus, who failed to be chosen among the best three hundred men, and who went away, "with a very glad countenance, as if rejoicing that the city had three hundred better men than himself."[6] It was the Spartan custom that the king marched into battle in close company with the man who had been the victor in the games. Plutarch tells of a certain Spartan athlete who refused to be bought off from a contest at Olympia by a very large sum of money, and who after a bitter struggle outwrestled his opponent. Someone said to him: "What advantage, O Spartan, hast thou got from thy victory?" whereat he answered, with a smile: "I shall stand in front of my king when we fight our enemies."[7]

But there was another aspect of this, an aspect of shocking and horrifying savagery and cruelty. The Spartan way of life was based on slavery. The number of Spartan citizens was small. There were never more than from eight to ten thousand of them.[8] The slave population were called the "helots," and they outnumbered the free population many times over. The helots were therefore a constant danger; they had to be kept where they were, or the whole Spartan system would collapse. Aristotle said of the helots that they were "like an enemy constantly sitting in wait for the disasters of the Spartiates."[9] In regard to these helots there were certain very terrible customs, which were nothing less, as we shall go on to see, than an essential part of Spartan education. Whenever the Ephors, the chief magistrates of Sparta, entered into office, they officially declared war against the helots, so that it might be legal

[5] Plutarch: *Lycurgus* 25. 3. [6] Plutarch: *Lycurgus* 25. 3.

[7] Plutarch: *Lycurgus* 22. 4.

[8] Herodotus 7. 234: Aristotle: *Politics* 2. 6. 12.

[9] Aristotle: *Politics* 2. 6. 2.

to do anything at all to them. There was, as Plutarch tells, a custom called the *krupteia*, the Secret Service, which formed an integral part of the training of the young Spartans. The best of the young men were sent out into the country, equipped only with daggers, and enough food for the bare essentials of life. They scattered into the hills and the lonely places, where by day they lay hidden; but by night they came down and slaughtered every helot whom they found. Even by day they would invade the fields where the helots were working, and would slay the strongest and the best of them.[10] Thucydides relates an even more treacherous way of dealing with the helots:

> They made proclamation that all helots who claimed to have rendered the Lacedaimonians the best service in war should be set apart, ostensibly to be free. They were in fact, merely testing them, thinking that those who claimed, each for himself, the first right to be set free would be precisely the men of high spirit who would be the most likely to attack their masters. About two thousand of them were selected, and these put crowns on their heads and made the round of the temples, as though they were already free, but the Spartans not long afterwards made away with them, and nobody ever knew in what way each one perished.[11]

So it can be seen that there was at least a sense in which Spartan education could become education for murder.

There remain two further Spartan characteristics to be fitted into this picture. First, Sparta was the most conservative country which ever existed. The one aim was to keep things as they were. Up to 550 B.C. Sparta developed and progressed. About that time there was a popular uprising which was mercilessly crushed. And

[10] Plutarch: *Lycurgus* 28. 1–4. Plato refers to this custom of secretly sending out the young men, without relating the slaughter of the helots in the *Laws* 633 B. Cp. Isocrates: *Panathenaicus* 271 B (181), "The Ephors have the power to put to death without trial as many as they please, whereas in the other states of Hellas it is a crime against the gods to stain one's hands with the blood of even the basest of slaves."

[11] Thucydides 4. 80.

ever after that the one aim of the Spartan ruling class was to maintain the *status quo*. As Marrou has it: "Sparta voluntarily petrified herself at the stage of development which had made her the leader of progress."[12] Sparta was the one place where the Sophists, the wandering Greek educators, need not try to teach. Hippias agrees with Socrates that he will fare far better in Sicily and at Inycus, "for it is not the inherited usage of the Spartans to change their laws or to educate their children differently from what is customary."[13] That ultra-conservatism could be seen in the simplest things. The man who wished to make a change in the rules of the ball-game was publicly scourged. Terpander had introduced to Sparta long ago the seven-stringed lyre. In the Spartan council-chamber there hung, as a warning against change, the eleven-stringed lyre which Timotheos had brought to Sparta, only to have it publicly smashed, a fate which the nine-stringed lyre of Phrynis shared. What had once been introduced and accepted could not be changed.[14] In Sparta as things were so they must remain. In many ways the educational system of Sparta developed into a petrified anachronism.

The second significant Spartan characteristic was their hatred of strangers. They would neither tolerate strangers within their gates, nor would they permit their own citizens to visit other lands. Plutarch says of Lycurgus:

> He did not permit them to live abroad at their pleasure, and to wander in strange lands, assuming foreign habits and imitating the lives of peoples who were without training and lived under different forms of government. Nay more, he actually drove away from the city the multitudes which streamed in there for no useful purpose, not because he feared that they might become imitators of his form of government and learn useful lessons in virtue . . . but rather that they might not become in any wise teachers of evil.[15]

[12] H. I. Marrou: *A History of Education in Antiquity*, p. 18.

[13] Plato: *Hippias Major* 284 B.

[14] Pausanias 3. 12: quoted K. J. Freeman: *Schools of Hellas*, p. 12.

[15] Plutarch: *Lycurgus* 27. 3. Cp. Xenophon: *Constitution of the Lacedaimonians* 14. 4: "To live abroad was illegal, and I have no doubt that the purpose of these

Sparta had erected the iron curtain, that things might remain as they were.

It is against this background that we must go on to examine in detail the educational system of Sparta, a background of the deliberate obliteration of the individual in the service of the state, a background of the deliberate maintenance of the *status quo*, even if that meant a deliberate policy of domestic murder and of rigid exclusion of all foreign influence.

The truth is that Sparta was organised for war. Aristotle saw this; he writes: "In Sparta and in Crete both the system of education and the mass of the laws are framed in the main with a view to war." [16] It is a most significant fact that Lycurgus laid it down that no Spartan must even engage in a game or in an athletic contest which involved "the stretching forth of the hands," for such a gesture is the gesture of appeal, and that is a gesture that no Spartan might ever make.[17] Sparta was the country where everything in education was organised for war.

For our knowledge of Spartan ways and customs we are mainly indebted to two works. The first is Plutarch's *Life of Lycurgus*. Lycurgus may well be a figure of legend, but he was the king and law-giver to whom the Spartans traced back all their characteristic laws and customs. His place in the laws of Sparta may well be likened to the place of Moses in the laws of Israel. Nor could Lycurgus ever have had a more sympathetic biographer than Plutarch, "genial, garrulous, moral and sensible." [18] Plutarch was born in A.D. 50 when the great days of Greece were but a memory.

---

regulations was to keep the citizens from being demoralised by contact with foreigners." Cp. the speech of Pericles in Thucydides 2. 39. 1, where Pericles claims in deliberate contrast to Sparta: "We throw our city open to all the world."

[16] Aristotle: *Politics* 7. 2. 5. Cp. H. I. Marrou: *A History of Education in Antiquity*, p. 19: "Sparta became an out-and-out military barracks, a city in the hands of a closed military caste that was kept permanently mobilised, entirely absorbed in its threefold task of defence—national, political, social." Cp. A. S. Wilkins: *National Education in Greece*, p. 9: "Sparta was a garrison planted in the midst of enemies, and its laws and habits were those of a garrison."

[17] Plutarch: *Lycurgus* 19. 4.

[18] T. R. Glover: *The Conflict of Religions in the Early Roman Empire*, p. 85.

He was a native of Chæronea, then a little town, but he never left it, and he never grudged to serve his native town, even in the humblest tasks. As Glover tells us, Plutarch says that he was a citizen of a small town, and he did not wish to make it smaller by leaving it.[19] He believed a city to be an organism, like a human being,[20] and he did not think much of the men—like the Stoics—on whom the claims of their native city sat lightly.[21] He was the Telearch of Chæronea, an office which gave him the oversight of the public buildings, and which, in a town that was little more than a village, was a humble task. When men smiled to see him inspecting the measurement of tiles, and the carrying of cement and stones he would say: "It is not for myself, I say, that I am doing this, but for my native place."[22] Plutarch indeed was a man who could well understand the passionate love of Lycurgus for Sparta. Plutarch too was a conservative, a lover of the good old days; and he writes of Sparta as one who admired, and of Lycurgus as one who loved his subject.

Our other principal literary source of information is Xenophon in his *Constitution of the Lacedaimonians.* Xenophon was born about 430 B.C. He was one of the outer circle of the friends of Socrates. He took service in the army of Cyrus, the Persian king, and he will be for ever famous as the leader of the lost thirty thousand in their immortal march to the sea. The Athenians banished him, perhaps because they considered him too friendly with the Spartans. His own two sons were schooled in Sparta.[23] In his banishment the Spartans gave him an estate in Sparta, where he lived. Later he lost the estate, and went to Corinth; and at the end of his life the Athenians withdrew the decree of banishment from him. So Xenophon writes of Sparta at first hand, as one who knew and loved the institutions of that country.[24]

[19] Plutarch: *Demosthenes* 2. [20] Plutarch: *De Sera.*: 15, 559 A.

[21] Plutarch: *De Stoic. rep.* 2. 1033 B.C. [22] Plutarch: *Pol. Præc.* 15, 811 C.

[23] Plutarch: *Agesilaus* 20; Diogenes Laertius 2. 54.

[24] Xenophon's love for and admiration of Sparta appear repeatedly. In the *Memorabilia* when Socrates and the young Pericles are discussing the degeneracy of Athens, Pericles is made to say: "When will the Athenians show the Lacedaimonian reverence for age, seeing that they despise all their elders, beginning with their own fathers? When will they adopt the Lacedaimonian system of

Our information about Sparta therefore comes from one writer who is thoroughly sympathetic, and who had a gift for picking up all kinds of odd and out-of-the-way information; and from another writer, who was a practised historian, a transparently honest man and who had for years lived there himself. It is not necessary to argue that these accounts of Lycurgus are rigidly historically accurate, or that the description of life in Sparta in them is in every detail factually true. No doubt legend has crept in, and no doubt the picture has been idealised. But the fact remains that we are quite safe in using these accounts to draw material from them to construct a picture of the *ideal* of Spartan education; and that we propose to do. But before we do so in detail, it will be well to look briefly at Lycurgus himself, to see what manner of man Spartan and Greek tradition held him to be.

Lycurgus impressed Xenophon as being different from any other ruler. As we have already indicated, there are those who doubt that he ever existed, and who regard him as a purely legendary figure. But he probably did live somewhere in the eighth or ninth century B.C.; and although the reforms connected with his name cannot be dated much before 600 B.C. the Spartans none the less believed that it was Lycurgus who had stamped his name and ideals across all their constitution and all their customs and practices. In any event in a study like this we are dealing with ideals far more than we are dealing with men, and there is a sense in which it is true to say that nothing so well shows a man's ideals as the legends and the stories which gather around his name. Xenophon writes of Lycurgus:

---

training, seeing that they not only neglect to make themselves fit, but mock at those who take the trouble to do so? When will they reach that standard of obedience to their rulers, seeing that they make contempt of rulers a point of honour? Or, when will they obtain that harmony, seeing that, instead of working together for the general good, they are more envious and bitter against one another than against the rest of the world?" (3. 5. 15, 16). In the same work Socrates praises Lycurgus to Hippias: "Lycurgus the Lacedaimonian now—have you realised that he would not have made Sparta to differ from other cities in any respect, had he not established obedience to the laws most securely in her? Among rulers in cities, are you not aware that those who do most to make the citizens obey the laws are best?" (4. 4. 15).

> Lycurgus, who gave them the laws that they obey, and to which they owe their prosperity, I do regard with wonder; and I think that he reached the utmost limit of wisdom. For it was not by imitating other states, but by devising a system utterly different from that of most others, that he made his country pre-eminently prosperous.[25]

What then were the stories which men told about Lycurgus?

The great aim of the Spartan constitution was to build up a compact, unified community, able to defy any threat of war either from without or from within; it was, in other words, to build up a fellowship, and to produce a nation which was " a united band of brothers." When Lycurgus was asked how best an invasion of enemies could be warded off, he answered: " By remaining poor, and by not desiring to be greater the one than the other." And when asked the best way to fortify the city, he answered: " A city will be well fortified which is surrounded by brave men and not by bricks." [26] Everything therefore was designed to produce a fellowship of men. Let us then look at the traditional steps Lycurgus took to effect that object.

The first step was to redistribute the land equally among the citizens, where before there was a " dreadful inequality in this regard."

> Determined therefore to banish insolence and envy and crime and luxury, and those yet more deep-seated and afflictive diseases of the state, poverty and wealth, he persuaded his fellow-citizens to make one parcel of all their territory and divide it up anew, and to live with one another on a basis of entire uniformity and equality in the means of subsistence, seeking pre-eminence through virtue alone, assured that there was no other difference or inequality between man and man than that which was established by blame for base actions, and praise for good ones.[27]

The story went that once, when he had returned from a journey, and saw the land in harvest time, he said: " All Laconia looks like a

[25] Xenophon: *Constitution of the Lacedaimonians* I. 2.

[26] Plutarch: *Lycurgus* 19. 4. [27] Plutarch: *Lycurgus* 8. 2.

family estate divided among many brothers."[28] The basis of division was that the lot assigned to each man was sufficient to produce seventy bushels of barley for a man, and twelve for his wife, together with a proportionate amount of wine and oil, since " they needed sustenance enough to promote vigour and health of body, and nothing else."[29] The basis of everything, then, was a land which had ideally become an estate divided equally among brothers.

The next step was radically to alter the whole theory of money. All gold and silver money was withdrawn, and only iron money was left. Still further, a very small value was assigned to a very great weight of money. Ten *minas* worth of money—that is about £40—required a large storeroom in which to keep it, and a full yoke of oxen to carry it about. The result was that robbery, bribery and financial corruption became practical impossibilities. There was a further result. All luxury goods vanished, for Spartan money was worthless in the rest of Greece, and therefore there could be no imports. Plutarch says:

> It was not possible therefore to buy any foreign wares or bric-à-brac; no merchant seaman brought freight into their harbours; no rhetoric teacher set foot on Laconian soil,[30] no vagabond soothsayer, no keeper of harlots, no gold- or silver-smith, since there was no money there.[31]

The result of this was that money became an irrelevance, and therefore luxury died. A curious result was that the common objects in everyday use became extraordinarily beautiful. Bedsteads, chairs and tables were most excellently made; Spartan drinking cups were world-famous, " since their artisans were now freed from useless tasks, and displayed the beauty of their workmanship in objects of constant and necessary use."[32] Wealth had become " an object of no desire."[33] There remained one possible avenue in which ostentation could be displayed—in the building of a house. But even that was safeguarded against; for it was laid down that " every

[28] Plutarch: *Lycurgus* 8. 4. [29] Plutarch: *Lycurgus* 8. 4.
[30] Cp. Plato: *Hippias Major* 284 D. [31] Plutarch: *Lycurgus* 9. 3.
[32] Plutarch: *Lycurgus* 9. 4, 5. [33] Plutarch: *Lycurgus* 10. 2.

house should have its roof fashioned by the axe, and its doors by the saw only, and by no other tool." Thus elaboration in building was rendered impossible, and luxury inside the house was rendered extremely improbable, if for no other reason than the effect of sheer incongruity it would have produced.[34]

The third step which Lycurgus was said to have taken, to eradicate differences and to establish fellowship, was the introduction of common meals eaten in messes called *pheiditia*.[35] This effectively put an end to all luxury of the table. "The rich man could neither use nor employ nor even see or display his abundant means, when he went to the same meal as the poor man. . . . The rich could not even dine beforehand at home, and then go to the common mess with full stomachs, but the rest kept careful watch of him who did not eat and drink with them, and reviled him as a weakling, and one too effeminate for the common diet."[36] The companies in these messes numbered about fifteen. Each of them had to make a monthly contribution of a bushel of barley meal, eight gallons of wine, five pounds of cheese, two and a half pounds of figs, and a very small sum of money for such "relishes" as flesh or fish. If a man had been sacrificing, or had been hunting, he always sent part of the sacrifice or of the game to the mess.[37] Only supper might be eaten at home; all the other meals had to be eaten in the common mess. So rigid was this rule that once, when King Agis had returned from a victorious expedition against the Athenians, and wished to eat at home with his wife, he sent to the mess for his rations, and they were refused to him.[38] In Sparta gluttony had become an impossibility; the poor man and the rich man ate the same diet, united at the same table.

Such then were the steps which, it was said, Lycurgus took to produce a country in which citizen was bound to citizen in a fellowship in which virtue was the only distinction. And it was precisely here that there entered into the Lacedaimonian constitution the paramount importance of education. The tradition was that Lycurgus prohibited the use of written laws. The laws were not written down; they were implanted in the habits and the training

[34] Plutarch: *Lycurgus* 13. 3–5.
[35] Plutarch: *Lycurgus* 12. 1.
[36] Plutarch: *Lycurgus* 10. 3.
[37] Plutarch: *Lycurgus* 12. 1, 2.
[38] Plutarch: *Lycurgus* 12. 3.

of the citizens. They were " imparted to the young by education which performs the office of a law-giver for every one of them." [39] And therefore the inevitable conclusion followed in that Lycurgus was said to regard education " as the greatest and the noblest task of the law-giver." [40] And to the details of that education we are now in a position to proceed.

It might well be said that the education of a Spartan child began before he was born. In Sparta the marriage relationship was unique. Spartan women had a place in public life which women enjoyed in no other Greek state. " The rest of the Greeks," says Xenophon, " expect their girls to imitate the sedentary life that is typical of the handicraftsmen—to keep quiet and to do wool-work. How then is it to be expected that women so brought up will bear fine children? " [41] But in Sparta the girls underwent the same training as the boys.

> He made the maidens exercise their bodies in running, wrestling, casting the discus, and hurling the javelin, in order that the fruit of their wombs might have vigorous root in vigorous bodies, and come to better maturity, and that they themselves might come with vigour to the fullness of their times, and struggle successfully and easily with the pangs of child-birth.[42]

They wore the same short tunic as the boys did. It is the claim of Plutarch that by these very customs " modesty attended them and wantonness was banished; that the simplicity of their habits gave them an ardent desire for health and beauty of body." Nay more, it gave them a touch of lofty sentiment, " for they felt that they too had a place in the arena of bravery and ambition." [43] The Spartan girl had a share in life and a stake in her country that it was given to no other Greek woman to have.

It was the belief of Lycurgus that motherhood was the most important function of freeborn women.[44] The bachelor was a man under a stigma. The bachelors were forbidden to spectate when the young men and maidens performed their gymnastic and athletic

[39] Plutarch: *Lycurgus* 13. 1. [40] Plutarch: *Lycurgus* 14. 1.
[41] Xenophon: *Constitution of the Lacedaimonians* 1. 3.
[42] Plutarch: *Lycurgus* 14. 2. [43] Plutarch: *Lycurgus* 14. 4.
[44] Xenophon: *Constitution of the Lacedaimonians* 1. 4.

contests and displays. They were compelled to march round the market place, wearing only their tunics, singing a song which condemned themselves; and they were, when they grew older, deprived of the right of respect which was always paid to age.[45]

The marriage customs of Sparta were extraordinary, a queer mixture of almost sentimental romanticness, together with the eugenics of the stud-farm. Marriage was by capture, and the young man carried off his bride by force, when she was in the full bloom of her physical maturity and perfection. The bride's maid then took her, cut off her hair close, clothed her in a man's cloak and a man's sandals, laid her on a straw pallet and left her in the dark. Then the bridegroom slipped stealthily into the room, and after a brief time with his bride went back to the quarters where he lived with the other young men. Nor did this way of visiting happen only once; every visit was paid by stealth, and that only at infrequent intervals. "It was laid down that the bridegroom should be ashamed to be seen entering his wife's room or leaving it," as Xenophon tells; and Plutarch says: "And this they did not for a brief time only, but long enough for some of them to become fathers before they looked upon their own wives by daylight."[46] This self-imposed continence, and this stolen time of sweetness, kept marriage fresh and never left them sated and glutted and weary, with even the passions exhausted. In Plutarch's phrase, "there was always left behind in their hearts some residual spark of mutual longing and delight."[47]

But there were stranger customs than that. It is not strictly true to say that the Spartans practised community of wives. But it is true to say that they sought to set up a system in which all possessiveness and jealousy were eliminated. Both Xenophon and

[45] Plutarch: *Lycurgus* 15. 2. In that passage Plutarch tells an anecdote concerning Dercyllidas, who was a famous general, yet unmarried. He entered a certain company in which none of the younger men would rise and give him a seat, with the respect which age and experience would normally have commanded. One of the younger men said: "Indeed, thou hast begotten no son who will one day give his seat to me." And distinguished though Dercyllidas was, such treatment was considered entirely right, because he was unmarried.

[46] Xenophon: *Constitution of the Lacedaimonians* 1. 5; Plutarch: *Lycurgus* 15. 3–5.

[47] Plutarch: *Lycurgus* 15. 5.

Plutarch quote two practices. If an elderly husband had a handsome and healthy wife, it was natural and proper for him to introduce some virile young man to her, so that she might have children by him. If any man desired to have children by a woman who had proved herself to be a mother of fine sons, he was quite at liberty to do so, always provided her husband consented, and it was the husband's duty so to consent.[48] Lycurgus allowed this for two reasons. "He did not regard sons as the peculiar property of their fathers, but rather as the common property of the state, and therefore would not have his citizens spring from random parentage, but from the best there was." And further, as Lycurgus said: "In the breeding of dogs and horses they insist on having the best sires which money or favour can secure, but they keep their wives under lock and key, demanding that they have children by none but themselves, even though they be foolish, or infirm, or diseased." And the claim was that the whole strange system was so far removed from licentiousness that adultery, in the sense of entering secretly into forbidden relationships, was completely unknown.[49]

So, then, even before he was born the Spartan child belonged to his country; and all his life he continued to do so. "The training of the Spartans," wrote Plutarch, "lasted into the years of full maturity. No man was allowed to live as he pleased, but in their city, as in a military encampment, they always had a prescribed regimen and employment in public service, considering that they belonged entirely to their country and not to themselves."[50] It is literally true to say that Spartan education lasted unbroken from birth until thirty years of age; and it is also literally true to say that education was a whole-time activity, which filled all life. In order to understand the Spartan system, it must be remembered that the Spartan citizens did nothing at all in the nature of what we would call work. Their whole life was devoted to training for the service of the state, and indeed anything else was forbidden. The work was the concern of the slaves and of the helots, and did not enter into the life of the citizen at all. Aristotle laid it down: "Now it is a thing admitted that a state that is to be well governed must be

[48] Xenophon: *Constitution of the Lacedaimonians* 1. 7, 8; Plutarch: *Lycurgus* 15. 6, 7.

[49] Plutarch: *Lycurgus* 15. 8–10.

[50] Plutarch: *Lycurgus* 24. 1.

provided with leisure from menial occupations." [51] Nowhere was that ever carried out in such a total way as in Sparta. Plutarch writes: " One of the noble and blessed privileges which Lycurgus provided for his fellow-citizens was abundance of leisure, for he forbade their engaging in any mechanical art whatsoever." Xenophon writes: " In other states, I suppose, all men make as much money as they can. One is a farmer, another a ship-owner, another a merchant, and others live by different handicrafts. But in Sparta Lycurgus forbade freeborn citizens to have anything to do with business affairs." [52] For the Spartan life was education, for there was nothing else to do than to be educated for and in the service of the state.

The life of the child began with the state's decision as to whether the state had any use for him at all. Plutarch describes what did actually happen:

> Offspring was not reared at the will of the father, but was taken and carried by him to a place called Lesche, where the elders of the tribes officially examined the infant, and, if it was well-built and sturdy, they ordered the father to rear it . . . but, if it was ill-born and deformed, they sent it to the so-called Apothetæ, a chasm-like place at the foot of Mount Taygetus, in the conviction that the life of that which nature had not well equipped at the very beginning for health and strength, was of no advantage either to itself or to the state.[53]

When it had been decided that a child was to be kept, he was bathed in wine, for it was believed that wine so used sent the weakly into convulsions and unconsciousness, but tempered the

[51] Aristotle: *Politics* 2. 6. 2.

[52] Plutarch: *Lycurgus* 24. 1–4; Xenophon: *Constitution of the Lacedaimonians* 7. 1. In the same chapter Plutarch tells the following revealing anecdote. " Therefore it was that one of them who was sojourning at Athens, when the courts were in session, and learned that a certain Athenian had been fined for idleness, and was going home in great distress of mind, and attended on his way by sympathetic and sorrowing friends, begged the bystanders to show him the man who had been fined for living like a freeman."

[53] Plutarch: *Lycurgus* 16. 1. See Appendix A.

body of the strong like steel.[54] And there and then the child's education began. For the first seven years of his life, the child was left at home, under his nurse; but the Spartan nurses were world famous, and were in demand in every country.[55] It was with the nurse that the training began; for "they reared infants without swaddling bands, and this left their limbs and figures free to develop; besides, they taught them to be contented and happy, not dainty about their food, not afraid of the dark, not afraid to be left alone, not given to contemptible peevishness and whimpering." [56] So the nurse nursed the child, even in his earliest days, into physical excellence and into that self-contained courage for which the Spartans were justly famous.

We have seen that no Spartan parent had any private rights in his child. "It was not lawful for every father to rear and train his son as he pleased." [57] It would have been unthinkable for any Spartan to put his child into the charge of a slave, however cultured, as would be done in Athens. So when the child was seven years of age, he came directly under the care of the state. He came under the *Paidonomos*, the Director of Youth, or the Inspector of Boys. He was removed to something very like a boarding-school. There the boys were divided into troops called *ilai* and *agelai*. Even as young as this both obedience and responsibility were taught, for the boy "who excelled in judgment and who was most courageous in fighting" was appointed captain, *bouagor*, troop-leader, and his orders and punishments the others had to obey.[58] Their hair was close-clipped; they were taught to go bare-foot; and to play for the most part naked.[59]

One thing may be noted at this point, although it is true all through the training and the education of the Spartan boy. Every older Spartan citizen was actively engaged in the training of the young. Even in the boy's earliest days, "the elderly men used to watch their sports, and by ever and anon egging them on to mimic battles and disputes, learned accurately how each one of them was naturally disposed, when it was a question of boldness

[54] Plutarch: *Lycurgus* 16. 2.

[55] Alcibiades had a Spartan nurse named Amycla (Plutarch: *Alcibiades* 1. 2).

[56] Plutarch: *Lycurgus* 16. 3.

[57] Plutarch: *Lycurgus* 16. 4.

[58] Plutarch: *Lycurgus* 16. 5.

[59] Plutarch: *Lycurgus* 16. 6.

and aggressiveness in their struggles." As they grew older, "the elderly men kept close watch on them, coming more frequently to their places of exercise, and observing their contests of strength and wit, not cursorily, but with the idea that they were all in a sense the fathers and tutors and governors of all the boys. In this way, at every fitting time, and in every place, the boy who went wrong had some one to admonish him." In the absence of the *Paidonomos* "he gave authority to any citizen who chanced to be present to require them to do anything that he thought right, and to punish them for any misconduct." Xenophon notes it as one of the great differences between Sparta and other states, that in other states a man has control of his own children. But in Sparta "every father has authority over the other men's children as well as his own." And he must rule other children as he would wish his own to be ruled. If a son is whipped by another father, his own father must not resent it, but must himself whip him for the misdeed. In Sparta there was a situation when every father was the father of every child.[60]

When the boy reached the age of twelve, this training was intensified. It was of course under the direction of the *Paidonomos*; but it was actually carried out by the *Eirens*. These *Eirens* were the best of the boys who had finished their training; they had reached the age of twenty; and now they were put in charge of the smaller boys. The *Eiren* was rather like a prefect at a public school. He was in charge of the exercises, and could inflict all necessary punishment; the boys had to find his food and theirs, and they had to serve him with his, tasks being allotted to them in accordance with their strength and their age.[61] The process of strengthening and toughening the boys still went on, but now with more severity.

> When they were twelve years old, they no longer had tunics to wear; they received one cloak a year; they had hard, dry bodies, and knew little of baths and ointments; only on certain days of the year, and few at that, did they indulge in such

[60] Plutarch: *Lycurgus* 16. 5; 17. 1; Xenophon: *Constitution of the Lacedaimonians* 2. 10; 6. 1.

[61] Plutarch: *Lycurgus* 17. 2, 3.

> amenities. They slept together in troops and companies, on pallet-beds, which they collected for themselves, breaking off with their hands—no knives allowed—the tops of the rushes which grew along the river Eurotas. In the wintertime they added to the stuff of these pallets the so-called "lycophon," or thistle-down, which was thought to have warmth in it.[62]

It can be seen already that there was little that was cultural or technical in Spartan education; it was designed to produce a certain kind of physical and mental constitution, a certain kind of character exercised through a certain kind of body. "It was calculated," as Plutarch said, "to make them obey commands well, endure hardships and conquer in battle."[63]

We must now turn to education in the more technical sense of the word.

In the technical sense of the term the Spartans were notoriously uneducated. So far from being a cultured people, they hardly possessed the bare rudiments of education. The basic Greek system of education had three sections.

There was letters. "Of reading and writing," says Plutarch, "they learned only enough to serve their turn."[64] Marrou quotes the unknown author of the *Dissoi Logoi*, who was a Dorian sophist, who had been a pupil of Protagoras, as saying: "The Lacedaimonians consider it a bad thing for children to learn music and reading and writing, whereas the Ionians think it shocking, if they do not know these things."[65] Isocrates declares that the Lacedaimonians are more backward than barbarians. He says that "they have fallen so far behind our common culture and learning that they do not even try to instruct themselves in letters." In the *Panathenaicus* there are many complimentary things said about Sparta; "but they will pay no more attention to what is written in Athens than to what is said beyond the pillars of Hercules." The more intelligent of them may listen to the speech, "if they can find

[62] Plutarch: *Lycurgus* 16. 6, 7.

[63] Plutarch: *Lycurgus* 16. 6. [64] Plutarch: *Lycurgus* 16. 6.

[65] *Dissoi Logoi* 2. 10: quoted H. I. Marrou: *A History of Education in Antiquity*, p. 21.

some one who will read it to them."[66] The cultured Isocrates has his doubts as to whether the Spartans can even read, but there is more of literary snobbery than of accuracy here. In the *Hippias Major* Socrates and the sophist Hippias are speaking about what the Spartans will listen to by way of teaching. Socrates suggests that Hippias might lecture on the stars and the phenomena of the heavens. But Hippias answers that they would not stand it for a moment. Socrates suggests that a course on geometry might suit. But Hippias rejects that on the grounds that the Spartans do not even know how to count.[67] They knew and liked Homer as the best of the poets,[68] and they enjoyed the martial and patriotic poems of Tyrtaeus. They liked to hear about the genealogies of heroes and the foundation of cities and about antiquity in general.[69] There is no doubt that the cultured Athenians exaggerated the barbarity of the Spartans, but it is certainly true that they did reduce culture to a bare minimum. Even Aristotle accuses the Spartans of being "untrained in necessary things."[70]

In music there had been a time in the seventh and sixth centuries when Sparta had been the musical capital of Greece.[71] Among her great musicians were Terpander, and the lyric poets Alcman and Tyrtaeus. The Spartans were still famous for their choral singing. They used their music for three purposes. They used it to keep alive the memory of the past and all its heroes. "Their themes were for the most part praises of men who had died for Sparta, calling them blessed and happy; censure of men who had played the coward, picturing their grievous and ill-starred life."[72] They used it to waken emulation in those of the present. They had a kind of festival of three choirs, at which the three choirs corresponded to the three ages. The choir of old men would sing:

"We once did deeds of prowess, and were strong young men."

The choir of the young men would respond:

"We are so now, and, if you wish, behold and see."

[66] Isocrates: *Panathenaicus* 276 D, 285 C.

[67] Plato: *Hippias Major* 285 C. [68] Plato: *Laws* 630 C.

[69] Plato: *Hippias Major* 285 D. [70] Aristotle: *Politics* 8. 3. 5.

[71] Plutarch: *Mus.* 1134 B: quoted, H. I. Marrou: *A History of Education in Antiquity*, p. 17.

[72] Plutarch: *Lycurgus* 21. 1.

And then the choir of the boys would answer:

"We shall be sometime mightier men by far than both."[73]

And they used it in battle. They went into battle singing marching songs to the accompaniment of the flute. Plutarch has a magnificent description of the Spartans entering battle:

> And when at last they were drawn up in battle array and the enemy was at hand, the king sacrificed the customary she-goat, commanded all the warriors to set garlands on their heads, and ordered the pipers to pipe the strains of the hymn to Castor; then he himself led off in a marching pæan, and it was a sight equally grand and terrifying when they marched in step with the rhythm of the flute, without any gap in their line of battle, and with no confusion in their souls, but calmly and cheerfully moving with the strains of their hymn into the deadly fight.[74]

There was nothing effeminate or voluptuous in Spartan music; it was music used to awaken noble memories of the past, and to inspire to great deeds in the present.

They were equally famous for their dancing; but their dancing was in the main training in unified and co-ordinated movement, which made them able to manœuvre and to fight with precision in battle. They had a famous dance of the Dioscuri, Castor and Pollux, of which Plato approved.[75] Lucian tells of a dance of the Spartan young men in which they danced military and choral dances, moving with precision in serried ranks.[76] From Xenophon we learn that at the Festival of the Gymnopædia there was a combination of gymnastic and mimetic dancing which great numbers of strangers came to see.[77] As with their music, so with their dancing, there was nothing voluptuous or even merely artistic; at the back of it there was preparation for war.

The third great branch of Greek education was gymnastics. Here the Spartans were famous. Between 720 and 576 B.C. eighty-one Olympic victors are known to us; and forty-six were Spartans. In the all-important stadium race twenty-one of the thirty-six

[73] Plutarch: *Lycurgus* 21. 2.

[74] Plutarch: *Lycurgus* 21. 3; 22. 2, 3.

[75] Plato: *Laws* 796 B.

[76] Lucian: *De Salt.* 10, 11.

[77] Xenophon: *Memorabilia* 2. 61.

known champions were Spartans.[78] Spartan gymnastics had certain principles. They would have nothing to do with specialisation; they despised the athlete over-developed in one direction. They were specially famous for boxing and wrestling.[79] Once again the same basic fact emerges; the Spartans did not practise athletics for their own sake; they did not even practise them for the sake of the fame of Olympic victories; they practised them in order that the athlete should be not a better athlete, but a fitter man in order that he might be a better soldier.

This then was technical Spartan education—and it was meagre enough. There was a bare minimum of reading and writing, and a wider culture did not enter into their horizon at all; there was music whose aim was moral far more than æsthetic; there was dancing which was nearer to military movement than to anything else; there were athletics, which indeed produced champions, but which foreswore specialisation for the all-round development, which would make a man a better soldier of his country.

But the real Spartan education was not technical at all; it was education in character; and we must go on now to examine it. The whole Spartan discipline was not aimed at producing scholars; it was aimed at producing men. However they may have failed, the Spartan schools were intended to be schools of manhood. When Agesilaus, the Spartan king, was asked what things boys ought to learn, he answered: "What will be useful to them when they are men."[80] Plutarch tells of a Spartan who met with a defeat in the wrestling-match in the Olympic Games. It was said to him that his adversary had proved himself a better man. "Not a better *man*," he answered, "only a better *thrower*."[81] Quite genuinely the Spartan entered upon athletics, not to vanquish his adversary, but to make *himself* a better man. One of the simplest and the most revealing of all their regulations, mentioned both by Plutarch and Xenophon, is that after an evening spent at the *pheiditia* no Spartan was allowed to use a torch to walk in the dark.[82] The Spartan was

[78] Cp. H. I. Marrou: *A History of Education in Antiquity*, p. 16.

[79] Xenophon: *Constitution of the Lacedaimonians* 4. 6; 6. 9.

[80] Plutarch: *Ap. Lac. Ages.* 67. [81] Plutarch: *Diaph. Apoph.* 69.

[82] Plutarch: *Lycurgus* 12. 7; Xenophon: *The Constitution of the Lacedaimonians* 5. 4.

a man who was not afraid of the dark. No non-Spartan can ever have known Sparta better than Xenophon for Xenophon spent years as a resident in Sparta; and Xenophon writes of the kind of boy that Lycurgus wished to produce:

> Moreover wishing modesty to be firmly rooted in them, he required them to keep their hands under their cloaks, to walk in silence, not to look about them, but to fix their eyes on the ground. . . . You would expect a stone image to utter a sound sooner than these lads; you would sooner attract the attention of a bronze figure; you might think them more modest than even a young bride in the bridal-chamber.[83]

The Spartan aim was to produce a certain kind of character in which courage and modesty were disciplined into a harmonious whole. Let us then see the various elements which were used to build up such a character.

At a very early stage in life the Spartans laid responsibility on their boys and demanded disciplined obedience from them. Even the seven-year-olds had their *bouagor*, their pack leader; and after the age of twelve the lads were trained and commanded by the Eiren, who was himself a lad of twenty who had distinguished himself in leadership. To these leaders obedience was due, and punishment was inflicted if it was not forthcoming. From the beginning the Spartans trained their young people in the acceptance of responsibility and the acceptance of discipline, and by so doing they were laying a good foundation for manhood.

It is not to be thought that the Spartan lads were enveloped in a constant shy silence. Part of their training was training in expressing sound judgments in concise language. Plutarch describes the Eiren with his circle of boys after supper. One of the boys would have to sing a song to entertain the company. To another a question would be put: " Who is the best man in the city? " or, " What do you think of that man's conduct? " An answer had to be given, which was both reasonable and concisely expressed. The punishment for failing to give such an answer was a bite in

[83] Xenophon: *The Constitution of the Lacedaimonians* 3. 4, 5.

the thumb from the Eiren![84] Thus the boys were taught to use a way of speaking "which combined pungency with grace and condensed much observation into a few words. . . . For as sexual incontinence generally produces unfruitfulness and sterility, so intemperance in talking makes discourse empty and vapid."[85] "It was never their wont," says Plutarch, "to talk at random, or to let slip a speech which had not some thought or other worth serious attention."[86] To this day we use the word *laconic* to describe speech which is brief and pungent; and in that kind of speech the Spartan boy was taught and encouraged to express himself.

The Spartan boy was educated into a kind of universal endurance of body and of mind. His diet was of the most meagre; the idea was to make him slim and tall, and to enable him some day to endure a campaign when the rations were short. A Spartan boy must have spent most of his life hungry.[87] The boy was initiated into a kind of mental endurance also. As we have already seen, the boys were sometimes brought as guests to the *pheiditia* or messes. They would listen to discussions about things which mattered. "There they themselves became accustomed to sport and jest without scurrility, and to endure jesting without displeasure." Indeed it seems to have been especially characteristic of a Spartan to endure jesting.[88] The picture is that of a lad, who, in the modern phrase, had physically and mentally learned to take it.

The Spartan lad was trained in initiative. We have already referred to what was called the *krupteia*, the secret service. According to Plutarch the lads were let loose on the country, and attacked and slaughtered the helots chiefly by night, but also by day.[89] Even for Sparta that seems a most improbable custom. It is much more

[84] Plutarch: *Lycurgus* 18. 2, 3. [85] Plutarch: *Lycurgus* 19. 1.

[86] Plutarch: *Lycurgus* 20. 5. Plutarch gives a selection of epigrammatic Spartan sayings. "Men of few words," said Charilaus, "need few laws." When Hecatæus, the sophist, had been a guest in a public mess, and had kept silence, he was criticised by some, but Archidamidas said: "He who knows how, knows also when to speak." (Plutarch: *Lycurgus* 19. 3–20. 6.)

[87] Plutarch: *Lycurgus* 17. 4; Xenophon: *The Constitution of the Lacedaimonians* 2. 5, 6.

[88] Plutarch: *Lycurgus* 12. 4. But Plutarch goes on to say: "But if anyone could not bear up under it, he had only to ask it, and the jester ceased."

[89] Plutarch: *Lycurgus* 28. 2, 3.

likely that in the *krupteia* the lads were sent out into the country with the minimum of provisions, to live off the land, and to get from place to place on their own initiative, just as the modern soldier is trained to do. That is the more likely, since in Plato's *Laws* Megillus, the Spartan, describes the *krupteia* without any mention of the slaughter of the helots: "The *krupteia*, as it is called, affords a wonderfully severe training in hardihood, as the men go barefoot in winter and sleep without coverlets and have no attendants, but wait on themselves, and rove through the whole countryside by night and by day."[90] The lads were trained to initiative and independence by being sent out in all kinds of weathers to support themselves.

There is then much on the credit side of the picture, but there is another side to all this. Not only were the boys trained in initiative; they were also trained in cunning, and in actual theft. As we have seen, the boys must always have been hungry, and both Plutarch and Xenophon tell how they were encouraged—indeed it was part of their training—to steal their food. And, if they were discovered, they not only remained hungry, but received a severe flogging for their inefficiency.[91] The boys would go to any length

[90] Plato: *Laws* 633 B.C.

[91] Plutarch: *Lycurgus* 17. 3, 4: "They steal what they fetch (when the *eiren* sent them out to get food for the common meals), some of them entering the gardens, and others creeping right slyly and cautiously into the public messes of the men. . . . They steal too whatever food they can, and learn to be adept in setting upon people when asleep or off their guard. But the boy who is caught gets a flogging and must go hungry. For the meals allowed them are scanty, in order that they may take into their own hands the fight against hunger, and so be forced into boldness and cunning." Xenophon: *The Constitution of the Lacedaimonians* 2. 6–9 reports the same practice, stressing its use as a training for war. "Obviously a man who intends to take to thieving must spend sleepless nights, and play the deceiver, and lie in ambush by day, and moreover, if he means to make a capture, he must have spies ready. There can be no doubt then that all this education was planned by him in order to make the boys more resourceful in getting supplies, and better fighting men." Isocrates refers with contempt to this custom in the *Panathenaicus* 277: "Every day they send out their boys, from the very cradle, as it were, with such companions as each may prefer, ostensibly to hunt, but in reality to steal the property of the people who live in the country. In this practice those who are caught are punished with fines and with blows, while those who have accomplished the greatest number of thefts

to escape detection, and it is indeed from this very custom that one of the most famous Spartan stories comes. Plutarch tells us that one of them was carrying under his cloak a young fox which he had stolen; and rather than allow his theft to be detected he allowed the animal " to tear out his bowels with its teeth and claws," and so died.[92] Here indeed was a curious part of the education of the Spartan boy. Training in theft is indeed an educational oddity; but, as in everything in the Spartan system, it is to be explained by the fact that the whole system was designed for successful warfare. It is that very fact which must have saved this custom from having a ruinous effect on the character of the boys. It looks like a deliberate attempt to raise a race of juvenile delinquents; it did not in fact turn out like that, because of its military intention.

There is still worse to come. There were two Spartan customs which cannot have been anything else than brutalising. It was the charge of Aristotle that Spartan training made the boys *thēriodēs*, like wild beasts.[93] There was organised flogging. At a certain time of the year there was a kind of competition in flogging at the altar of Artemis Ortheia. The young men deliberately submitted to flogging. No matter what the pain they uttered never a groan; Plutarch

---

and have been able to escape detection enjoy a higher esteem among their fellow youths than the others, and when they attain to manhood, provided they remain true to the ways they have practised in youth, they are in line for the most important offices."

[92] Plutarch: *Lycurgus* 18. 1. Aulus Gellius also knew of this training in theft. He reports that, " Among the Spartans thieving was lawful and customary, and it was practised by their young men, not for base gain or to furnish means for indulgence, or amassing wealth, but as an exercise and training in the art of war; for dexterity and practice in thieving made the minds of the youth keen and strong for clever ambuscades, and for endurance in watching, and for the swiftness of surprise." (*The Attic Nights*, 11. 18. 17.) It is of interest to note that, when Xenophon was commanding the Thirty Thousand on their march to the sea, if he had a difficult and dangerous reconnaissance duty to assign, he assigned it to a Spartan, trained in this way. This Xenophon passage also implies that the law laid down definite limits in regard to what could and could not be stolen by the boys (*Anabasis* 4. 6. 14, 15).

[93] Aristotle: *Politics* 8. 3. 3.

says that he saw some of them dying under the lash with never a word.[94] This lasted down to the time of Cicero and even of Pausanias. The lad who bore most without a murmur was called the *bōmonikēs*, and an inscription was erected in his honour.[95] Lucian, in the *Anacharsis* (38) tells how in the imaginary dialogue Solon counsels Anacharsis, the Scythian, not to laugh at the customs of the Spartans, if he goes there:

> Above all, do not laugh if you see them getting flogged at the altar and dripping blood while their fathers and mothers stand by and are so far from being distressed by what is going on that they actually threaten to punish them if they should not bear up under the stripes, and beseech them to endure the pain as long as possible and be staunch under the torture. As a matter of fact, many have died in the competition, not deigning to give in under the eyes of their kinsmen while they still had life in them, or even to move a muscle of their bodies; you will see honours paid to their statues, which have been set up at public cost by the state of Sparta.

This is done that those who are destined to preserve their country should be tremendously staunch and superior to every fear. If a man trained like that was captured in war, nothing would make him betray any secret to the enemy. He would laugh at the torturers, and take his flogging, matching himself against the flogger to see who would first give in. That indeed must have been a brutalising experience.

The second of these brutalising customs was deliberate fighting in mimic battles of the utmost savagery. In Plato's *Laws* Megillus, the Spartan, tells how the Spartan lads are trained in "hardy endurance of pain in manual contests."[96] This was much more than simply straightforward fighting. It was deliberately induced and fomented savagery. Cicero tells how he saw companies of youths in Sparta fighting with incredible fierceness, kicking with their heels, hitting with their fists, scratching with their nails, biting with their teeth, and actually dying rather than confess themselves

[94] Plutarch: *Lycurgus* 18. 1. Cp. Pausanias 3. 16. 6, 7; Cicero: *Tusc. Dis* 2. 34.

[95] Cp. K. J. Freeman: *Schools of Hellas*, p. 29. [96] Plato: *Laws* 633 B.

vanquished.[97] Pausanias adds further grim details, and tells how they fought with their hands, leaped on each other with their heels, bit each other, and dug out each other's eyes.[98] Here we see training for war at its worst. To produce good soldiers like that was to produce them at too high a cost.

Here then is the Spartan ideal of education. It had great values. It made the state a real family; it taught devotion to that family; it produced physical fitness; it inculcated discipline, obedience, courage; it made it well-nigh impossible for the sins of gluttony, of avarice, and of luxury to flourish. But the fact remains that basically it was a failure, and essentially it was wrong. What then were its fundamental mistakes?

It was an education which was based on war. In Plato's *Laws* the Athenian stranger says: "It was with a special view to war that Lycurgus laid down all the legal usages in Sparta."[99] As K. J. Freeman put it: "Every one at Sparta was a part of a beautifully organised machine, designed almost exclusively for military purposes."[100] That was exactly the charge of Aristotle, when he said that in Sparta and in Crete both the system of education and the mass of the laws were framed in the main with a view to war.[101] It is, therefore, true to say, that, however active Spartan education looked, it was none the less, education, and even civilisation, based on idleness. A man either fought, or prepared to fight, or did nothing. It was a way of life in which there was literally no future. War must in the nature of things be an emergency; it must be the abnormal state of affairs; and just because the Spartan trained and prepared for nothing but war there was no such thing as routine life. It was an education and a civilisation doomed to extinction for that, if for no other, reason.

Because it was an education which was based on war, it was ultimately a brutalising education. When Aristotle is thinking about Spartan education, and when in his mind there is the battle-training that was normal for the Spartan youth, he says: "Honour and not animal ferocity should play the first part (in education); for it is not a wolf or one of the wild animals that will venture upon

[97] Cicero: *Tusc. Disp.* 5. 27. 27. [98] Pausanias 3. 14. 8.
[99] Plato: *Laws* 630 D. [100] K. J. Freeman: *Schools of Hellas*, p. 12.
[101] Aristotle: *Politics* 7. 2. 5.

any noble hazard, but rather a good man."[102] Aristotle saw the Spartan training in the end producing wolves instead of men. Marrou has it: "The Spartan ideal is the ideal of a barrack-room sergeant-major."[103] The very stress on obedience and on discipline brought the charge to Sparta, even among her contemporaries, that Spartans knew how to obey, but not to command.[104] Essentially Spartan education was the elimination of personality, and the obliteration of the individual.

Spartan education was the education of the "iron curtain." It was the fact that Sparta was an armed garrison that dominated everything. A. S. Wilkins writes: "It cannot be doubted that the Dorians of Sparta carried on for years, and it may be for generations, a kind of *epiteichismos*—an erecting of fortified walls—against the surrounding Achæan towns."[105] No Spartan might leave Sparta without special permission under penalty of death; no stranger was welcome within Sparta. This extraordinary Spartan life and education could only go on, so long as an iron curtain was erected against the world.[106] One of the tragedies of ancient history was that when Spartan leaders and generals were taken out of Sparta and faced with the wider world, again and again their whole moral fibre collapsed.[107] Any civilisation which depends on the protection of an iron curtain is essentially artificial and insecure, and cannot permanently last.

Finally, Spartan education and civilisation were based on slavery. Never was there such a clear differentiation between the privileged few and the unprivileged many. "In Sparta," said Plutarch, "the

[102] Aristotle: *Politics* 8. 3. 5.

[103] H. I. Marrou: *A History of Education in Antiquity*, p. 24.

[104] Plutarch: *Lycurgus* 30. 3. Plutarch himself does not agree with this criticism.

[105] A. S. Wilkins: *National Education in Greece*, p. 9.

[106] "The Spartan discipline was only possible so long as all the citizens subjected to it were kept in narrow isolation from the rest of Hellas" (A. S. Wilkins: *National Education in Greece*, pp. 58, 59).

[107] "The obedience to the law which had been inculcated in the vale of Eurotas was forgotten as soon as the Spartan generals passed into a wider field; the simplicity and scorn of luxury, which the whole of their training had been intended to produce, was changed into a venality and greed for gold almost unparalleled." A. S. Wilkins: *National Education in Greece*, p. 42.

freeman is more of a freeman than anywhere else in the world, and the slave more of a slave." [108] It is impossible to speak with any certainty about the size of the population of Sparta, and about the proportion of the various elements within it, but the estimate of A. S. Wilkins is that there were in Sparta about nine thousand families of citizens; there were about thirty thousand *perioikoi*, or resident-aliens; and there were about a quarter of a million helots,[109]; and everything existed for the sake of the nine thousand. No civilisation so based can last. It is quite certain that sooner or later the privileged will degenerate and the under-privileged will rise. In any civilisation like that there is a tension which will sooner or later become intolerable, and a volcano which will sooner or later erupt. That indeed is why Spartan education has left little permanent mark on western civilisation; and it is of the greatest interest to compare and contrast the ideal of Jewish education, which has left so great a mark. Isidore Epstein writes of the sheer democracy of Jewish education. "The Law belongs to all Israel; it is the inalienable patrimony of every child, irrespective of social status or position. . . . An attempt to monopolise knowledge would be inimical to the idea of a Jewish mission. . . . It is a democratic mission, and against any tendency towards forming an exclusive class, which finally degenerates into an oligarchy or a gang." [110] No system which is designed to enable a small minority to possess everything and to compel a large majority to possess nothing can possibly last.

Spartan education failed, because it made the fundamental mistake of working on the assumption that man is the exclusive property of the state, and that therefore he has neither any individual rights of his own, or in the last analysis, any duty to God. Spartan education failed because basically it was founded on an impossible doctrine of man.

[108] Plutarch: *Lycurgus* 28. 5.

[109] A. S. Wilkins: *National Education in Greece*, pp. 11, 12.

[110] Isidore Epstein: *The Jewish Way of Life*, p. 202.

III. *Education Among the Athenians*

THE TRAINING OF THE INDIVIDUAL IN THE SERVICE OF CULTURE

THE GREEKS never doubted the essential character of education. " Education," said Heraclitus, " is a second sun to its possessors "; and that saying, as Kathleen Freeman reminds us, is the first recorded mention of education attributed to a Greek philosopher.[1] Antiphon writes:

> The first thing, I believe, for mankind is education. Whenever anyone does the beginning of anything correctly, it is likely also that the end will be right. As one sows, so can one expect to reap. If in a young body one sows a noble education, this lives and flourishes through the whole of his life, and neither rain nor drought destroy it.[2]

There are two incidents in history which vividly show the importance which the Greeks attached to education. Under the threat of Xerxes the Athenians decided to evacuate their women and their children. Most of them went to Troezen. " They were received," Plutarch tells us, " with eager good-will by the Troezenians, who passed a vote that they should be maintained at the public charge, by a daily payment of two obols to everyone, and leave be given to the children to gather fruit where they pleased, and schoolmasters paid to instruct them." [3] Schooling was an essential thing even in the life of a refugee, and must be provided as one of the necessaries of life. Ælian tells us that when the people of Mitylene ruled the

[1] Kathleen Freeman: *God, Man, and State, Greek Concepts*, p. 170.
[2] Kathleen Freeman: *God, Man, and State, Greek Concepts*, p. 180.
[3] Plutarch: *Themistocles* 10.

sea, the penalty they laid on any of their allies who revolted was that they forbade their children to be taught letters or music, for they believed that the heaviest penalty which could be inflicted was to condemn people to a life without music and without letters.[4] To the Greek education was the birthright of the child, and an essential part of anything which could be called civilisation.

But one thing must be clearly remembered. For the Athenian education was never technical education. It was never education in the sense of teaching a young person to make a living. As K. J. Freeman put it: "To do anything to extract money was vulgar and ungentlemanly."[5] Anything which was aimed at making money, anything which was designed to enable a man to follow a trade or a profession for the Greek was not education at all. Greek civilisation was founded on slavery, and in Greek life the tradesman was always despised. So much so was this the case that there were many who believed that no tradesman should ever be allowed to be a citizen. The Greek ideal was unlimited leisure, in which unlimited culture could be acquired. Sir H. Idris Bell relates an incident from the life of Sir Arthur Pickard-Cambridge. When Sir Arthur was Vice-Chancellor of Sheffield University, he applied to the town council for a subvention towards the augmentation of the classical library. One of the councillors, whom he approached, replied: "If you can explain to me how a boy is helped by learning Latin and Greek, I am prepared to support you." "Well," said Pickard-Cambridge, "I can't say that learning Latin and Greek will help a boy to earn five shillings a week more, but I am sure that it ought to make him a better man." "My idea of a better man," was the reply, "*is* a man who earns five shillings a week more."[6] That councillor's view was the exact and precise opposite of the Greek ideal of education.

Herodotus knew well the objection to trade, though he held it to be of foreign origin. He writes:

[4] Aelian: *Var. Hist.* 7. 15.

[5] K. J. Freeman: *Schools of Hellas*, p. 43. Cp. Plato: *Protagoras* 312 B: "When you took your lessons from each of these (the language-master, the harp-teacher, and the sports-master) it was not in the technical way with a view to becoming a professional, but for education, as befits a private gentleman."

[6] H. Idris Bell: *The Crisis of our Time and Other Papers*, pp. 68, 69.

> I know that in Thrace and Scythia and Persia and Lydia and nearly all foreign countries those who learn trades are held in less esteem than the rest of the people, and those who have least to do with artisan's work, especially men who are free to practise the art of war, are highly honoured. Thus much is certain, that this opinion, which is held by all the Greeks, and chiefly by the Lacedaimonians, is of foreign origin. It is in Corinth that artisans are held in least contempt.[7]

This is a point of view which the greatest voices in Greek literature are always stating. In the *Laws* Plato puts his own view-point into the mouth of the Athenian stranger:

> At present, when censuring or commending a man's upbringing, we describe one man as educated, and another as uneducated, though the other may often be uncommonly well educated in the trade of a pedlar or skipper or some other similar education. . . . The education we speak of is training from childhood in goodness, which makes a man eagerly desirous of becoming a perfect citizen, understanding how both to rule and to be ruled righteously. This is the special form of nurture to which, as I suppose, our present argument would confine the term " education "; whereas an upbringing which aims only at money-making, or physical strength, or even some mental accomplishment devoid of reason and justice, it would term vulgar and illiberal and utterly unworthy of the name " education."[8]

Later in the same work Plato lays it down: " No resident citizen shall be numbered among those who engage in technical crafts."[9] The whole conception of education as something which enables a man to develop crafts and skills and abilities which will enable him to pay his way and to make a living is quite foreign to the thought of Plato. To him any alliance between trade and citizenship is inconceivable. This comes out very clearly and definitely in the regulations for the education of the Guardians in the *Republic*. The Guardian is the defender of the state. The Guardian must be

[7] Herodotus 2. 167.

[8] Plato: *Laws* 643 E, 644 A. [9] Plato: *Laws* 846 D.

"soldier and philosopher." The Guardians will therefore learn mathematics. But they must be induced to approach it, not in an amateur spirit, but perseveringly, until, by the aid of pure thought, they come to see the real nature of numbers. They are to practise calculation, not like merchants and shopkeepers for purposes of buying and selling, but with a view to war and to help in the conversion of the soul itself from the world of becoming to truth and reality.[10] The last reason on earth for which mathematics is to be learned is to cast up accounts. It is to be learned as a pure science for the good of a man's soul.

Even the practical-minded Xenophon has the same ideas. In the *Œconomicus* he depicts Socrates talking to Critobulus about what he calls the "illiberal arts," what we would call the trades and crafts:

> Very good, Critobulus; for, to be sure, the illiberal arts, as they are called, are spoken against, and are, naturally enough, held in utter disdain in our states. For they spoil the bodies of the workmen and the foremen, forcing them to sit still and live indoors, and in some cases to spend the day at the fire. The softening of the body involves a serious weakening of the mind. Moreover, these so-called illiberal arts leave no spare time for attention to one's friends and city, so that those who follow them are reputed to be bad at dealing with friends and bad defenders of their country. In fact, in some of the states, and especially in those reputed warlike, it is not even lawful for any of the citizens to work at illiberal arts.[11]

Here is the same point of view, the point of view which simply cannot see how a person engaged in any kind of trade can either be educated, or have any claims to citizenship, or even be able to perform the duties of a citizen.

Even Aristotle, who has much more common sense than Plato has, has the same point of view. He says, we might translate it: "To seek for usefulness everywhere is entirely unsuited to a gentleman."[12] He agrees that there are certain useful arts and crafts and

[10] Plato: *Republic* 525 C.

[11] Xenophon: *Œconomicus* 4. 2, 3.

[12] Aristotle: *Politics* 8. 3. 2.

abilities which the young person must be taught, for, after all, life must go on, but always with the greatest care. They must never participate in any of the useful arts which render a person vulgar (*banausos*). " A task, and also an art or a science, must be deemed vulgar, if it renders the body or soul or mind of free men useless for the employments and actions of virtue. Hence we entitle vulgar all such arts as deteriorate the body, and also all the industries which earn wages, for they make the mind preoccupied and degraded." [13] If this is true, then leisure becomes the most important of all things; it is in fact more desirable and more of an end than business.[14] He goes on to conclude that education is given, not because it is either useful or necessary, but because it is liberal and noble.[15] He takes two illustrations. Music is included in education. It is not a necessity, for there is nothing necessary about it; it is not useful, in the way that reading and writing and household management are useful; it is not useful in the sense that gymnastics are useful for health and fitness. It is of no practical use whatever, and yet in spite of that—or even because of that—it is an essential part of education.[16] Aristotle would include drawing in primary education; not that people may be saved from going wrong in making private purchases, and not that they may avoid being cheated in buying furniture, or in selling it, but " because this study makes a man observant of bodily beauty." [17] The test of utility is anathema to the cultured Greeks; anything that is learned to be used for practical purposes is not education; anything which enables a man to make money is necessarily an ungentlemanly thing; and anyone engaged in making money is *ipso facto* unfit to be a citizen.

One would have thought that this Greek attitude to practical knowledge would have been unintelligible to a practical Roman; and, as we shall go on to see,[18] the main stream of Roman thought did think music valuable only as it helped the delivery of the orator, and geometry to be learned only in so far as it enabled lawyers to settle the boundaries of estates. But it sometimes happens that a convert can state the new outlook which he has learned with even more precision than those from whom he learned it. And

[13] Aristotle: *Politics* 8. 2. 1.
[14] Aristotle: *Politics* 8. 2. 4.
[15] Aristotle: *Politics* 8. 3. 1.
[16] Aristotle: *Politics* 8. 2. 6.
[17] Aristotle: *Politics* 8. 3. 2.
[18] See pp. 188, 189.

this point of view can be found in the Roman writers. Quintilian, near the end of the first book of the *Institutio Oratoria*, says primly: "I trust there is not even one among my readers who would think of calculating the monetary value of such studies."[19] Cicero, in *De Officiis* has a detailed discussion of all this, which might have been written by a full-blown Victorian snob. It is worth while quoting it in full:

> Now in regard to trades and other means of livelihood, which ones are to be considered becoming to a gentleman and which ones are vulgar, we have been taught, in general, as follows. First, those means of livelihood are rejected as undesirable which incur people's ill-will, as those of tax-gatherers and usurers. Unbecoming to a gentleman, too, and vulgar are the means of livelihood of all hired workmen whom we pay for mere manual labour, not for artistic skill; for in their case the very wage they receive is the pledge of their slavery. Vulgar we must consider those also who buy from wholesale merchants to retail immediately; for they would get no profits without a great deal of downright lying: and verily there is no action which is meaner than misrepresentation. And all mechanics are engaged in vulgar trades; for no workshop can have anything liberal about it. Least respectable of all are those trades which cater for sensual pleasures:
>
> Fishmongers, butchers, cooks, and poulterers,
> And fishermen,
>
> as Terence says. Add to these, if you please, the perfumers, dancers, and the whole *corps de ballet*.
>
> But the professions in which either a higher degree of intelligence is required, or from which no small benefit to society is derived—medicine and architecture, for example, and teaching—these are proper for those whose social position they become. Trade, if it is on a small scale, is to be considered vulgar; but if wholesale and on a large scale, importing large quantities from all parts of the world and distributing to many without misrepresentation, is not to be greatly disparaged. Nay, it even

[19] Quintilian: *Institutio Oratoria* I. 12. 17.

> seems to deserve the highest respect, if those engaged in it, satiated, or rather, I should say, satisfied with the fortunes they have made, make their way from the port to a country estate, as they have often made it from the sea into port. But of all the occupations by which gain is secured, none is more profitable, none more delightful, none more becoming to a freeman, none better than agriculture.[20]

There again all trade is condemned, unless it be on a big enough scale to end up with a country estate, or unless it works on the farm.

If, then, education is not for the amassing of knowledge—and long ago Heraclitus had correctly said, " Polymathy does not give a man sense " [21]—and if education has nothing to do with teaching a man to learn a trade, and to make a living, what is it for? At the widest it may be said that education among the Athenians was education for culture. " To a Hellene education meant the training of character and taste, and the symmetrical development of body, mind and imagination." [22] To put it in a more definite way, and to fit it into a historical situation, in Athens education was designed to produce an Athenian. It was designed to produce an Athenian citizen. As T. R. Glover wrote: " The work of the Greek is, above all things, the discovery of the individual." [23] The aim of Athenian education was to produce Athenians, who loved beauty and who loved Athens, and who were prepared to serve Athens in peace and in war. It was a great ideal. Paul Monroe points out that from the very beginning of Greek history, right back to the days of the *Iliad* and the *Odyssey* there had always been a twofold ideal of Greek education. On the one hand there was the man of valour, typified by Achilles, and on the other side there was the man of wisdom, typified by Odysseus.[24] But in the Athenian ideal these two ideals were united, and, at its highest, the Athenian ideal united these two ideals and sought to produce the man, who, at one and the same time, was the philosopher and the man of action. Dr. Johnson dismissed the Athenians as ignorant barbarians, but Mac-

[20] Cicero: *De Officiis* I. 42. 150, 151. [21] Bywater: *Heraclitus* fragment 16.

[22] K. J. Freeman: *Schools of Hellas*, p. 43.

[23] T. R. Glover: *The World of the New Testament*, p. 18.

[24] Paul Monroe: *Source Book of the History of Education*, p. 2.

aulay in his *Essay on the Athenian Orators* put the matter in a truer light, when he said that for an Athenian "to be a citizen was to be a legislator—a judge,—one upon whose voice might depend the fate of the wealthiest tributary state, of the most important public man." [25]

In one place above all this Athenian ideal comes most nobly to light, in the funeral oration of Pericles over the Athenian dead.[26] There Pericles praises the institutions which brought greatness to Athens (2. 36. 4). Athens is a city sufficient for every claim that peace or war can make upon it (2. 36. 3). She has imitated none, and she is a pattern for all to follow (2. 37. 1). She is a true democracy in which merit alone is supreme, and in which neither class nor poverty is any barrier to greatness in service (2. 37. 1). In her there is perfect personal liberty, in which a man can follow his own ways and desires, and yet that liberty never becomes anarchy for there is reverent fear, and a deep-seated respect for the unwritten laws which are the greatest of all laws (2. 37. 2). She knows how to relax in her games, and in her sacrifices, and in homes where there is always taste and elegance (2. 38. 1). It is characteristic of Athens that in her the stranger is welcome and that she is open to all. She does not need to fear that any alien can spy out her stratagems; she does not have prearranged plans and schemes and systems, for she depends on "the courage which springs from our souls, when we are called to action" (2. 39. 1); for in her education is not a barbarous and tyrannical discipline, but something which equips a man to meet any hazard which presents itself. In Athens ease and courage are combined (2. 39. 4). Her people are lovers of beauty without extravagance. It was Plato who held that the most effective kind of education is that a child should play amongst lovely things.[27] In Athens wealth is not a matter for boasting, but a challenge to action to fit its privilege. It was Aristotle who was to draw the picture of the vulgar man, as distinct from the great-souled man, who in his vulgarity makes a tasteless display of wealth on unimportant occasions, who gives a dinner party in his club on the scale of a wedding-feast, who clothes a chorus in purple, who spends little when he ought to spend much, and much when

[25] Quoted A. S. Wilkins: *National Education in Greece*, p. 91.

[26] *Thucydides* 2. 35–46. [27] Plato: *Republic* 558 B.

he ought to spend little.[28] But in Athens wealth is not a reason for ostentation but a challenge to service, while honest poverty is no shame, if it comes unavoidably upon a man (2. 40. 1). In Athens a man is prepared to serve in public affairs. Such affairs are discussed by the whole democracy, and are settled by democratic decision; and therefore in Athens action always follows reflection, and is taken in a full knowledge of the issues involved (2. 40. 3). Athens is generous to all, and not with any calculating generosity, whose only object in giving is some day to get back (2. 40. 4, 5). In Athens there is an amazing versatility in the ordinary man. The Athenians are no race of narrow specialists, but " each individual amongst us could in his own person, with the utmost grace and versatility, prove himself self-sufficient in the most varied forms of activity " (2. 41. 1). Therefore, says Pericles, the duty of every Athenian is to become a lover of Athens and to walk with his eyes fixed upon her (2. 43. 1). It is indeed a noble picture; and this was the aim and end of Athenian education. It aimed not to produce Athenian scholars, and certainly not to produce Athenian tradesmen, but to produce Athenian men. If the Athenian was truly taking advantage of his own educational ideal, he would be indeed obeying the advice of Plotinus: " Be always at work carving your own statue." [29]

Herein was not so much what we would call education in the technical sense of the term, but initiation into a way of life. We shall understand some of that way of life better, if we see some of the simple things which it involved, and if we listen to some of the laments for it, in the days when the greatest men felt that it was passing away.[30] It is the very unexpected simplicity of the demands which show the kind of life that Athenian education sought to produce. Hesiod in the *Works and Days* [31] lays down some of these rules of conduct, simple things, yet with the sanctions of the gods behind them. A man must never be taunted with his poverty, for the gods send it. Good men must never be slandered; a guest must never be boorish at a meal where all contribute; " nor at a feast of the gods cut the withered from the quick from off the five-branched with gleaming iron," that is to say, a man must not cut

[28] Aristotle: *Nicomachean Ethics* 4. 2. 20.

[29] Plotinus: *Enn.* 1. 6. 9.

[30] T. R. Glover: *Greek Byways*, pp. 160 ff.

[31] Hesiod: *Works and Days*, 706–64.

his fingernails at table. No man must pray with unwashed hands or the gods spit back his prayers, nor lay the ladle across the mixing-bowl. When Plato speaks of the lost things which the lads of the ideal state must recover, they are simple things, " matters," he calls them, " supposed to be of little importance; how the young should be silent in the presence of their elders, give up their seats to them, and take dutiful care of parents; not to mention details of personal appearance, such as the way their hair is cut, and the clothes and shoes they wear." [32] Xenophon has the same story. In the *Memorabilia* he depicts Socrates as saying: " Is not the general opinion that a young man should make way for an older, offer his seat to him, honour him with a comfortable couch, and allow him to have the first word? " [33] When Xenophon draws the picture of Cyrus in the *Cyropædia* the picture is far more that of a Greek gentleman than of a Persian king. So Cyrus tells his sons: " I too was thus trained by my country and yours to give precedence to my elders—not merely to brothers but to all fellow-citizens—on the street, in the matter of seats and in speaking." This is what is approved " by time, by custom and the law." [34] So in the *Clouds* Aristophanes paints the picture of the good old days in contrast with the new-fangled ideas of Socrates and his crew. Incidentally, it is worth noting, as T. R. Glover does, that there is surely something remarkable about a community in which a philosopher in middle life is singled out as the central figure in a popular comedy on the subject of education.[35] The education of any community in which that could happen must have been indeed a remarkable thing. The *Dikaios Logos* is describing the great days which are behind:

> To hear then prepare of the Discipline rare which flourished in
> Athens of yore
> When honour and truth were in fashion with youth and sobriety
> bloomed on the shore;
> First of all the old rule was preserved in our school that " boys
> should be seen and not heard: "

[32] Plato: *Republic* 423. [33] Xenophon: *Memorabilia* 2. 3. 16.

[34] Xenophon: *Cyropædia* 8. 7. 13, 14.

[35] T. R. Glover: *Greek Byways*, pp. 102, 103.

And then to the home of the Harpist would come decorous in action and word
All the lads of one town, though the snow peppered down in spite of all wind and all weather:
And they sang an old song as they paced it along, not shambling with thighs glued together. . . .
You therefore, young man, choose me while you can; cast in with my method your lot;
And then you shall learn the forum to spurn, and from dissolute baths to abstain,
And fashions impure and shameful abjure, and scorners repel with disdain;
And rise from your chair if an elder be there, and respectfully give him your place,
And with love and with fear your parents revere, and shrink from the brand of disgrace." [36]

Isocrates in the *Areopagiticus* paints the same picture of the good old days with the same complaints: "The young men did not waste their time in the gambling-dens and with the flute-girls or in the kind of company in which they now spend their days, but remained steadfastly in the pursuits to which they had been assigned, admiring and emulating those who excelled in these. And so strictly did they avoid the market-place that even at times when they were compelled to pass through it, they were seen to do this with great modesty and sobriety of manner. To contradict one's elders or to be impudent to them was then considered more reprehensible than it is nowadays to sin against one's parents; and to eat and drink in a tavern was something, which no one, not even an honest slave, would do; for they cultivated the manners of a gentleman, and not those of a buffoon; and as for those who had a turn for jesting and playing the clown, whom we to-day speak of as clever wits, they were then looked on as sorry fools." [37] There was the kind of man who can do all kinds of menial services but who is not even enough of a gentleman to know how to wear his robe draped in the right way.[38]

[36] Aristophanes: *The Clouds*, 960–1023: B. B. Rogers's translation.

[37] Isocrates: *Areopagiticus* 49 (149 C. D.).

[38] Plato: *Theætetus* 175 C.

The picture is the picture of a certain way of life, with all its conventions, little things maybe, and yet lending a certain character and flavour to life. Greek education so often dealt not with the knowledge which can be bought and sold, or served up in an examination paper, but with the intangibles which, when added up, produce what the Greek would call an Athenian and a gentleman.

It is quite clear that an education like this will depend far more on home training than it does on educational institutions. If the teaching be, not teaching in facts and crafts and abilities, but initiation into a certain atmosphere and way of life, then the home in which the child lives will be by far the biggest factor in it. Plutarch was very much alive to that fact, for he begins his essay *On The Education of Children* by saying in effect that the greatest educational advantage that a child can have is good parents and a good home. He quotes Euripides' *Hercules Furens*:

> The home's foundation being wrongly laid,
> The offspring needs must be unfortunate.

and then he goes on to lay it down: " A goodly treasure, then, is honourable birth." [39] He says that, as in the cultivation of the soil to produce a good harvest three things are necessary—good soil, a wise husbandman and sound seed—so in the upbringing of children three factors combine to produce the perfect result—good stock, a wise teacher, and sound teaching.[40]

It was the tragedy of Athens that on the whole home circumstances were not good, and were not favourable to the sound upbringing of the child. Because the human heart does not change, there were in Athens, as there must always be, gracious and faithful marriages. But in Greek thought there is a curious strain in which the relationship between husband and wife is not the highest relationship. Antigone, well-knowing that it has been forbidden by Creon, and well aware that she is courting death, resolves to bury her brother Polynices, slain at Thebes. Creon demands her

[39] Plutarch: *On the Education of Children* 1 B, C. (1, 2); Euripides: *Hercules Furens* 1261.

[40] Plutarch: *On the Education of Children* 2 B (3).

imprisonment and death; Antigone answers, addressing her dead brother:

> For with these hands, I laved and decked your limbs
> In death, and poured libations on your grave.
> And last, my Polynices, unto thee
> I paid due rites, and this my recompense.
> Yet am I justified in wisdom's eyes.
> For even had it been some child of mine,
> Or husband mouldering in death's decay,
> I had not wrought this deed despite the State.
> What is the law I call in aid? 'Tis thus
> I argue. Had it been a husband dead
> I might have wed another, and have borne
> Another child, to take the dead child's place.
> But now my sire and mother both are dead,
> No second brother can be born for me.[41]

The relationship of brother and sister is dearer and more precious than that of husband and of wife. The same strain of thought appears in a story which Herodotus tells. Darius had arrested Intaphernes and his friends in the suspicion that they were plotting against him. The wife of Intaphernes came weeping bitterly to the palace gates; Darius, moved with compassion, offered to release to her anyone of her kinsmen whom she might choose; and she chose—to the king's surprise—the life of her brother. The king asked her why she passed over the lives of her husband and her children in order to save her brother. She answers: " O King, another husband I may get, if heaven so will, and other children, if I lose these; but my father and mother are dead, and so I can by no means get another brother; that is why I have thus spoken."[42] Marriage among the Greeks was in fact often arranged by parents or near relations, sometimes with the help of a professional matchmaker,[43] and it must often have happened that, at least at the beginning, there was little love in the marriage tie, although equally there must have been many a love-match. It may well

[41] Sophocles: *Antigone* 900–12. [42] Herodotus 3. 119.

[43] L. Whibley: *A Companion to Greek Studies*, p. 593.

be, therefore, that many a Greek marriage lacked the essential love.

But further, a Greek woman was in normal circumstances entirely uneducated. There were no provisions at all for her schooling. If she was of the respectable classes, she lived alone in the women's apartments, not even joining her family for meals, and not even able to go out into the streets unaccompanied. K. J. Freeman says: "The mother was a nonentity, living in the women's apartments; the child probably saw little of her."[44] The mother was in fact quite unequipped to be of any help to her child in the matter of education. At the end of his funeral oration Pericles has a word for the women: "If I am to speak also of womanly virtues, referring to those of you who will henceforth be in widowhood, I will sum up all in a brief admonition: Great is your glory if you fall not below the standard which nature has set for your sex, and great also is hers of whom there is least talk among men, whether in praise or blame."[45] However much freedom the Athenian husband might claim for himself, an isolated seclusion was the lot of his wife.

Xenophon has two pictures of the kind of life which women lead. One is one of the most charming pictures in Greek literature, the picture of Ischomachus, the *kalos kagathos*, the Greek gentleman, and the girl wife, whom he married and loved, and who loved him.[46] Socrates asks whether Ischomachus had instructed his own wife in household duties, or whether she came to him equipped with the necessary knowledge of how to run a house. "How could she have sufficient knowledge when I took her," answers Ischomachus, "since she came to my house when she was not fifteen years old, and had spent the preceding part of her life under the strictest restraint, in order that she might see as little, hear as little, and ask as few questions as possible?" (7. 5). All that she knew was how to take wool and to make a garment, and to apportion the tasks of spinning among the maid-servants (7. 6). So Ischomachus bided his time until the girl was tame enough to carry on a conversation with him (7. 10). Then he began to talk to her with his grave, ingenuous charm, far more like a father than a husband. Providence

[44] K. J. Freeman: *Schools of Hellas*, p. 282.

[45] Thucydides 2. 45. [46] Xenophon: *Œconomicus* 7–10.

has given to husband and wife their several duties, and they must carry them out, for Ischomachus was a religious man, and he and his wife had prayed together before they talked together of the house (7. 8). Broadly speaking the work of the wife lies indoors, and the work of the husband lies outdoors (7. 22). "It is more becoming for the woman to stay within doors than to roam abroad, but to the man it is less creditable to remain at home than to attend to things out of doors" (7. 30). Nature has made woman physically weaker than man, and has made her more timid, for she is the guardian of the home; but nature has given the woman more of love, for hers is the care of the little child. But nature has made man and woman equal in memory and in powers of attention; they are therefore complementary to each other (7. 23–8). The wife must take charge of the house; she must carefully divide out what is needed so that what is meant to last a year will not be expended in a month; she must look after the wool and the garments; she must care for any servant who falls ill. Ischomachus must go out and earn and bring in the necessaries; but she must look after them in the house, for there is little point in putting water in a bucket which is full of holes (7. 36–40). She must look after the spinning-maids and teach them their job, and supervise the housekeeper, and her greatest thrill will be to show herself so efficient that finally she will render Ischomachus himself her humble servant (7. 41, 42).

Ischomachus goes on to teach her to be orderly, all because one day she could not find what he asked for. Order is everything. You cannot run a chorus, build a house, command an efficient army, sail a ship unless there is a place for everything, and everything is in its place (8. 1–17). So Ischomachus goes on to sing the praises of order with a kind of old-maidish tidiness, which cannot but make us smile. How beautiful are boots and shoes when they are lined up in order, and clothes when they are hung in disciplined array. Even pots and pans can look like a chorus when you line them in order, graduating them according to size. In a city of tens of thousands of citizens you can find any citizen, for each citizen has a home and stays in it—and a house should be the same (7. 18). So Ischomachus went on to teach the girl what the various rooms of the house were for—the inner rooms for the valuables, the dry rooms for the corn, the cool rooms for the wine, the well-lit rooms for furnishings which need the light (9. 3, 4). So, the instruction finished, Ischomachus desired his wife " to consider herself the guardian of the laws established in the house, and to inspect the household furniture, whenever she thought proper, as the commander of a garrison inspects the sentinels; to signify her approbation if everything was in good condition, as the senate signified its approval of the horses and the horse-soldiers; to praise and honour the deserving like a queen, according to her means, and to rebuke and disgrace anyone who required such treatment" (8. 15). No wonder Socrates gravely—or, was it with a Silenus-like smile —closed the conversation by saying: " It is a far greater pleasure to hear of the merit of a living woman, than if Zeuxis were to exhibit to me the most beautiful representation of a woman in a painting" (10. 1).

It is indeed a charming picture. It shows the complete ignorance in which a young girl came to her husband in Greece. Oddly enough in only one thing was she well instructed. " As to what concerns the desires, Socrates," said Ischomachus, " which seems to me a most important part of instruction for a man and for a woman, she came to me extremely well instructed" (7. 6). The wife had no education whatever, and in this case she was fortunate, for the grave and gentle Ischomachus was bent on giving her a place in the household which a richer and an idler woman would not have held. A child would have more than a chance in the home of an Ischomachus, but if a totally uneducated woman was rich enough to leave everything to her slaves, she was bound to degenerate physically and mentally until she became such that she could be of no help to her child.

Xenophon in the *Memorabilia* [47] tells another story which well illustrates the position of women in a normal Greek upper-class household. Socrates met Aristarchus and Aristarchus was sunk in gloom. Socrates invites him to share his troubles as friendship demands (2. 7. 1). Aristarchus's trouble is quite simple; the revolution has driven people from Athens to the Peiræus; and he has been left with no fewer than fourteen female relatives on his hands—sisters, nieces and cousins for whose support he has become responsible, not counting slaves. House-property has become valueless;

[47] Xenophon: *Memorabilia* 2. 7.

land is in the hands of the invaders; borrowing has become impossible; and Aristarchus is at his wits' end to make ends meet (2. 7. 2). "It's hard, Socrates, to let one's people die, but it is impossible to keep so many in times like these." Socrates asks how Ceramon, who has so many mouths to feed, manages to exist in riches and comfort, while Aristarchus is on the verge of ruin. Aristarchus gives what is to him the obvious explanation: "My dependents are gentlefolk, his are slaves" (2. 7. 3). Socrates, being Socrates, goes on probing. Aristarchus would agree that his gentlefolk are better than Ceramon's slaves? Well, then, is it not an odd thing that Ceramon's full household of inferior people keep him in comfort, while Aristarchus's full household of superior gentlefolk have brought him nearly to starvation? Aristarchus again gives the obvious reason: "Of course his dependents are artisans, while mine have had a liberal education" (2. 7. 4). Socrates suggests that you might define an artisan as someone who knows how to produce something useful (2. 7. 5), with which Aristarchus agrees. Well, then, Aristarchus's houseful of women can produce groats, can't they, and bread? They can make clothes, can't they, men's and women's cloaks, shirts, capes, smocks? Oh yes, they can do that; these are domestic duties. Well, then, says Socrates, Cyrebus keeps his family in luxury by baking bread and running a baker's business; Demeas and Menon are tailors and are wealthy with their tailoring. The idea is beginning to dawn on Aristarchus, but he is shocked: "They buy foreign slaves. . . . My household is made up of gentlefolk and relations" (2. 7. 6). The idea of gentlewomen working is one that has never struck Aristarchus. Are then gentlefolk, asks Socrates, to do nothing but eat and sleep? If Aristarchus does not take a grip of things, these women are going to see that they are a burden; gratitude will turn to dislike; and things will be wretched. Set them to work; they will feel useful; they will know that Aristarchus is pleased with them; the atmosphere of the overcrowded house will be changed. After all he is not setting them a task that is worse than death; he is only asking them to do what they have been trained all their lives to do (2. 7. 9, 10).

Aristarchus is convinced, and goes off to borrow capital to set his womenfolk working. Wool was purchased and Aristarchus's house was turned into a kind of clothing factory. "The women worked during dinner and only stopped at the supper hour. There were happy instead of gloomy faces; suspicious glances were changed to pleasant smiles. They loved him as a guardian and he liked them because they were useful" (2. 7. 12). But the troubles of the wretched Aristarchus were not yet finished. The next time he met Socrates he had a new complaint. "One objection the women have to me," he complains, "I am the only member of the household who eats the bread of idleness" (2. 7. 12). Socrates' resource is not inadequate to meet even this situation. Tell them the story of the sheep and the sheep dog. The sheep complained to the shepherd that they gave wool and lambs and cheese, and the dog gave nothing. Yet the master shared his food with the dog, and left them to find their own food. The dog heard it: "Of course that is what the master does. Do not I keep you from being stolen by thieves and carried off by wolves? But for my protection you could not even eat for fear of being killed." The sheep admitted the justice of the way in which the dog was treated. Let Aristarchus tell his fourteen women that he is the watch-dog, who protects them in safety and comfort that none may harm them (2. 7: 13, 14).

It is the implications of that story which are so significant. For respectable women to work was a revolutionary idea; left to himself Aristarchus would never have conceived of it even as a possibility; and yet when the ordinary domestic skills of the women were turned to profit, it was so extraordinary an adventure that they were thrilled by it. The story of Ischomachus and the story of Aristarchus show us the picture of this domestic isolation of women, this complete lack of training, which meant that there would be little or nothing that a mother could do to educate her child; and the older the child grew, the more he would necessarily grow away from his mother.

Both Plato and Aristotle saw quite clearly that by the complete neglect of the education of women one-half of the whole population of the state was being totally neglected, an obviously dangerous and foolish situation.[48] Plato went the whole way. In the *Republic* he insists that the only criterion must be ability to receive education and to hold office in the service of the State. He therefore insists

[48] Aristotle: *Politics* 1. 5. 12; 2. 6. 5.

that women must have precisely the same education as men, whenever they are able to receive it.[49] In the *Laws* he writes: "I affirm that the practice which at present prevails in our districts is a most irrational one—namely, that men and women should not all follow the same pursuits with one accord and with all their might." For thus from the same taxation and trouble there arises and exists half a state only instead of a whole one, in nearly every instance; yet surely this would be a surprising blunder for a law-giver to commit. His conclusion is that "the female sex must share with the male, to the greatest extent possible, both in education and in all else." It is the custom in Thrace to set the women to tilling the soil and minding the sheep and oxen and toiling like slaves. In Athens men huddle all their goods together in their houses, and then hand over the dispensing of them to the women, and give them the wool work to do. In Sparta there is a kind of half-way house towards equal education. To Plato it is the height of folly that the law-giver should allow the female sex to "indulge in luxury and expense and disorderly ways of life, while supervising the male sex; for thus he is actually bequeathing to the state half only, instead of the whole, of a life of complete prosperity." [50] In point of fact women were admitted to the Academy. But to the ordinary Greek this was far too revolutionary, and even unnatural, a demand. The ordinary Greek women received no kind of education, and was immured in her own home so that the more her child grew up, the less she was able to help him.

When a boy reached the age of seven, he came more directly under the care of his father; but the Athenian father was far too busy with the affairs of the state. The *boulē*, the *ekklēsia*, his duties as a *dikastēs*, or juryman, his absence on embassies or on military or naval service, left him little time to look after his son. So at the age of seven the boy was handed over to the care of the *paidagōgos*. The word is difficult to translate. It certainly does not mean "teacher," for the *paidagōgos* had no technical teaching duties whatsoever. The *paidagōgos* might well be with the lad from the time he was seven until the time when he was sixteen or even eighteen. Wherever the lad went, the *paidagōgos* had to go; he and the lad were inseparable companions. The *paidagōgos* was responsible for

[49] Plato: *Republic* 455. [50] Plato: *Laws* 805 A, C; 806 B, C.

conveying the lad to school each day, for carrying his books and his lyre, unless the family was wealthy enough to employ a separate slave for these duties, and for taking him home again. The *paidagōgos* was responsible for the training of the lad in both morals and manners. It was his duty to see that the boy walked in the streets with modesty and downcast head; that he was well-mannered at table and that he wore his clothes with grace; that he was always silent in the presence of his elders and gave place to them. It was under the hands of the *paidagōgos* that the boy's conduct was directed and his character moulded and formed. The *paidagōgos* was, as K. J. Freeman puts it, " a mixture of nurse, footman, chaperon and tutor." [51] There is no English word which will cover all this, because there is nothing in the English educational system which really corresponds to it. The word " tutor " is the word which is commonly used as a translation, even if it is an inadequate one.

It is quite clear that a most heavy responsibility for the formation of the lad's character lay on the shoulders of the tutor. One would have thought it obvious that only the best and the wisest men would have been chosen for such a position; and indeed sometimes it was so. We hear of a tutor who was asked: " What is your duty ? " and who answered: " To make the good pleasant to the boy." We know that when Themistocles wished a most trusted man to carry to Xerxes the message which was to lure him to his doom, he chose the tutor of his children, one Sikinnos by name, as the most trusted man whom he could find; and we know that this Sikinnos was afterwards rewarded with the citizenship and became a wealthy and respected man.[52] There is a third century papyrus letter from a mother to her absent son in which she writes: " Let you and your tutor see to it that you attach yourself to the most fitting teacher," and which ends with personal greetings, to " Eros, the most honoured *paidogōgos*." [53]

Greek literature has many references to the *paidagōgos* and his duties. The tutor was an absolute necessity. From his earliest childhood the nurse, the mother, the tutor, and the father strive

[51] K. J. Freeman: *Schools of Hellas*, p. 66. [52] Herodotus 8. 75.

[53] J. H. Moulton and G. Milligan: *The Vocabulary of the Greek New Testament*, p. 473.

that the child may excel.[54] Plato writes in the *Laws* that just as no sheep can exist without a shepherd no child can exist without a tutor. "Of all wild creatures," he writes, "the child is the most intractable; for in so far as it, above all others, possesses a fount of reason that is yet uncurbed, it is a treacherous, sly and most insolent creature. Wherefore the child must be strapped up, as it were, with many bridles—first, when he leaves the care of nurse and mother, with tutors to guide his childish ignorance, and after that with teachers of all sorts of subjects and lessons."[55] The tutor never leaves the lad's side. Plato compares the tutor's constant watching of the lad to the way in which a man who is seriously ill has to look after his health. Just as the invalid has to watch every symptom, and every action and every article of diet, so the tutor must constantly watch the actions of the lad.[56] When Quintus Fabius Cunctator pursued his policy of biding his time and of refusing direct engagement with Hannibal till the right moment should come, those who wished for more direct action called him Hannibal's *paidagōgos* "since he did nothing but follow him up and down and wait on him."[57] In the *Lysis* Plato describes the scene when Socrates is trying to teach the lad the necessity of discipline and training and control. "Do they let you control yourself?" asks Socrates. "Of course not," says the lad. "But some one controls you?" says Socrates. And the answer is: "Yes, my tutor here."[58] It is clear how great a responsibility the tutor had and how great an influence he must have exercised on the growing and developing lad.

As we have already said, one would have thought that the man who was chosen for the position of *paidagōgos* would have been selected with the greatest care, not so much for his academic attainments, as for his personal qualities. Sometimes it was so; but far too often the precise opposite was the case. J. P. Mahaffy says of the *paidagōgos*: "He was often old and trusty, often old and useless, always ignorant and never respected."[59] In speaking of the same situation in Rome, Warde Fowler points out that the *paidagōgos* was usually a slave and usually a Greek, and at best a freedman. There-

[54] Plato: *Protagoras* 325 C. [55] Plato: *Laws* 808 D, E.
[56] Plato: *Republic* 406 A. [57] Plutarch: *Fabius* 5.
[58] Plato: *Lysis* 208 C. [59] J. P. Mahaffy: *Old Greek Education*, p. 29.

fore the boy had to submit to oversight and punishment from men whom he despised, men whose station was low and whose morals were often inferior.[60] That in itself made for a most unsatisfactory relationship. Plutarch unsparingly condemns parents for their lack of care in tutors for their sons: "When boys attain to an age to be put under attendants, then especially great care must be taken in the appointment of these, so as not to entrust one's children inadvertently to slaves taken in war, or to barbarians, or to those who are unstable. Nowadays the practice of many persons is worse than ridiculous; for some of their trustworthy slaves they appoint to manage farms, others they make masters of their ships, others their factors, others their house stewards, some even money-lenders; but any slave whom they find to be a wine-bibber, and a glutton, and useless for any kind of business, to him they bring their sons, and put them in his charge."[61]

These tutors were notoriously unsatisfactory characters. At the end of the *Lysis* Plato tells how the tutors broke up the discussion, when they came to take their charges, Lysis and Menexenus, away: "Like spirits from another world there came upon us the tutors of Menexenus and Lysis; they were bringing along the boys' brothers, and called out the order to them to come home, for it was quite late. At first we tried, with the help of the group around us, to drive the tutors off. But they took no notice of us at all, and went on angrily calling as before, in their foreign accent. We decided that they had taken a drop too much at the festival and might be awkward customers, so we gave in to them, and broke up our party."[62] It is not a pretty picture, for these tutors of Lysis and Menexenus were clearly uncouth and drunken creatures, the last kind of men to be put in charge of sensitive and high-spirited boys. In the *First Alcibiades* Plato contrasts the Persian practice with the Greek. In Persia, when the boy reaches the age of fourteen, he is given four tutors; these tutors are the wisest one, the justest one, the most temperate one, and the bravest one. The wisest one teaches him the worship of the gods; the justest one teaches him to be truthful all his life long; the most temperate one teaches him

[60] W. Warde Fowler: *Social Life at Rome in the Age of Cicero*, pp. 183, 184.
[61] Plutarch: *On The Education of Children* 4 D (7).
[62] Plato: *Lysis* 223 A, B.

never to be mastered by any pleasure, so that he may be a truly free man; the bravest one teaches him to be fearless and undaunted. How different in Greece! "But you, Alcibiades," says Socrates, "had a tutor set over you by Pericles from amongst his servants, who was so old as to be the most useless of them, Zopyrus the Thracian."[63] It is indeed said that, when Pericles saw a slave fall from a tree and break his leg, he said: "Lo, he is now a *paidagōgos*!"

It was the tragedy of the Greeks, in the greatest days of Athens, that the boy did not get off to a good start in life. His mother was so uneducated, so isolated, so secluded that she could be of little help to him; and often in the more wealthy families she was so lazy that she would not even nurse her own child.[64] His father was so busy being an Athenian citizen that he had little time to know him. And his *paidagōgos* might be a faithful slave, but was more likely to be a worthless creature, whose influence was bound to be bad rather than good.

Before we go on to look at the details of the education of the Greek boy, one question arises. If education and making a living were entirely dissociated, if education to the Greek had nothing to do with learning a craft, and fitting oneself to earn money, where in fact did the Greeks learn the necessary trades and skills which are needed for the support of life and home and family?

These things—even what we would call the professions—were learned by a process of apprenticeship. In the *Cleitophon* Plato at one point in the argument lays it down that any craft or profession has two aims—to practise the craft itself, and to produce others who can practise it. So the joiner's art produces houses and it produces those who know joinery; medicine produces doctors and it produces health. It was the duty of any man who had a skill to pass on that skill to others, as well as to practise it himself.[65] We may in fact see that principle operating in the famous Hippocratic oath, which is the moral law of the medical profession to this day, for in it the doctor makes the promise:

> I swear by Apollo the physician and Asclepius and Hygeia and

[63] Plato: *Alcibiades I* 122 A, B.

[64] Plutarch: *On The Education of Children* 2 C, D. (5).

[65] Plato: *Cleitophon* 409 A, B.

> Panacea, invoking all the gods and goddesses to be my witnesses, that I will fulfil this oath and this written covenant to the best of my power and of my judgment.
>
> I will look on him who shall have taught me this art even as on mine own parents: I will share with him my substance, and supply his necessities, if he be in need: I will regard his offspring even as my own brethren, and will teach them this art, if they so desire it, without fee and covenant. I will impart it by precept, by lecture, and by all other manner of teaching, not only to my own sons but also to the sons of him who has taught me, and to disciples bound by covenant and oath according to the law of the physicians, but to none other.[66]

In the *Protagoras* Plato speaks of the crafts " which men of course have learned from their fathers, in so far as they were competent to teach them,"[67] thereby implying that this was the normal way in which trades, and crafts and skills were learned. Twice at least in the *Republic* Plato makes mention of the custom whereby the potter taught his son his trade. If the potter becomes too poor, he will lack the tools and the equipment to practise his trade adequately, " and he will not make such good craftsmen of his sons and apprentices." Again, he points out how children learn what some day

[66] The oath may be found in the Loeb edition of the works of Hippocrates and conveniently in English in *The Legacy of Greece*, ed. R. W. Livingstone, pp. 213, 214. The oath goes on: " The regimen I shall adopt shall be for the benefit of the patients to the best of my power and judgment, not for their injury or for any wrongful purpose. I will not give a deadly drug to anyone, though it be asked of me, nor will I lead the way in such counsel; and likewise I will not give a woman a pessary to procure abortion. But I will keep my life and my art in purity and in holiness. Whatsoever house I enter, I will enter for the benefit of the sick, refraining from all voluntary wrong-doing and corruption, especially seduction of male or female, bond or free. Whatsoever things I see or hear concerning the life of men, in my attendance on the sick or even apart from my attendance, which ought not to be blabbed abroad, I will keep silence on them, counting such things to be as religious secrets.

If I fulfil this oath and confound it not, be it mine to enjoy life and art alike, with good repute among all men for all time to come; but may the contrary befall me if I transgress and violate my oath." (This translation is by Professor Arthur Platt.)

[67] Plato: *Protagoras* 328 A.

they must do by watching their elders do it: "You must have noticed how, in the potter's trade for example, the children watch their fathers, and wait on them, long before they may touch the wheel."[68]

It was the duty of every craftsman, not only to practise his art or craft himself, but to pass it on. We have seen how the Jews had a saying that the father who did not teach his son a trade taught him to steal. According to Plutarch, Solon passed a similar law in Athens. In his day Athens was becoming crowded by those who sought the security which a city can give. Because of that the necessary imports of Athens were steeply increasing. Solon perceived the elementary law that no one will bring goods into a city without receiving something desirable in exchange. "He therefore turned the attention of the citizens to the arts of manufacture, and he enacted a law that no son who had not been taught a trade should be compelled to support his father."[69] The Greek law was insistent on the duty of the son to support an aged parent; but, if the parent had not fulfilled his duty by teaching the son some art or craft or skill, then the child also was absolved from his duty. So then the actual means of making a living were taught by a system of apprenticeship, and were commonly passed down from father to son.

Before we turn to the detail of Athenian education, let us look once again at the ideal behind it. Nowhere is that ideal better set out than in the speech of Protagoras in Plato's *Protagoras*. It is a long speech, but it must be set down in full, for it sets out the whole educational ideal, and the educational process of the child:

> Education and admonition begin in the first years of childhood, and last to the very end of life. Mother and nurse and father and tutor are quarrelling about the improvement of the child as soon as ever he is able to understand them: he cannot say or do anything without their setting forth to him that this is just and that is unjust; this is honourable, that is dishonourable; this is holy, that is unholy; do this and abstain from that. And if he obeys, well and good; if not, he is straightened by threats

[68] Plato: *Republic* 421 E; 467 A. [69] Plutarch: *Solon* 22. 1.

and blows, like a piece of warped wood. At a later stage they send him to teachers, and enjoin them to see to his manners even more than to his reading and his music; and the teachers do as they are desired. And when the boy has learned his letters and is beginning to understand what is written, as before he understood only what was spoken, they put into his hands the works of the great poets, which he reads at school; in these are contained many admonitions, and many tales and praises, and encomia of ancient famous men, which he is required to learn by heart, in order that he may imitate or emulate them and desire to become like them. Then again the teachers of the lyre take similar care that their young disciple is temperate and gets into no mischief; and, when they have taught him the use of the lyre, they introduce him to the poems of other excellent poets, who are the lyric poets; and these they set to music, and make their harmonies and rhythms quite familiar to the children's souls, in order that they may learn to be more gentle, and harmonious, and rhythmical, and so more fitted for speech and action; for the life of man in every part has need of harmony and rhythm. Then they send them to the master of gymnastic, in order that their bodies may better minister to the virtuous mind, and that they may not be compelled through bodily weakness to play the coward in war or on any other occasion. This is what is done by those who have the means, and those who have the means are the rich; their children begin education soonest, and leave off latest. When they have done with masters, the state again compels them to learn the laws, and live after the pattern which they furnish, and not after their own fancies; and, just as in learning to write, the writing master first draws lines with a stylus for the use of the young beginner, and gives him the tablet and makes him follow the lines, so the city draws the laws, which were the invention of good law-givers who were of old time; these are given to the young man, in order to guide him in his conduct, whether as ruler or ruled; and he who transgresses them is to be corrected, or in other words, called to account, which is a term used not only in your country, but also in many others. Now when there is all this care about virtue private and public, why,

Socrates, do you still wonder and doubt whether virtue can be taught? Cease to wonder, for the opposite would be far more surprising.[70]

This is one of the most significant of all passages for the Greek ideal. Education for the purpose of taking a degree would have been just as unintelligible to the Greek as education for making money. A boy read the great poets that he might become like the great heroes; he sang and recited the great lyrics that something of their rhythm and harmony might enter into his own life; he exercised his body in gymnastics that the healthy body might be the willing servant of the virtuous mind. It is character rather than erudition at which the teacher must aim. It is what is just and unjust, honourable and dishonourable, holy and unholy that is instilled into the child from his very earliest years, even from his birth. No one would claim that that ideal was wholly realised—very far from it; but equally no one would deny that it is a very great ideal, an ideal as different as night is from day from the utilitarian ideal of education which

[70] Plato: *Protagoras* 325 C–326 D. Cp. Lucian: *Anacharsis* 20: "Their early upbringing we entrust to mothers, nurses, and tutors, to train and rear them with liberal teachings; but when at length they become able to understand what is right, when modesty, shame, fear, and ambition spring up in them, and when at length their very bodies seem well-fitted for hardships, as they get firmer and become more strongly compacted, then we take them in hand and teach them, not only prescribing them certain disciplines and exercises for the soul, but in certain other ways habituating their bodies also to hardships. We have not thought it sufficient for each man to be as he was born, either in body or soul, but we want education and disciplines for them by which their good traits may be much improved and their bad altered for the better. We take example from the farmers, who shelter and enclose their plants while they are small and young, so that they may not be injured by the breezes; but when the stalk at last begins to thicken, they prune away the excessive growth, and expose them to the winds to be shaken and tossed, in that way making them more fruitful.

Their souls we fan into a flame with music and arithmetic at first, and we teach them to write their letters, and to read them trippingly. As they progress, we recite for them the sayings of wise men, deeds of olden times, and helpful fictions, which we have adorned with metre that they may remember them better. Hearing of certain feats of arms and famous exploits, little by little they grow covetous and are incited to imitate them, in order that they too may be sung and admired by men of after time."

prevails in our own time. The Greek was not concerned to give the boy something which he could sell in some academic, professional or commercial market-place; he was concerned to give him the means and the opportunity to make himself a certain kind of person, who would make Athens a certain kind of city—and who shall say that the Greeks were wrong?

In Greece the school went very far back in history. At least twice the historians mention schools, and both times in connection with disaster. Herodotus tells how warnings from heaven are sent when great ills threaten a city or a nation. A little before the Chian time of national disaster "the roof fell in on boys at school, insomuch that of a hundred and twenty of them one alone escaped."[71] Thucydides tells how the Thracians burst into the city of Mycalessus. "The Thracian race, like the worst barbarians, is most bloodthirsty when it has nothing to fear. And so on this occasion, in addition to the general confusion, which was great, every form of destruction ensued, and in particular they fell upon a boys' school, the largest in the town, which the children had just entered, and cut down all of them. And this was a calamity inferior to none that had ever fallen upon a whole city, and beyond any other unexpected and terrible."[72]

In Greece there were always schools; and for anything to happen to these schools and to their children was a disaster than which none could be greater. The child and the school were precious in Greece.

There was no definite age in Athens at which children began school, nor at which they ended schooling. When they began and when they ended depended very largely on the financial position of the parents. The richer the parents were, the sooner the child went to school and the longer he remained there. Poorer parents did not wish to send their children until they were able to learn quickly, for the shorter the time they were there, the less the fees would amount to; and they removed them from school as quickly as possible, in order that they might become contributors to the family exchequer. In the richer families the child was often sent to school as soon as he could look on. In the *Hermotimus* Lucian relates how nurses often say that the child might as well go to school

[71] Herodotus 6. 27. [72] Thucydides 7. 29. 5.

to get him out of the way; he probably will not learn anything but at least at school he will not get into mischief.[73] Xenophon, speaking from the Spartan point of view, is vague. He says that "as soon as they can understand what is said to them" they are sent to learn letters, music and gymnastics.[74] Aristotle lays it down that up to the age of five "it is not well as yet to direct them to any study or to compulsory labours, in order that their growth may not be hindered."[75] Plato, in the *Laws*, restricts the child's education to games up to six years of age.[76]

But one thing must be noted—all the great Greek thinkers are perfectly certain that education does not start with going to school, but that for better or for worse it begins long before that. One of the most interesting features of the educational theory both of Aristotle and Plato is the importance which they attach to games or to play in education. Aristotle lays it down that the exercise which the young child needs must be obtained "by various pursuits, particularly play." But that play must not be unfit for freemen; it must not be laborious; and it must not be undisciplined. "Most children's games," he says, "should be imitations of the serious occupations of later life."[77] Plato is even more insistent upon this. He says: "To form the character of the child between three and six there will be need of games." In these games there must be punishment for those who break the rules; but that punishment must never be such that it is degrading. A wise course is to be steered between too much and too humiliating punishment which will degrade the child, and no punishment at all which will pamper the child. Play, as Plato sees it, is an instinct. "Children of this age have games which come by natural instinct; and they generally invent them of themselves whenever they come together." So the children between three and six are to be taken by their nurses to the temples, where they are to indulge in what can only be called disciplined play.[78]

Plato takes this matter of games and discipline in them with the greatest seriousness. He says that in all states there is a complete

[73] Lucian: *Hermotimus* 82.

[74] Xenophon: *Constitution of the Lacedaimonians* 2. 1.

[75] Aristotle: *Politics* 7. 15. 4.

[76] Plato: *Laws* 793 E.

[77] Aristotle: *Politics* 7. 15. 4–6.

[78] Plato: *Laws* 794 A, B.

ignorance about children's games, and their decisive importance for legislation. Plato argues that change in children's games should be absolutely forbidden; the child must always play the same games and delight in the same toys in exactly the same way. There can be no worse kind of pest than the man who introduces innovations in children's games. "Nothing," says Plato, "is more perilous than change in respect of everything except what is bad." Plato's argument is that if the child is allowed or encouraged to innovate in his games and to make changes in them, he will grow up into a man who loves innovations, and who is impatient of the laws and resentful of discipline, and who is therefore a dangerous citizen.[79]

But there is another pre-school influence. That is the tales which nurses tell to children. Aristotle is clear that the stories which are told to children must be controlled and regulated by the state officials who are in charge of the training of the child.[80] Plutarch makes the same point: "Youth is impressionable and plastic, and while such minds are still tender lessons are infused deeply into them; but anything which has become hard is with difficulty softened. For just as seals leave their impression in soft wax, so are lessons impressed upon the minds of children when they are young. And it seems to me that Plato, that remarkable man, quite properly advises nurses, even in telling stories to children, not to choose at random, lest haply their minds be filled at the outset with foolishness and corruption. Phocylides, too, the poet appears to give admirable advice in saying:

> Should teach while still a child
> The tale of noble deeds."[81]

The Greek nurses had their tales of bogey-men to scare the children into being good—Mormo, Ephialtes, Empousa, Lamia, and the rest of them.[82] Chrysippus blames those who would try to keep men from sin by the fear of the gods. He says that it is not any different from Acco and Alphites, by whom women try to

[79] Plato: *Laws* 797, 798. [80] Aristotle: *Politics* 7. 15. 5.

[81] Plutarch: *On The Education of Children* 3 E, F (5).

[82] W. Murison: *E.R.E.* 5. 186.

keep little children from mischief.[83] The Greek educational thinkers had no doubt as to the damage that these stories could do to the child mind, and would have had the nurses strictly controlled.

Although it ought to come later, it may be simplest to take here the famous attack of Plato on the stories which are told to children. Plato does not dispute that stories must be told to children; but there are two kinds of stories, the true and the false, and the tragedy is that it is the false stories with which we so often begin. The stories which poets and composers of fables and nurses tell must be strictly controlled. The law-giver cannot write them—but he can and must control them. And many must be discarded, for they only teach what some day the child must unlearn. In particular Plato launches his attack against Homer and Hesiod. They are not only guilty of lies, they are guilty of the ugliest of lies which is " when anyone imagines badly in his story about the gods and heroes." No young listener must be taught stories which will one day enable him to justify an outrage by saying that the gods have done it. These stories show the gods engaged in adulteries and immoral actions; they show children and parents at variance; they tell of internecine wars; and they must be rooted out. The law-giver cannot and must not consent when Homer or any other poet " insanely runs into this error about the gods."

So Plato lays down two canons by which all stories of the gods must be judged. First, " God is not the cause of all things, but only of the good." Second, " The gods are neither themselves wizards, metamorphosing themselves, nor do they mislead us by falsehood of word or of deed." To tell stories of Proteus, Hera, Thetis and their metamorphosing of themselves is quite wrong. We cannot even say that the gods send these stories in dreams, for God could not even send a deceiving dream. These two canons must become the canons by which all stories are judged in the ideal state.[84] The very

[83] Quoted by A. S. Wilkins: *National Education in Greece*, p. 63. Xenophon said that the Spartans said of the Mantineans that they feared the peltasts as the children fear *mormonas* (*Hellenica* 4. 4. 17). Theocritus paints the picture of Praxinoa refusing to take the child to the festival—" Horsey-bogey bites little boys " (*mormō hippos*); Theocritus 15. 40. Lucian has a hair-raising ghost story in *Philopseudes* 31. 2.

[84] Plato's lengthy discussion of this question is in the *Republic* 377 B–385.

fact that Homer was the educational bible of the Greeks shows how important and revolutionary this attack of Plato was; and the very fact that Homer continued to be the educational bible of the Greeks as long as education lasted shows how unavailing Plato's criticism was.

So then the Greek educationalists were clear that often the damage could be done before ever the boy reached school; and they were wishful to control the games children play and the stories children hear, although it cannot be said that their aim was ever carried out. This is the very problem which Lucian's Menippus states:

> While I was a boy, when I read in Homer and Hesiod about wars and quarrels, not only of the demi-gods but of the gods themselves, and besides about their amours and assaults and abductions and lawsuits and banishing fathers and marrying sisters, I thought that all these things were right, and I felt an uncommon impulsion to them. But when I came of age, I found that the laws contradicted the poets and forbade adultery, quarrelling and theft. So I was plunged into great uncertainty, not knowing how to deal with my own case; for the gods would never have committed adultery and quarrelled with each other, I thought, unless they had deemed these actions right, and the law-givers would not recommend the opposite course unless they supposed it to be advantageous.[85]

More than Plato were aware of the impropriety of the stories schoolboys learned; but still the stories remained as the basis of early education.

It is not certain how far primary education was compulsory in Athens. A law is attributed to Solon that every boy should learn swimming and his letters.[86] In the *Crito* Socrates carries on an imaginary conversation with the laws, in which the laws demand why he should wish to destroy them. The laws ask if he has any fault to find with the laws which have to do with the nurture and the education of the child. "Did those of us assigned to these matters not give good directions when we told your father to edu-

[85] Lucian: *Menippus* 3. [86] K. J. Freeman: *Schools of Hellas*, 57.

cate you in music and gymnastics?"[87] It may well be that in the case of primary education *nomos* is much more "accepted custom" than it is "legal law"; it is certainly true that, whether or not education was compulsory in the primary stage, it was certainly universal. It is equally true that such regulations as the state did lay down were in no sense technical; they had nothing to do with the curriculum of the school, and the academic qualifications of the teacher; they were only concerned with the moral welfare of the boy. Æschines quotes the laws which affected schools—he seems to refer them back to Solon—in his speech *Against Timarchus*:

> Consider the case of the teachers. Although the very livelihood of these men, to whom we necessarily entrust our children, depends on their good character, while the opposite conduct on their part would mean poverty, yet it is plain that the lawgiver distrusts them; for he expressly prescribes, first, at what time of day the free-born boy is to go to the school-room; next, how many other boys may go there with him, and when he is to go home. He forbids the teacher to open the school-room, or the gymnastic-trainer the wrestling-school, before sunrise, and he commands them to close the doors before sunset; for he is exceedingly suspicious of their being alone with a boy, or in the dark with him. He prescribes what children are to be admitted as pupils, and their age at admission. He provides for a public official who shall superintend them, and for the oversight of the *paidagōgoi*. He regulates the Festival of the Muses in the school-rooms, and of Hermes in the wrestling-schools. Finally he regulates the companionships which the boys may form at school, and their cyclic dances. He prescribes, namely, that the *chorēgos*, a man who is going to spend his own money for your entertainment, shall be a man of more than forty years of age when he performs this service, in order that he may have reached the most temperate time of life before he comes into contact with your children.[88]

The law clearly accepted moral oversight over the child, but equally

[87] Plato: *Crito* 50 D. [88] Æschines: *Against Timarchus* 9–11.

clearly it laid down and insisted on no special educational curriculum for him.

The inevitable consequence of this was that schools were private; they were neither state-controlled nor state-provided; and again the inevitable consequence was that they varied very considerably, according to the fees that were charged. In the *Memorabilia* Xenophon shows us Socrates implying that parents would make sacrifices to obtain for their children as good an education as possible. He says to the young man: "Nor are parents content only to supply food, but as soon as their children seem capable of learning they teach them what they can for their good, and if they think that another is more competent to teach them anything, they send them to him at a cost, and strive their utmost that the children may turn out as well as possible."[89] The school must have been very much what the teacher made it.

Commonly the elementary school-teacher was poorly paid. In the *Menippus* Lucian paints the picture of the underworld after death in which fortunes are reversed, and the great are humbled: "You would have laughed much more heartily, I think, if you had seen our kings and satraps reduced to poverty there, and becoming so poor that they had either to sell kippers or become elementary school-teachers."[90] It appears that fees were paid at the end of the month, and that teachers even had difficulty in getting the pittance which was due to them. Theophrastus in his character of the Mean Man tells us of the man who deducts so much from the fee for every day the lad was off school ill, and who will not send the lad to school at all in the month of Anthesterion, because in it there were so many public festivals which were all holidays, and on which the teacher would expect a present.[91] The average elementary school-teacher was ill-paid and ill-respected, for he had to sell education at cut prices to attract the children of those who either wished or had to educate their children as cheaply as possible.

It was indeed this uncontrolled character of education against

[89] Xenophon: *Memorabilia*. 2. 2. 6.

[90] Lucian: *Menippus* 17. "He is dead, or he is teaching letters" was a proverbial expression to describe someone who had unaccountably vanished. (W. Murison, *E.R.E.* 5. 188.)

[91] Theophrastus: *Characters* 30. 14.

which both Plato and Aristotle protested. Socrates says to Alcibiades: " About your birth, Alcibiades, or nurture or education, or about those of any other Athenian, one may say that nobody cares, unless it be some lover whom you chance to have." [92] Aristotle held that since the aim of education is one—to produce good citizens—then education itself must be one and that " the superintendence of this must be public, and not on private lines, in the way in which at present each man superintends the education of his own children, teaching them privately, and whatever special branch of knowledge he thinks fit." His conclusion is that " It is clear that there should be legislation about education, and that it should be conducted on a public system." [93]

But although education was uncontrolled by the state, there was nevertheless a standard system and curriculum which was to all intents and purposes universal. Almost every Greek boy went to three teachers who taught him the three basic subjects of education. He went to the *Grammatistēs*, who taught him reading, writing, and a little arithmetic, and with whom he learned to read the great poets, and to learn their poetry by heart. He went to the *Kitharistēs*, with whom he learned to play the seven-stringed lyre and to sing the songs of the lyric poets. He went to the *Paidotribēs*, who cared for his physical development, and from whom he learned wrestling, boxing, the pankration, running, jumping, throwing the javelin and the discus. That was the basic curriculum of Greek education.[94]

[92] Plato: *First Alcibiades* 122 B.

[93] Aristotle: *Politics* 8. 1, 2, 3.

[94] This curriculum is frequently referred to in Greek literature. In the *Protagoras* Socrates speaks to Hippocrates of the training which he received from his *grammatistēs*, his *kitharistēs* and his *paidotribēs*, which W. R. M. Lamb translates, "language-master,""harp-teacher" and "sports-instructor" (312 B). In the *Euthydemus* the teachers of the learners are the *kitharistēs* and the *grammatistēs* (276 A). In the *Charmides* 159 C the same three teachers are mentioned one after another. In the *Cleitophon* it is said that children are instructed in letters and music and gymnastic, which is regarded as a complete education in virtue (407 C). Isocrates speaks of boys labouring through their lessons in grammar, music and the other branches (*Antidosis* 267). Xenophon speaks of parents sending their children to school to learn letters, music, and the exercises of the wrestling ground as soon as they can understand (*Constitution of the Lacedaimonians* 2. 1). Aristotle speaks of

Instruction in letters and in music were to all intents and purposes universal; only the very uneducated did not know music. The Sausage-seller in Aristophanes's *Knights* has to admit that he only knows his letters, and of them but little,[95] and that he understands nothing of *mousikē*. And in the *Wasps* the plea is made that a thief should be let off punishment because " he never learned the lyre." [96] But in the *Laws* Plato can lay it down in the mouth of the Athenian stranger: " Shall we assume that the uneducated man is a man without choir-training, and that the educated man is fully choir-trained? " [97] To be trained in a choir meant to be trained both in singing and dancing. Those who had never been to the *grammatistēs* would not exist at all; and only the completely uneducated would have failed to have attended the *kitharistēs* in the days of their youth.

Let us then see the curriculum which was followed at the schools of the three teachers. It must be remembered that the three subjects did not come, as it were, in series one after another. They were taught simultaneously, except that the musical side began a little later than the other two. Let us then begin with the work of the *Grammatistēs*, the teacher of letters. We have already seen that schools could not open until it was light, and must close before it was dark; but it would seem that the schoolboy had a long day. In Lucian's *Parasite* Tychiades ends by saying: " Hereafter I shall go to you like a schoolboy both in the morning and after luncheon to learn your art." [98] Lucian gives us a sketch of a schoolboy's day:

> He gets up at dawn, washes the sleep from his eyes, and puts on his cloak. Then he goes out from his father's house with his eyes fixed upon the ground, not looking at anyone who meets him. Behind him follow attendants and *paidagōgoi*, bearing in their hands the implements of virtue, writing-tablets,

---

the " four customary subjects of education "—reading and writing, gymnastics, music, to which some add drawing. Socrates in the *Theages* speaks of letters, harping and wrestling as comprising the education of a gentleman (122 E).

[95] Aristophanes: *Knights* 188, 189.

[96] Aristophanes: *Wasps* 959.

[97] Plato: *Laws* 654 B. [98] Lucian: *Parasite* 61.

> or books containing the great deeds of old, or, if he is going to a music-school, his well-tuned lyre.
>
> When he has laboured diligently at intellectual studies, and his mind is sated with the benefits of the school curriculum, he exercises his body in liberal pursuits, riding or hurling the javelin or spear. Then the wrestling school, with its sleek, oiled pupils, labours under the mid-day sun, and sweats in the regular athletic contests. Then a bath, not too prolonged; then a meal, not too large, in view of afternoon school. For the schoolmasters are waiting for him again, and the books which openly or by allegory teach him who was a great hero, who was a lover of justice and purity. With the contemplation of such virtues he waters the garden of his young soul. When evening sets a limit to his work, he pays the necessary tribute to his stomach and retires to rest, to sleep sweetly after his busy day.[99]

His holidays cannot have been very many; there was of course no Sunday rest in the ancient world. The great festivals were holidays, and the seventh and the twentieth of each month were holidays for these days were sacred to Apollo. We have already seen that the stingy parent kept the boy from school altogether in the month of *Anthesterion*, because there were so many festivals. That month is the equivalent of February-March. In that month there were the three days of the *Anthesteria*, the great wine festival; there were the Lesser Mysteries of Demeter; and there was the *Diasia*, the greatest festival of gracious Zeus.[100]

First, the boy must be taught his letters. For that there would be nothing for it but hard memory work; but the Greeks had a way of making school pleasant; and there were aids to learning. There were for instance metrical alphabets of which Athenæus [101] gives a specimen.

> ἔστ᾽ ἄλφα, βῆτα, γάμμα, δέλτα, τ᾽, εἶ τε, καί
> ζῆτ᾽, ἦτα, θῆτ᾽, ἴωτα, κάππα, λάβδα, μῦ,
> νῦ, ξεῖ, τὸ οὖ, πεῖ, ῥῶ, τὸ σίγμα, ταῦ, τὸ ὖ,
> πάροντα φεῖ τε χεῖ τε τῷ ψεῖ εἰς τὸ ὦ.

[99] Lucian: *Lovers* 44, 45, quoted by K. J. Freeman.
[100] Theophrastus: *Characters* 30. 14. See R. C. Jebb's note, p. 133.
[101] Athenæus: *Deipnosophistæ* 453 C, D.

There was a remarkable spelling drama by a poet called Kallias; in this there was a chorus of twenty-four. Each member of the chorus represented a letter in the alphabet, and postured as far as possible in the shape of that letter. The first strophe runs so:

Beta	Alpha	Ba
Beta	Ei	Be
Beta	Eta	Bē
Beta	Iota	Bi
Beta	Ou	Bo
Beta	U	Bu
Beta	Ō	Bō

And as they sang the members of the chorus moved into position to form the syllables which they were singing.[102] There seems even to have been some kind of plot in this remarkable drama; and no doubt it made spelling a most interesting occupation.

There were also alphabetical puzzles, which even Euripides wrote, in which the letters were described in poetry and from the description the word had to be discovered. The following, which is by Euripides is on the word *Theseus*.

Θ	First such a circle as is measured out By compasses, a clear mark in the midst.
H	The second letter is two upright lines, Another joining them across their middles.
Σ	The third is like a curl of hair. The fourth
E	One upright line, and three crosswise infixed.
Υ	The fifth is hard to tell: from several points Two lines run down to form one pedestal.
Σ	The last is with the third identical.

There is a fragment of terra-cotta, found at Athens, containing on it:

[102] This and the following aids to spelling are given in K. J. Freeman: *Schools of Hellas*, pp. 88–90.

αρ, βαρ, γαρ, σαρ,
ερ, βερ, γερ, σερ.

It is probably a fragment of a kind of spelling-book.

As the boy learned to recognise the letters of the alphabet, he learned to write them. Plato in the *Protagoras*, in a passage which we have already quoted, outlines the method of teaching. W. R. M. Lamb's translation of the passage is: " Writing-masters first draw letters in faint outline for the less advanced pupils, and then give them the copybook, and make them write according to the guidance of the lines." [103] It is not completely clear what the method was; but there seem to be three different ways involved. It was on wax-tablets that the scholars wrote. Papyrus and vellum were expensive and it was more economical to write on the wax tablet which could be smoothed over and used again and again. It seems that sometimes the master divided the surface of the wax into squares, thereby providing guiding lines within and between which the scholar must write. Sometimes, again, he sketched the outline of the letter lightly in the wax, or parts of the outline and the scholar had to fill it in. Sometimes, again, correctly written copyheads were supplied, which the pupil had to copy as best he might. In the *Stromateis* of Clement of Alexandria we have a nonsense sentence which was used as a copyhead, because it contained every letter in the Greek alphabet.[104]

μάρπτε σφὶγξ κλὼψ ζβυχθηδόν.

In schools where books were few writing was important, because many notes would have to be taken. In the *Charmides* Plato indicates that the aim was to learn to write quickly, because it was quick writing that was specially prized.[105] But in the *Laws* Plato warns against spending too much time on learning exceptional speed and beauty of handwriting: " They must work at letters sufficiently to be able to read and to write. But superior speed or

[103] Plato: *Protagoras* 326 D.

[104] Clement of Alexandria: *Stromateis* 5. 8. It is this custom to which Peter refers in *I Peter* 2. 21, when he said that Christ left us a *hupogrammos*, a copyhead or sketch outline, that we should follow in his steps.

[105] Plato: *Charmides* 159 C.

beauty of handwriting need not be required in the case of those whose progress within the appointed period is too slow." [106]

Soon the boy would move on to dictation.[107] But there was one interesting stage, before the boy had acquired enough facility with letters to read, and enough ability with his stylus to write. At this stage the schoolmaster read to the class passages from the great poets, to which the boys listened, and which they then recited after him, and finally memorised. Here is the most characteristic thing about Greek elementary education. Apart only from Æsop, there were no children's books as such. The boy began with the immortal works of the masters. As soon as he heard anything in school the "surge and thunder" of the *Odyssey* was sounding in his ears. The Greeks were well aware that the boy would not understand it all; but they believed that, even when he did not understand, the beauty would permeate his mind and would leave an impression upon it. The Greek boy did not have to discover that literature was not about cats sitting upon mats; he knew it from the beginning.

What might well surprise us almost more than anything else in the Greek scheme of education is the fact that, when the boy began to read, it was the poets that he read. In the elementary school very little prose was read at all. It was Orpheus, Musæus, Hesiod, Epicharmus, Choirilos, Æschylus, Sophocles, Euripides who were read, and above all Homer, whose works were the bible of the Greeks. That was so because the Greeks believed that the poets were the great teachers. Strabo wrote: "The ancients assert that poetry is a kind of elementary philosophy, which takes us in our boyhood and introduces us to life and teaches us of character, feeling, action, and does it to our enjoyment. . . . That is why the states of the Greeks begin the education of the young with poetry, not merely to stir their souls but to train them." [108] Aristophanes in the *Frogs* makes Æschylus say that the poets are the teachers of men:

> First, Orpheus taught you religious rites and from bloody
> murder to stay your hands;

[106] Plato: *Laws* 810 B. [107] Xenophon: *Œconomicus* 15. 7.

[108] Strabo: 15; quoted T. R. Glover: *Greek Byways*, p. 122.

Musæus, healing and oracle lore; and Hesiod all the culture of lands,
The time to gather the time to plough. And gat not Homer his glory divine
By singing of valour, and honour, and right, and the sheen of the battle-extended line,
The ranging of troops and the arming of men? . . .
And thence my spirit the impress took, and many a lion-hearted chief I drew . . .
The tale may be true, but the tale of vice the sacred poet should hide from view,
Nor ever exhibit and blazon forth on the public stage to the public ken.
For boys a teacher at school is found; but we, the poets, are teachers of men.[109]

The Greeks went even further than that; they declared that the poets were the teachers of all things. In Xenophon's *Symposium* Niceratus says: " You know doubtless that the sage Homer has written about practically everything pertaining to man. Anyone of you, therefore, who wishes to acquire the art of the householder, the political leader, the general, or to become like Achilles, or Ajax, or Nestor, or Odysseus, should seek my favour for I understand these things." Homer teaches him how to be a king, and how to drive a chariot, and even how to use an onion as a relish for a drink.[110] It was the Greek view that there is nothing that the poets do not teach; and that it is the study of them which prepares a lad for manhood and for manhood's tasks.

There were two ways of presenting the poets to boys, as Plato tells in the *Laws*—he disapproves of both of them. The one is to present the boy with the whole of them so that he is " reared and soaked " in the poets, so that he becomes " a lengthy listener and a large learner " and can repeat whole poets by heart. The other is to prepare summaries of the poets, illustrated by purple passages, which the boy must get by heart.[111] The amount of memorising

[109] Aristophanes: *Frogs* 1030 ff.; B. B. Rogers's translation slightly adapted by T. R. Glover.

[110] Xenophon: *Symposium* 4. 6. [111] Plato: *Laws* 810 E, 811 A.

which was done would be by our standards fantastic. In the *Symposium* of Xenophon, Antisthenes asks Niceratus in what kind of knowledge he takes pride, and Niceratus answers: "My father was anxious to see me develop into a good man, and as a means to this end he compelled me to memorise all of Homer: and so even now I can repeat the whole *Iliad* and *Odyssey* by heart."[112] It is true to say that the printed book has killed the memory; in ancient times to possess a thing it was necessary to have it in the memory, and therefore it had to be memorised; now it is only necessary to look it up.

Greek education certainly did one thing—it turned out boys soaked and saturated in the poets of the past, and with their minds stored with greatness. But there is something further to be remembered. Not only did the Greek boy memorise; he also recited; and for the Greek recitation was not simply a repetition of the words; it was a living and an acting of the part. The Greeks are "a nation of actors."[113] And the sensitive boy threw himself heart and soul into the passage which he was reciting. Here he had his model in the rhapsodists, the professional reciters of Homer. Ion tells Socrates that when he is reciting Homer, "At the tale of pity my eyes are filled with tears, and when I speak of horrors, my hair stands on end and my heart throbs."[114]

It is against this background that we must understand and evaluate Plato's violent attack on the poets in general and on the dramatic poets in particular.[115] Let us see Plato's objections to the poets. It is the aim of education to make the Guardians of the state brave, and to see to it that they have the least possible fear of death. Therefore all the terrible and the gloomy and the terrifying pictures which Homer and all the rest of them draw of Hades must be excised (386). All the names which make men shudder must be removed (387 B). All outbursts of grief must go; never must an

[112] Xenophon: *Symposium* 3. 6. T. R. Glover, in commenting on this passage, says: "I have met young Finns who learned the whole *Kalevala* at school in Finland—20,000 lines in three years. Finland means to have a national consciousness, as Greece did; and Homer gave it to the Greeks" (*Greek Byways*, p. 120).

[113] K. J. Freeman: *Schools of Hellas*, p. 97.

[114] Plato: *Ion* 535 B. [115] Plato: *Republic* 386–98.

illustrious man be seen in tears and wailings and lamentations. A good man will never think death terrible for a good man; and he will be so self-sufficient and independent that it will never be terrible for him to lose a friend (387 C, D). Nor is laughter any better. Violent laughter implies a violent reaction; the gods must never be shown as giving way to laughter (388 D). Truth must be valued above all things and never must falsehood be shown (389 B). Temperance is above all things and any story which glorifies food or drink, or palliates intemperance must go (389 D, 390 A). No man must ever be shown to be venal, or to be a prey to ambition (390 E). Plato quotes an illustration of what he means from Pindar. Asclepius, the god of healing, was said to be the son of Apollo. It was said that he was persuaded by gold to restore to life a man who was dead, and that for this action he was struck by a thunderbolt. Plato insists that, " if he was the son of a god, he was not meanly covetous; and, if he was meanly covetous, he was not the son of a god " (408 B, C). All such stories are injurious to the hearer, for they make him pardon his own badness, if he thinks that the gods, and those near to the gods, are like that. If these stories are taught to young people, they cannot do other than produce " a great facility of viciousness " (391 B–E). Even in telling stories of human beings, it must never be made to seem that the unjust man is happy and the just man miserable; no story must ever seem to indicate that injustice is advantageous so long as it is not found out; and that justice is another's good and one's own loss (392 A, B). As he goes on, Plato illustrates each of his points by the quotation of passages from the *Iliad* and the *Odyssey* which he regarded as objectionable until there is little left for approval. Only passages about fine endurance are to be loved and quoted (390 D).

But Plato goes further; there are two ways in which a story can be told, by plain *narrative* and by *imitation*. In imitation the teller puts himself in the place of the person he is telling about and imitates him; all drama is imitation; and epic poetry is partly plain narrative and partly imitation (392 C, D). Now a man can only imitate one thing successfully; an actor is in fact an actor either of comedy or tragedy; he cannot excel in both; and the Guardians of the state, who must be brave, free, temperate and religious must on no account be permitted to imitate that which is unfree and ugly, lest they be infected with the reality (394 A–C). Here is a hammer-blow at the whole system of recitation and repetition. The Guardian must never be allowed to imitate a woman, a slave, an inferior man, a tradesman, a madman—they must have nothing to do with these things (395 D–396 B). For Plato it is unthinkable, let us say, that anyone should imitate Medea, the passionate fool of Euripides, or Prometheus the God-defier of Æschylus. There must be one man, one thing. The man who in his poems can and will imitate everything has no place in the ideal state, however popular he may be elsewhere; he must imitate only the good (397 E–398 A).

That is the most sweeping and trenchant criticism of ancient education—and it was quite unavailing.

One other significant fact may be noted. When the Greek boys were taught the works of the great poets, they were not much troubled with questions of grammar and syntax and vocabulary and the like; they were taught them for their beauty. In spite of Plato, we may say that the great good fortune that the Greek boy had was that he began with the best, and he learned it in a way that must have made it impossible ever totally to forget it.

While he was with the *grammatistēs*, the boy would also learn a certain amount of arithmetic. He would not learn anything in the nature of what might be called higher mathematics for that belonged to the next part of his schooling, and is outside our present scope. A certain amount of calculating knowledge was an absolute necessity. In the *Republic* the question is asked: "So we may conclude that a soldier must know how to count and calculate?" and the answer is: "He must, or he could not be a human being at all, to say nothing of marshalling an army."[116] Some kind of ability to count is a basic human qualification. Plato was impressed by the excellence of mental training that mathematical discipline brings. In the *Republic* it is said: "You see that this study is really indispensable for our purpose, since it forces the mind to arrive at pure truth by the exercise of pure thought." And then Plato asks: "Have you noticed, too, how people with a talent for calculation are naturally quick at learning almost any other subject; and how a training in it makes a slow mind quicker, even if it does no other good?"[117] This is a favourite contention with Plato, for he recurs

[116] Plato: *Republic* 522 B. [117] Plato: *Republic* 526 B.

to it in the *Laws*: "In relation to economics, to politics, and to all the arts, no single branch of educational science possesses so great an influence as the study of numbers: its chief advantage is that it wakes up the man who is by nature drowsy and slow of wit, and makes him quick to learn, mindful, and sharp-witted, progressing beyond his natural capacity by art divine."[118]

But at this point in education all that was required and all that was given was enough arithmetic for practical purposes. In the *Laws* Plato, speaking through the Athenian stranger, lists arithmetic as part of his educational curriculum, "of which I said that there ought to be as much as everyone needs to learn for purposes of war, house-management and civic administration; together with what is useful for these same purposes to learn about the courses of the heavenly bodies—stars and sun and moon—in so far as every state is obliged to take them into account." He means that enough arithmetical knowledge must be gained to calculate correctly the dates of the Feasts and Festivals which the community must observe if the duties of religion are to be correctly performed.[119]

So, then, at the elementary stage the idea is to teach the boy just as much arithmetic as will be practically useful, and indeed essential, for the life of a citizen. But here is where Greek education again shows its special genius. We have already noted the importance which the Greek educationalists attached to games and to play; and it is of the greatest interest to note how Plato suggests that arithmetic should be taught as a game far more than as a science. Early in the *Laws* he makes the interesting suggestion that the best way to educate a child is to set him playing at what he is aiming to be when he is a man. The passage is fairly long but it is worth quoting in full:

> What I assert is that every man who is going to be good at any pursuit must practise that special pursuit from infancy, by using all the implements of his pursuit both in his play and in his work. For example, the man who is going to make a good builder must play at building toy houses, and to make a good farmer he must play at tilling land; and those who are rearing them must provide each child with toy tools modelled on the

[118] Plato: *Laws* 747 B. [119] Plato: *Laws* 809 C.

> real ones. Besides this, they ought to have elementary instruction in all the necessary subjects—the carpenter, for instance, being taught in play the use of the rule and measure, the soldier taught riding or some similar accomplishment. So, by means of their games, we should endeavour to turn the tastes and desires of the children in the direction of that object which forms their ultimate goal. First and foremost education, we say, consists in that right nurture which most strongly draws the soul of the child when at play to a love for that pursuit of which, when he becomes a man, he must possess a perfect mastery.[120]

It is obvious that the child who is to be a builder or a carpenter will be set to playing at arithmetic. Later in the *Laws* Plato commends the game form of teaching arithmetic which, he says, is used among the Egyptians. His description is highly compressed, and we shall state it first and then, with the help of K. J. Freeman, expand it:

> First, as regards counting, lessons have been invented for the merest infants to learn, by way of fun and play—ways of dividing up apples and chaplets, so that the same totals are adjusted to larger and smaller groups, and ways of sorting out boxers and wrestlers, in byes and pairs, taking them alternately, or consecutively in their natural order. Moreover, by way of play, the teachers mix together bowls made of gold, bronze, silver, and the like, and others distribute them, as I said, by groups of a single kind, adapting the rules of elementary arithmetic to play.[121]

We know that a favourite game with Greek boys was knucklebones,[122] and playing that game must have meant the calculation of how many pieces were payable by the loser and owing to the winner. K. J. Freeman conjectures that the other games which Plato mentions may have been played out somewhat as follows.[123] The master took, say, sixty apples. First, he divided them among

[120] Plato: *Laws* 643 B–D. [121] Plato: *Laws* 819 A–C.

[122] Plato: *Lysis* 206 E. [123] K. J. Freeman: *Schools of Hellas*, p. 106.

two boys, who were made to count their share, thirty each; then among three boys, twenty each; then among four, fifteen each; then among five, twelve each; and then among six, ten each. This would teach the system of factors. Then a real, or imaginary, contest in wrestling or boxing would be arranged, say in a class of nine. The boys would work out, no doubt by actual experiment, if each boy had to fight every other boy at least once, how many rounds and byes were necessary; and thus permutations and combinations would be absorbed. Again, bowls of coins, some containing mixed coins, gold, silver and bronze, some containing coins all of one sort might be handed round the class; and the scholars would have to add and subtract them, and so learn arithmetic and the handling of money at the same time. The learning of arithmetic would be a most engaging pastime in a Greek school.

So, then, from the *grammatistēs* the boy would learn how to read and how to write; he would be introduced to the great works of the great poets, and would have to listen to them, recite them, and memorise them until he was soaked and saturated in them; and he would learn enough arithmetic for the ordinary uses of everyday life. It was no bad basic training; and it was not beaten into a boy, for much of the work was modelled on play, and often the boy would not know the difference between learning a lesson and playing a game.

We now come to the second of the great departments of elementary education in Athens, that which was presided over by the *kitharistēs*, and which was called *mousikē*. *Mousikē* is, as we shall see, much wider than the English word " music," for it included the poems of the great lyric poets, and also all rhythm of movement as in dancing.

We must remember two basic facts about Greek music. The first is the quite simple fact that the Greek had no use for music without words. Instrumental music never stood by itself; it was always an accompaniment to some form of words. The second fact is even more basic—the Greek had an extraordinary sense of the moral, and even the physical, power of music over men. To him music was a dynamic power, and that is why the great educationalists spend so much time laying down how it must be taught.

It is the complaint of Socrates in the *Gorgias* that in his day music "is only aiming at our pleasure, and at naught else." He complains that a musician and dithyrambic poet like Cinesias does not care "a jot about trying to say things of a sort that might be improving to his audience," but "only what is likely to gratify the crowd of the spectators." Men like that make the mistake of thinking that "music is invented for the sake of pleasure."[124] Aristophanes compares the ancient with the modern music:

> And then to the home of the Harpist would come decorous in action and word
> All the lads of the town, though the snow peppered down, in spite of all wind and all weather:
> And they sang an old song, as they paced it along, not shambling with thighs glued together:
> "O the dread shout of war how it peals from afar," or, "Pallas the stormer adore,"
> To some manly old air, all simple and bare, which their fathers had chanted before.
> And should anyone dare the tune to impair and with intricate twistings to fill,
> Such as Phrynis is fain, and his long-winded train, perversely to quiver and trill,
> Many stripes would he feel in return for his zeal, as to genuine music a foe.[125]

In the *Timæus* Plato writes of the formative power of music that "harmony is not regarded by him who intelligently uses the muses as given by them with a view to irrational pleasure, but with a view to the disharmonious course of the soul and as an ally for the purpose of reducing this into harmony and agreement with itself; and rhythm was given by them for the same purpose, on account of the irregular and graceless ways which prevail among mankind generally, and to help us against them."[126] In the *Protagoras* he writes: "They make rhythm and harmony familiar to the souls of boys, that they may grow more gentle, and graceful, and harmonious, and so be of service both in words and deeds; for the whole life of man

[124] Plato: *Gorgias* 501 E–502 A.

[125] Aristophanes: *Clouds* 964–72.

[126] Plato: *Timæus* 47 D.

stands in need of grace and harmony."[127] Plutarch in his essay *On Music* writes: "Whoever he be that shall give his mind to the study of music in his youth, if he meet with a musical education, proper for the forming and regulating of his inclinations, he will be sure to applaud and embrace that which is noble and generous, and to rebuke and blame the contrary, as well in other things as what belongs to music. And by that means he will become clear from all reproachful actions, for now having reaped the noblest fruit of music, he may be of great use, not only to himself but to the commonwealth; while music teaches him to abstain from everything that is indecent, both in word and deed, and to observe decorum, temperance, and regularity." "The right moulding or ruin of ingenuous manners and civil conduct lies in a well-grounded musical education."[128] It is Plato's conviction that the absence of grace, rhythm, and harmony, and baseness of thought, expression and character go together. So he goes on:

> Hence, Glaucon, I continued, the decisive importance of education in poetry and music; rhythm and harmony sink deep into the recesses of the soul and take the strongest hold there, bringing that grace of body and mind which is only to be found in one who is brought up in the right way. Moreover, a proper training in this kind makes a man quick to perceive any defect or ugliness in art or nature. Such deformity will rightly disgust him. Approving of all that is lovely, he will welcome it home with joy into his soul, and, nourished thereby, grow into a man of a noble spirit. All that is ugly and disgraceful he will rightly condemn and abhor while he is still too young to understand the reason; and when reason comes, he will greet her as a friend with whom his education has made him long familiar.[129]

When good music with noble rhythms is sung it challenges all who hear it to accompany the singers in acquiring virtue by means of these representations.[130]

[127] Plato: *Protagoras* 326 B.

[128] Plutarch: *On Music* 41 and 31. This and the previous two passages are quoted in A. S. Wilkins: *National Education in Greece*, pp. 76, 77.

[129] Plato: *Republic* 401. [130] Plato: *Laws* 812 C.

K. J. Freeman has made a collection of passages in which the Greeks show their sense of the actual power of music.[131] Theophrastus, the pupil of Aristotle, and a notable philosopher in his own right, goes the length of saying that the Phrygian harmony played on the flute is the correct cure for lumbago (*Athenæus* 624 B). Pindar says that Apollo, "gives to men and women cures for grievous sickness, and invented the harp, and gives the Muse to whom he will, bringing warless peace into the heart" (*Pythians* 5. 60–3). Athenæus tells how Cleinias, the Pythagorean philosopher, when he was in a bad temper, used to take the harp, saying: "I am calming myself" (*Athenæus* 624 A). The oddest of all these instances comes from Plutarch's *Lycurgus*. Lycurgus visited Crete and knew that the Cretan laws were good. He wished to introduce them into Sparta, but knew that his people were not ready for them. So he persuaded Thales to visit Sparta. "Now Thales passed as a lyric poet, and screened himself behind this art, but in reality he did the work of one of the mightiest law-givers. For his odes were so many exhortations to obedience and harmony, and their measured rhythms were permeated with ordered tranquillity, so that those who listened to them were insensibly softened in their dispositions, insomuch that they renounced the mutual hatreds which were so rife at that time, and dwelt together in a common pursuit of what was high and noble."[132] As Plutarch has it, it was nothing other than the music of Thales which produced the laws of Sparta.

With this belief the Greeks very naturally divided music into various modes, each of which had its own effect. There was the Lydian mode, which Plato approved, but which none the less was soft and enervating. There was the Mixed-Lydian and Synton-Lydian, which was melancholy and depressing. There was the Ionian, which was luxurious and pleasure-loving and altogether effeminate. There was the Æolic or Hypo-Dorian, which was haughty and arrogant, inflated and confident. There was the Phrygian, which was hysterical and orgiastic and maddening. And there was the Dorian, which, as Plato said, "suitably represented the notes and accents of a brave man in the presence of war or any

[131] K. J. Freeman: *Schools of Hellas*, p. 243.

[132] Plutarch: *Lycurgus* 4. 1, 2.

other violent action, going to meet wounds or death or fallen into any other misfortune, facing his fate with unflinching resolution."[133]

Plato in the *Republic* shows himself fascinated by this conception of rhythm which lies at the heart of music. Every craft needs its rhythm and its form, and nothing can bring it as music can. Craftsmen must be found who follow the graceful and the beautiful; they must live in beautiful surroundings " so that something may strike upon their seeing and their hearing like a breeze bearing health from wholesome places." Unconsciously children must be brought " to likeness and to friendship and harmony with the law of beauty." And for this music is the sovereign medicine, for nothing sinks into the soul like rhythm and tune, till they make a man as graceful as themselves. Through music he can absorb beauty into his soul.[134]

Aristotle, too, is sure that music is capable of producing a certain kind of character. He is clear that music " has the power of producing a certain effect on the moral character of the soul." [135]

If all this is so, nothing can be clearer than that music must be controlled and regulated by the wise law-giver. Neither the public nor the poets can be trusted. Dancing, singing and the whole of choristry must be brought under control. In the *Laws* Plato writes: " In truth every unregulated musical pursuit becomes, when brought under regulation, a thousand times better, even when no honeyed strains are served up: all alike provide pleasure. For if a man has been reared from childhood up to the age of steadiness and sense in the use of music that is sober and regulated, then he detests the opposite kind whenever he hears it, and calls it vulgar; whereas if he has been reared in the common honeyed kind of music, he declares the opposite of it to be cold and unpleasing." [136] In connection with this Plato has a lovely thought. He suggests

[133] Plato: *Republic* 399 A. The various modes are described in K. J. Freeman: *Schools of Hellas*, pp. 241–4. The classification is attributed by Athenæus (624 C) to Heracleides of Pontus.

[134] In the *Republic* the discussion of *mousikē* runs from 398 A to 402 D, from which section the quotations are taken.

[135] Aristotle: *Politics* 8. 4. 4; 8. 5. 9. Aristotle's main discussion of *mousikē* is in the *Politics* 8. 4. 3–8. 7. 11.

[136] Plato: *Laws* 802 C.

that all music should be consecrated; that it should be used in hymns and dances at the great festivals of the gods, and that no note of the singing and no movement of any limb must be changed.[137]

In one particular there was one accepted custom; the flute was barred from all respectable music. In the *Republic* Plato will not even allow the flute to be manufactured in the ideal state.[138] Aristotle sets out the reasons for its banishing. It is not a moralising, but an exciting instrument. It had for the Greek the supreme disadvantage that the player could not sing as he played it. And its playing distorts the face. It was said that Athene, the goddess, found a flute and flung it away because it so distorted her face.[139] Alcibiades, Plutarch tells us, refused to learn to play on the flute, calling it a sordid thing.[140] And Athenæus quotes the ancient proverb:

> A flautist's brains can never stay:
> He puffs his flute, they're puffed away.[141]

Flute-playing was left to flute-girls, and Pratinas bids the flute to be content "to lead young men in their carousals and their brawls." [142]

What then was the actual training in *mousikē* that the Greek lad received? According to Plato in the *Laws* he did not begin his actual training in *mousikē* until he was thirteen; and that, as a general rule, may well be true in view of the technical difficulty of playing his instrument.[143] The instrument that the lad played was the seven-stringed lyre, which was actually the *lura*; the *kithara* was in fact a professional instrument. So universal was this lyre-playing that even Socrates began it in his middle age to the great amusement of the class, and not with very notable success.[144]

But it was not so much the playing of the lyre which was important. As the boy learned to play, he learned to know and sing

137 Plato: *Laws* 799 A–800 A. 138 Plato: *Republic* 399 E.
139 Aristotle: *Politics* 8. 6. 5–8. 140 Plutarch: *Alcibiades* 2. 5.
141 Athenæus 377 F; quoted K. J. Freeman: *Schools of Hellas*, p. 111.
142 Quoted K. J. Freeman: *Schools of Hellas*, p. 110 (footnote).
143 Plato: *Laws* 810 A. 144 Plato: *Euthydemus* 272 C.

the poems of the great lyric poets like Alcæus and Anacreon; it was indeed for that that he learned. He was never intended to reach the standard of a professional; that would have been quite wrong; but, when the Athenians met for dinner, and after the dinner was passed, he was able to take his share in the songs which went round the table, which was part of the duty of an Athenian gentleman.

The whole conception of *mousikē* was not to produce technically perfect, solo musicians; it was to produce those who knew and loved the great lyric poets; and to move the soul to greatness by great music. It is told that the Earl of Kinnoull came to Handel after the first performance of his *Messiah*, and thanked him for the magnificent entertainment which he had given the audience. " My Lord," said Handel, " I did not mean to entertain them, I meant to make them better men and women "; and that would be no inaccurate description of the aim of Athenian *mousikē*.

There remains the third basic department of the education of the Greek boy, *gumnastikē*, and to it we must now turn our attention. As the first two departments were designed to train the mind, so this third department was designed to train the body, and in particular to train it as the servant of the mind.

Of the necessity for it the Greek had no doubt. As Plato saw it, physical fitness was a necessity for life. He draws a picture of the young men of his day, particularly among the wealthier classes, whom " luxurious indolence of body and mind " makes " too lazy and effeminate to resist pleasure or to endure pain." He speaks of such a man in battle " panting under his burden of fat, and showing every sign of distress." He pours contempt on the person " so unhealthy that the least shock from outside will upset the balance or, even without that, internal disorder will break out." [145] In the *Memorabilia* Xenophon shows us Socrates dealing sternly with the young Epigenes who was in poor condition. Socrates told him that he needed exercise, and Epigenes retorted that he was no athlete. Socrates points out to him that he may well have to become a soldier and fight his battles; and in battle " many thanks to their bad condition lose their life in the perils of war, or save it disgracefully." Many are taken prisoner because they are not fit enough to

[145] Plato: *Republic* 556.

escape. On the other hand the fit are healthy and strong; they can save themselves and help their friends; they can get themselves honour, live more pleasantly, and leave their children a better heritage. Not only is physical fitness a necessity for war; it is also a necessity for study. " Because, when the body is in a bad condition," insists Socrates, " loss of memory, depression, discontent, insanity often assail the mind so violently as to drive out whatever knowledge it contains." And finally Socrates utters a wise warning saying: "It is a disgrace to grow old through sheer carelessness." [146] A person who neglects his body by serving pleasure and neglecting discipline " in war and all important crises gives courage to his enemies, and fills his friends, and even his lovers themselves, with fear." [147]

It is with *gumnastikē* that Plato would begin education at the age of six when the boys must go to teachers of riding, archery, javelin-throwing and slinging. Plato has a curiously urgent appeal that children should all be taught to be ambidexterous. He points out that in the feet there is no difference in what he calls working capacity; and he says that it is through the follies of nurses and mothers that " we have all become limping, so to say, in our hands." He insists on the obvious advantage the ambidexterous person has, not only in war, but also in all the activities of life.[148]

But, convinced as the Greeks were of the necessity of physical training, they were equally convinced of the dangers which attended an undue stressing of athletics. To the Greek athletics were never an end in themselves. The cultured Greek had nothing but contempt for the specialised athlete, whose only care was his body. Plato speaks of the man who cultivates the body exclusively: " Suppose he does nothing else and holds aloof from all kinds of culture, then, even if there was in him something capable of desiring knowledge, it is starved of instruction and never encouraged to think for itself by taking part in rational discussion or intellectual pursuits of any kind; and so it grows feeble from lack of nourishment, and deaf and blind because the darkness that clouds perception is never cleared away. Such a man ends by being wholly uncultivated and a hater of reason." [149] In the *Lovers* there is the description

[146] Xenophon: *Memorabilia* 3. 12. 1–8. [147] Plato: *Phædrus* 239 C.
[148] Plato: *Laws* 794 C–795. [149] Plato: *Republic* 411 C, D.

of the athletic young man who has spent the whole of his life in practising the neckhold, and stuffing himself, and sleeping.[150] The body must have its proper nourishment, and the soul its proper learning and moral training, but the man who aims at being an Olympian or a Pythian victor has not time for anything but physical training, and he has lost that essential leisure for the other tasks which most truly deserve the name of "life."[151] Aristotle declares that up to the age of puberty physical training must be light; and even after that the boy must never be over-trained. He points out that in the list of Olympic victors you will not find more than two or three people who won the victory both as boys and men, because their training as boys ruined their bodies in the end. In any event, he says, no one can work hard with the body and the mind at one and the same time. The overstressing of athletics in effect renders men untrained and vulgar, not lions with the strength of gentleness, but wolves with animal ferocity.[152] Aristotle was very conscious of the brutalising effect of too severe physical training, as used, for instance in Sparta.

In the *Symposium* Socrates points out that athletic over-specialisation can result not in physical fitness, but in a certain deformity of body. He talks of the long-distance runners who develop their legs at the expense of their shoulders, and the prize-fighters who develop their shoulders but become thin-legged.[153] The really specialised athlete became torpid for other purposes, unable to withstand vicissitudes of heat and cold, and physically upset whenever he was unable to obtain his carefully chosen diet. Athenæus tells us that both Milo and Theagenes ate a whole ox in a day, and that Astyanax, the pankratiast, ate a meal which was intended for nine people.[154]

As in so many civilisations, the professional athlete was pampered and petted and fêted. Plutarch tells us that Solon laid it down that the victor in the Isthmian games was to be paid one hundred drachmæ, and the victor in the Olympic games five hundred

[150] Plato: *The Lovers* 132 C. [151] Plato: *Laws* 807 C, D.

[152] Aristotle: *Politics* 8. 4. 1, 2; 8. 3. 3–5.

[153] Xenophon: *Symposium* 2. 17.

[154] Athenæus: *Deipnosophistæ* 412 F; 413 B. For further instances, see K. J. Freeman: *Schools of Hellas*, pp. 120, 121.

drachmæ.[155] And we have only to read the odes of Pindar to see in what honour a victor in the games was held.

There were not wanting even in the early times voices to protest against this exaggerated athleticism. K. J. Freeman quotes two of them.[156] Xenophanes of Colophon wrote his protest in an elegiac poem:

> If a man wins a victory at Olympia . . . either by speed of foot or in the pentathlon, or by wrestling, or competing in painful boxing, or in the dread contest called the pankration, his countrymen will look upon him with admiration, and he will receive a front seat at the games, and eat his dinners at public cost, and be presented with some gift that he will treasure. And this he will get, even if he only win a horse race. Yet he is not as worthy as I; for my wisdom is better than the strength of men and steeds. Nay this custom is foolish, and it is not right to honour strength more than excellence of wisdom. Not by good boxing, nor by the pentathlon, nor by wrestling, nor yet by speed of foot, which is the most honoured in the contests of all the feats of human strength—not so would a city be well governed. Small joy would it get from a victory at Olympia: such things do not fatten the dark corners of a city.

The other voice of protest is the voice of the rebel Euripides:

> Of countless ills in Hellas, the race of athletes is quite the worst. . . . They are slaves of their jaw and worshippers of their belly. . . . In youth they go about in splendour, the admiration of their city, but when bitter old age comes upon them, they are cast aside like worn-out coats. I blame the custom of the Hellenes who gather together to watch these men, honouring a useless pleasure. Who ever helped his fatherland by winning a crown for wrestling, or speed of foot, or flinging the discus, or giving a good blow on the jaw? Will they fight the foe with the discus, or smite their fists through shields? Garlands should be kept for the wise and the good, and for him who best rules the city

[155] Plutarch: *Solon* 23. 3.

[156] K. J. Freeman: *Schools of Hellas*, pp. 121, 122.

> by his temperance and justice, who by his words drives away evil deeds, preventing strife and sedition.[157]

It is extremely interesting and significant to set beside all this Plato's conception of the function of *gumnastikē*. "There is," he says, "perhaps no greater hindrance than the supererogatory care of the body, which goes beyond gymnastic."[158] Plato's view of gymnastic is quite simple and very wise. Its primary aim is to keep a man in such a constant state of physical fitness that he will never need the medical art, except under some special compulsion.[159] He is convinced that *gumnastikē* and *mousikē* must go together and be complementary to each other. *Gumnastikē* by itself will produce too much fierceness; *mousikē* by itself will produce too much softness; but when they combine in the correct proportion the ideal body and character emerge. When both combine, the spirited and the wisdom-loving part of the mind are wrought into a perfect harmony.[160]

There were those in Greece who made a god of athletics; but the Greek ideal was to use athletics to make the perfectly symmetrical body the servant of the perfectly equipped mind.

Let us now see the actual gymnastic curriculum through which the boy passed. This was carried out in two centres. There was the *palaistra*, the wrestling-school. It was very simple, being little more than a wide, sandy playground, with the minimum of equipment. It was there that most of the boys' exercises were carried out. And there was the much more elaborate *gymnasium*, complete with all kinds of equipment and buildings, which, as we shall see, was not only the exercising-ground, but was also the social and intellectual centre of Athens. Let us then first follow the boy to the *palaistra*.

The teacher in charge of the *palaistra* and its training was the *paidotribēs*, literally "the boy-rubber." He was so called because of the great part that rubbing and anointing with oil took in these exercises. The *paidotribēs* was a thorough expert in his own line. He had to know what kind of exercise suited each particular boy, fitting the exercise to the boy's strength and skill and bodily ability.

[157] Euripides: A fragment of the *Autolycus*. [158] Plato: *Republic* 407 B.
[159] Plato: *Republic* 410 B. [160] Plato: *Republic* 410, 411.

He had to know what kind of exercises suited the largest number of people. He had to know what kind of exercises were required to enable an athlete to excel at any given sport or branch of sport.[161] Aristotle uses the work of the *paidotribēs* as an illustration of how the constitution of a city must be carefully wrought out to meet the needs of the city. The *paidotribēs* was so much an expert in physical things that he was not unworthy to be named in the same breath as the doctor. Plato in the *Gorgias* mentions the doctor and the trainer together.[162] Socrates says that if a *paidotribēs* were asked what his work was, his answer would be: "My work is making men's bodies beautiful and strong."[163] As we have already seen, Plato would have said that the function of the doctor is to cure disease, but the function of the *paidotribēs* would be to make a man so healthy and fit that disease would not attack him. His function was prevention, as the function of the doctor was cure. The *paidotribēs* was carefully chosen, for "people send their sons to a trainer that, having improved their bodies, they may perform the orders of their minds, which are now in condition, and that they may not be forced by bodily faults to play the coward in wars and other duties."[164]

The exercise was taken in the open air, and it was taken stripped naked. The ideal of the Greek was to have a body hardened and tanned by exposure to the weather and to the sun. Plato pours scorn on the man who has been so softened by devotion to pleasure that he is effeminate and not virile, who has not been brought up in the pure sunshine, but in mingled shade, who is unused to manly toils and the sweat of exertion, who is accustomed to a delicate and unmanly way of life, who is adorned by a bright complexion of artificial origin, since he has none by nature.[165] It was told of Agesilaus, the famous Spartan king, that he stripped his eastern captives naked, that men might see the whiteness of their bodies and despise them; to the Greek a white body was effeminate, and his aim was a body tanned by the sun.

What then were the exercises, and what was the training which the boy received?

[161] Aristotle: *Politics* 4. 1. 1.

[162] Plato: *Gorgias* 504 A.

[163] Plato: *Gorgias* 452 B.

[164] Plato: *Protagoras* 326 C.

[165] Plato: *Charmides* 239 C.

He began by learning proper deportment, how to sit correctly, and how to stand straight. To the Greek it was a sign of *agroikia*, boorishness, to sit in such a way that the ill-placed knees and ill-disposed robe revealed more than they concealed.[166] He was taught what is called *gesticulation*, that is exercises in which the arms were moved in a rhythmical way, a kind of exercise which was half-way between drill and dancing. The athletic activities comprised five different things.

First, there came *wrestling*. For it the ground was broken up with a pick-axe, so that the boy's body would not be bruised when he fell, or was thrown. His body was rubbed with oil, so that he would be slippery and hard to grip. There were two kinds of wrestling. In the one kind the victor was he who threw his opponent three times, without himself being dragged down; the other was a much more rough and tumble affair, in which the two struggled upright and rolled on the ground until one was pinned down. There is one rather interesting point to be noted. The wrestling was not primarily for victory. It consisted of a series of *schēmata*, grips and holds and positions. Under the direction of the master the combatants would use now one *schēma* and now another; they would move from gambit to gambit, and from hold to hold. They were learning the theory of that which would be used in earnest later on. Isocrates uses that method as an illustration of the way in which a rhetorician teaches his pupils.[167] He teaches them the theoretical gambits and moves, which in later days they will have to apply in the dust and heat of the court. This exercising in the theory of wrestling would obviously have none of the brutalising effect of the Spartan method of fighting in earnest.

Lucian in the *Anacharsis*, his essay on athletics, says of the Greek methods: " We rub the boys with olive oil and supple them in order that they may be more elastic, for, since we believe that

[166] Theophrastus in his character of the Boorish Man says that such a man " will sit down with his cloak above his knee, and thus expose too much of himself" (*Characters* 4. 4). Aristophanes in *The Clouds* (973) says that that is the kind of thing that the well-trained boy of the good old days would never have done.

[167] Isocrates: *Antidosis* 184.

leather when softened by oil is harder to break and far more durable, lifeless as it is, it would be extraordinary if we did not think that the living body would be put in better condition by oil." [168] He explains that it is the Greek custom to strip the boys, in order to habituate them to the weather, and to make them used to the several seasons, so that they will not be distressed by the heat or give in to the cold. "They show no white and ineffective corpulence or pallid leanness . . . they have a ruddy skin, coloured darker by the sun." [169]

There was *boxing*. In the real boxing contests at the great games the contestants wore heavy gloves with balls of lead in them; but the boys wore coverings of string worn round their hands and wrists and fingers. Boxing was taught in the same way as wrestling, by the use of *schēmata*, figures. As the boys boxed, the master called out the leads and the checks that they must use, so that the boxing never descended into a real fight, but prepared the boys for the real fight when it should come.

There was the *pankration*. This was easily the most ferocious of the exercises, and was not for small boys at all. It combined boxing and wrestling; it was often fought with bare hands; and it was more of a rough and tumble, with nothing barred, than anything else. In it the contestants wore dog-skin caps to protect their ears. Lucian's *Anacharsis* is an imaginary conversation on Greek athletics between Solon, the great Greek law-giver, and Anacharsis, the famous Scythian. It opens with the amazed comments of Anacharsis, for he and Solon must have arrived on the scene when the *pankration* was in progress. "And why are your young men doing this, Solon? Some of them, locked in each other's arms, are tripping each other up, while others are choking and twisting each other and grovelling together in the mud, wallowing like swine. . . . They push one another about with lowered heads and butt their foreheads together like rams. And see there! That man picked the other one up by the legs, and threw him to the ground, and then fell down upon him and will not let him get up, shoving him all down into the mud; and now after winding his legs about his middle and putting his forearm underneath his throat, he is choking the poor fellow, who is slapping him sideways on the shoulder, by way of

[168] Lucian: *Anacharsis* 168. [169] Lucian: *Anacharsis* 24, 25.

begging off I take it, so that he may not be strangled completely." To Anacharsis it looks like insanity, and the conduct of men who are out of their minds. "For my part," he says, "if one of you should treat me like that, he will find out that we do not carry these daggers in our belts for nothing!"[170] The lengths to which the pankration could go may be seen in the famous story of Alcibiades, as Plutarch tells it: "Once, when he was a boy, being hard-pressed in wrestling, and fearing to be thrown, he got the hand of his antagonist to his mouth, and bit it with all his force. The other loosed his hold immediately and said: 'You bite, Alcibiades, like a woman.' 'No,' replied Alcibiades, 'like a lion!'"[171] The *pankration* was the most ferocious of athletic activities, and clearly not for the younger and the smaller boys.

There was *running*. In Greek athletics running was the greatest sport of all. There were three main races. There was the *stadion*, of which the length was two hundred yards. There was the *diaulos* which was a quarter of a mile. There was the long distance race which varied from three-quarters of a mile to almost three miles; but the standard distance was twenty-four *stadia*, four thousand, eight hundred yards. Two things are to be noticed about these races. For men, they were often run in full armour, for they were in reality training for war. And they were apparently always run in soft sand, for that was thought to be a better training. "The running is not done on hard resisting ground," says Lucian in his *Anacharsis* (27), "but in deep sand, where it is not easy to plant one's foot solidly or to get a purchase with it, since it slips from under one as the sand gives way beneath it." He goes on to say that they were set to jumping across ditches, carrying heavy weights as they jumped.

There was the *long jump*. There seems to be no trace of a high jump in Greek athletics. The long jump was performed with the aid of *haltēres*, which were a kind of dumb-bells; no doubt they were swung in the hands to give the jumper momentum. The long jump was performed to the music of the flute, in order to give the jumper rhythm as he came to the take off. If the figures are true, the Greek record for the long jump still stands. For Chionis, a Spartan, is recorded to have jumped fifty-two

[170] Lucian: *Anacharsis* 1, 5, 6. [171] Plutarch: *Alcibiades* 2. 3.

feet in 660 B.C., and Phayllos of Croton fifty-five feet a little later.[172]

There was *throwing the discus.* The discus was a bronze or other metal circle eight or nine inches across. It was thrown to the music of the flute; and the movements preparatory to throwing were complicated and rhythmic; in it both distance and direction were taken into account in assessing the winner.

There was *throwing the javelin.* For the boy the javelin was an unpointed cane of wood; and it was thrown at a hoop in the ground a certain distance away.

We are told that the whole athletic course cost one *mina*, that is about five pounds; and that that contribution covered admission to the *palaistra* apparently for life.[173]

Finally we follow the athlete to the *gymnasium.* As we have said the *gymnasium* was a much more elaborate place. The *palaistra* was privately owned; but the *gymnasium* was built and owned by the state; and it was the social club, and the intellectual centre of Greek life. The following account of it is based on the description by K. J. Freeman.

It was generally in the afternoon that the Greek went to the gymnasium, and from it, bathed and anointed, he would go straight on to dinner.[174] First, there was the stripping and the dressing-room. When Socrates returned from Potidæa, he sought his wonted conversations. It was to the wrestling-school of Taureas he went; and there he talked with Charmides about *sōphrosunē.*[175] When Socrates met Hippothales and his friends, they invited him to the wrestling-school where Miccus, the sophist, was discoursing, and where the dialogue which is known as the *Lysis* ensued.[176] It was in the undressing-room that Socrates was sitting, and which he was just intending to leave, when his daemon bade him stay,

[172] J. P. Mahaffy: *Old Greek Education*, p. 34.

[173] Most of the facts regarding gymnastics have been taken from K. J. Freeman's account of the subject in *Schools of Hellas*, pp. 129–34. It would scarcely be possible to write without being indebted to his invaluable work.

[174] In his *Symposium* Xenophon tells how Callias invited Socrates and his friends to dinner. The guests arrived " some having first taken their exercise and their rub-down; others with the addition of a bath " (I. 7).

[175] Plato: *Charmides* 153 A. [176] Plato: *Lysis* 204 A.

when he met Euthydemus, and where the dialogue of that name took place.[177]

Out of the dressing-room there opened the cloister. Exercise was taken always in the open air, but people could walk in the cloister when the weather was too severe or the sun too hot; it was in the cloister that Euthydemus and Dionysodorus were talking when Socrates saw them.[178] It was in the cloister that Theodorus the mathematician from Cyrene was working out his problems in the sand, and talking about geometry.[179] The dressing-room and the cloister of the gymnasium were places where anyone might be met, and where there would be free lectures at any time by the greatest scholars.

Next there was the oiling-room and the dusting-room where they anointed their bodies with oil, and powdered them with dust, later to be scraped off with the scraper, the *stleggis*.

Next there were the baths, to which the Athenian would go before he went on to dinner. The baths were not baths in the English sense of the term. The water stood in great jars, and was poured over the head in beakers. Socrates speaks of Thrasymachus deluging the ears of the company with a torrent of words, " as the man at the baths might empty a bucket over one's head."[180] It was customary to tip the man who poured the water over the bather's head, and Theophrastus describes the man who was shamelessly mean, " who loves to go up to the cauldrons at the baths, and dipping the ladle despite the cries of the bathing-man, do his own drenching, and exclaim as he runs off: ' I've had my bath, and no thanks to you for that.' "[181]

Within the cloister there was a great open space, where people might practise. In particular there was the *korukos*. The *korukos* was a kind of punch-ball. It was a sack swinging on a rope. The heavier kind was filled with sand; the lighter with grain. It was set swinging, and the idea was to stop it with the head, or the chest, or the back, without being bowled over. Round the wall there

[177] Plato: *Euthydemus* 272 E. [178] Plato: *Euthydemus* 273 A.

[179] Plato: *Euthydemus* 144 C; 147 D, E. [180] Plato: *Republic* 344 D.

[181] Theophrastus: *Characters* 9. 8. The phrase: " I will give myself a bath," was a proverb for doing something for oneself.

were lay figures, or dummies, on which a man might practise boxing, if he could find no partner with whom to practise. Plato in the *Laws* says: "If we chanced to be very short of training-mates, do you suppose that we should be deterred by fear of the laughter of fools from hanging up a lifeless dummy and practising on it?" [182]

All round there were rooms and these rooms were furnished with seats and it was often there that the famous sophists lectured, and first found a following. Outside there were places where the boxers and the wrestlers practised; where the runners trained; where the teams of the *ephēbi* prepared for their contests; where the archers and the discus- and the javelin-throwers practised. And it was not without danger for was Hyacinthus not slain by the discus of Apollo? And Antiphon had an imaginary case in which a boy was killed by a javelin as he crossed the open space. It was there that the ball games—in which Sophocles was a famous expert—were played.

Two further things must be noted. First, from all this women were totally excluded. Here was the man's preserve, where men met with men. Second, all this was free, with the exception of the oil and the scraper, for which a man must pay. In Greece athletics were more than athletics; they were the means to a liberal education.

Such then is the outline of Greek education. It began with the *grammatistēs* who taught the boy his letters, who guided his hand in writing, who taught him to count, and who set the great poets ringing in his ears; it went on to the *kitharistēs*, from whom the boy learned music, and the great lyric poets; and all the time he was going to the *paidotribēs* that his body might be made the fit servant of his mind. It is a lovely picture in many ways; but it has one basic disadvantage. It was based on slavery. To a man like Aristotle slavery was natural and essential, in the very nature of things. There are those for whom it is advantageous to be governed; there are those who by nature belong to someone else; the usefulness of the slave is like the usefulness of the domestic animal; "bodily service for the necessities of life is forthcoming from both." [183] This was an education which despised work. If

[182] Plato: *Laws* 830 B. [183] Aristotle: *Politics* I. 2. 13, 14.

a man could have walked in the sun all day, talking with those like-minded with himself, and if he could have dined at night, not only on things to eat, but on a feast of reason, and if he could have done that every day, then Greek education would have been perfect. But the fault of Greek education was that it remembered culture and forgot duty.

IV. Education Among the Romans

THE TRAINING OF THE INDIVIDUAL IN THE SERVICE OF THE STATE

T. R. Glover chose two vivid incidents as illuminating Roman life and character better than anything else in history.[1] Pyrrhus of Epirus could claim to have defeated the Romans in two great battles and to have left the field with honours even in a third, for he defeated the Roman arms at Heraclea and Asculum, and held his own at Beneventum. There was a time when Pyrrhus not unnaturally thought that he must have beaten the resistance out of the Romans; and to them he sent his envoy, the Thessalian Cineas. Cineas was no raw barbarian. He had been, as Plutarch tells, a disciple of Demosthenes, and when he spoke he revived in men the memory of the force and vigour of the eloquence of the master. So notable an orator and a diplomat was Cineas that Pyrrhus used to say of him that he had captured more cities with his words than he himself had with his arms. So this Cineas went on his embassy to Rome and offered a peace which Rome proudly refused, for although Rome could lose battles she could never lose a campaign in the days of her greatness. When Cineas was in Rome, he took the opportunity to study Rome and her institutions, to understand her methods of government, and to talk with the noblest of her citizens; and when he returned to Pyrrhus, and told him of his experiences, he said that to him the senate of Rome had seemed "a council of kings."[2] Here indeed was a tribute to the "grandeur that was Rome."

That incident happened in the first quarter of the third century

[1] He uses these incidents more than once. He uses them together in *The World of the New Testament*, pp. 63–6. In *Democracy in the Ancient World*, the Cineas incident is on p. 178, and the Popilius Lænas incident on pp. 194, 195.

[2] Plutarch: *Pyrrhus* 10.

B.C.; the second incident happened midway through the second century B.C., a hundred years later. Antiochus Epiphanes of Syria had set out on an expedition against Egypt. Rome well knew the inflammability of the Middle East, and decided that Antiochus must be called to order. Popilius Lænas, a senator, was sent to bid Antiochus retire. He had no army with him, but only a very small staff. He met Antiochus. There had been a time when Antiochus had lived for thirteen years as a hostage in Rome, and Antiochus and Popilius exchanged news and talked of this and that. Then Antiochus asked Popilius why he had come. Popilius gave him the tablets which told him that Rome did not wish him to proceed with his campaign against Egypt. Antiochus said that he would reflect upon his answer. Popilius Lænas took the vine stick which he was carrying, and with it he drew a circle round Antiochus as he stood. "Answer me," he said, "before you step out of that circle." Antiochus thought for a moment or two, and then he said: "I will go home." [3] There must have been something about a nation whose unarmed senators could send kings and their armies home, as if they had been disobedient and truant-playing schoolboys.

In the greatest days of Rome, Rome was characterised by that untranslatable quality called *gravitas*. That *gravitas* was a thing of character; and it was towards the production of character that early Roman education was entirely directed. Horace said: "It is by obeying the gods, O Roman, that you rule the world." [4] "The ideal education," says T. G. Tucker, "was a training which should fit a man for his duty to the gods, the state, and the family." [5] Warde Fowler insists that Roman education in the great days was mainly for character. "What was wanted was the will to do well and justly, and the instinctive hatred of all evil and unjust dealing." [6] A. S. Wilkins writes: "The education of her children aimed at no more than at the development of those virtues and capacities, the value of which was recognized in daily life. If a boy grew up healthy and strong in mind and body, if he revered the gods, his parents, and the laws and institutions of his country, if he was

[3] The story is told in Polybius 29. 27; Livy 45. 12; Cicero: *Philippic* 8. 8. 23.

[4] Horace: *Odes* 3. 6. 5.

[5] T. G. Tucker: *Life in the Roman World of Nero and St. Paul*, p. 320.

[6] W. Warde Fowler: *Social Life in Rome in the Days of Cicero*, p. 168.

familiar with the traditional methods of agriculture, and had some knowledge of conducting public business in times of peace and of serving in the field in time of war; if a girl learned from her mother to be modest, virtuous and industrious, skilled in the duties of the household, this was all that was needed, that children should grow up what their parents would have them to be."[7] As Cicero put it, the aim was to produce, "self-control, combined with dutiful affection to parents, and kindliness to kindred."[8] It was for this very reason that, in its greatest days, as Aubrey Gwynn has put it, the chief merit of Roman education was that "it fostered a reverence for childhood which made every boy and girl an object of almost religious veneration."[9] One of the noblest things that was ever said about childhood was Juvenal's "*maxima debetur puero reverentia,*" "the greatest reverence is due to the boy."[10] If the aim of education was character, then reverence for the child in his earliest days was an absolute essential.

[7] A. S. Wilkins: *Roman Education,* pp. 1, 2.

[8] Cicero: *De Officiis* 2. 13. 46.

[9] A. Gwynn: *Roman Education from Cicero to Quintilian,* p. 17.

[10] Juvenal: *Satires,* 14. 47. In his characteristically full and erudite note on this passage J. B. Mayor cites a selection of equally noble parallels. Plato in the *Laws* (729 B, C) writes: "To our children we should bequeath self-respect and not gold. This we think to do by rebuking their shameless acts; but we shall never succeed, if we inculcate the maxim now in vogue, 'The young should reverence all.' Rather will a wise law-giver charge the elder *to reverence the young,* and to beware above all things lest the young see or hear them doing or saying anything shameful; for where the old have no shame, there the young will be most unabashed. For the best instruction stands not in precept, but in the consistent practice of what we teach." Plutarch (*Roman Questions* 33) ascribes the ancient Roman practice of taking children out to dinner, not so much to a desire to control the child, as to make the fathers themselves behave with modesty and temperance because the children are present. Pliny (*Letters* 7. 24. 5) quotes an extraordinary example of this care in the presence of children. He writes of Ummidia Quadratilla, the grandmother of Quadratus, who had been one of his pupils: "I once heard her say . . . that it was her habit, being a woman, and as such debarred from active life, to amuse herself by playing at counters or backgammon, and to look on the mimicry of her pantomimes; but that before engaging in either diversion, she constantly sent away her grandson to his studies; a custom which, I imagine, she observed as much out of a certain reverence, as affection, for the youth."

There was a deep underlying reason for this Roman stress on character. Marrou writes: "Rome was never to emancipate herself entirely from the collective ideal whereby the individual is completely in the hands of the state—not even when in all her customs she had grown far away from it. She always looked back to it nostalgically. She was always making efforts to return to it." But to that, as Marrou rightly sees, there is something to be added. Again and again we saw how it was noted that this Roman character was to be expressed in the simple, ordinary, day-to-day virtues. As Warde Fowler has it: "It was to be an education in the family virtues, thereafter to be turned to account in the service of the state." [11] The reason was simply this—that Rome was built on a peasant foundation; the whole Roman system of early education was "not for knights but for peasants." The Romans were fundamentally a peasant race, who had acquired a world empire.[12] Therein lies the secret of its essential solidarity and its essential simplicity. Macaulay in his *Horatius* was not so very wrong about these early days when he wrote:

> Then none was for a party;
>   Then all were for the state;
> Then the great man helped the poor,
>   And the poor man loved the great:
> Then lands were fairly portioned;
>   Then spoils were fairly sold:
> The Romans were like brothers
>   In the brave old days of old.

The fact of its peasant origin gave early Roman education its two great characteristics.

It was an education which was founded on tradition. "It was an initiation into a traditional way of life." Its great watchword was *mos maiorum*, the customs of our ancestors. To follow the *mos maiorum* was the one way to virtue; to offend against it was the one way to sin. Cicero quotes the saying of Ennius: "The strength of Rome is founded on her ancient customs as much as on the

[11] W. Warde Fowler: *Social Life at Rome in the Age of Cicero*, p. 177.

[12] H. I. Marrou: *A History of Education in Antiquity*, pp. 229, 230.

strength of her sons." [13] Both Cato and Varro quote a custom which shows this force and call of tradition. Cato says: "At a party each guest was supposed to sing a song in praise of the heroes of old, for this was the special function of the goddess of song." [14] Varro says: "The well-trained boys used to sing ancient songs, in which were the praises of their ancestors." [15] When such a great Roman died, the boys were taken to hear the laudation which was pronounced over him. Polybius paints the scene. When such a Roman died, it was the custom that life-size statues of former members of the family should be carried in dignified procession through the forum, adorned with all the insignia of their rank. A panegyric was then pronounced both on the glory of the man himself and on the glory of his ancestors. "It would not be easy," writes Polybius, "to offer a fairer spectacle to an ambitious and generous boy. For who would not be moved to see the statues of men famous for their valour grouped together as though they were alive? What fairer spectacle could there be than this? And, best of all, the young are thus stimulated to bear all manner of hardship for the common weal, hoping thereby to gain the glory which is given to brave men." [16] The supreme force was the force of tradition; and the supreme aim was to continue the tradition and not to depart from it.

The second basic fact is that all early Roman education took place within the family. "The basis and backbone of this education was the family." [17] This was in fact inevitable because of the *patria potestas*, that unique power, extending even to the power of life and death, which a Roman father possessed over his child so long as that child should live. It is the amazing fact that under Roman law a Roman child never came of age, so long as the father was alive.[18]

It is easy to see from the very existence of the *patria potestas* that at least in the early days Roman education would centre round the home. "School-life was reduced to a minimum, where it existed

[13] *Moribus antiquis res stat Romana virisque*: quoted Cicero: *De Rep.* 5. 1.

[14] Cato; quoted Cicero: *Brutus* 19. 75. [15] Varro: *Ap. Non.* p. 77.

[16] Polybius 6. 53; quoted A. Gwynn: *Roman Education from Cicero to Quintilian*, p. 22.

[17] Cp. A. S. Wilkins: *Roman Education*, p. 2.

[18] For the *patria potestas* see Appendix B.

at all."[19] It was for that reason that Roman schooling was never really systematised and standardised as other educations were. It has been remarked that school was always a part of Greek life. Even in the *Iliad* Achilles was the pupil of Phœnix; the Greek mother was quite unable to teach her child, because normally she had no education herself; the Greek father was far too busy being a citizen of Athens to pay much attention to his child. But in Rome things were quite different. In the fourth book of his *De Republica* Cicero draws a contrast between Greek and Roman ideals. That book now only exists in fragments; and one of the extant fragments is a speech by Scipio into whose mouth Cicero put his own opinions:

> Let us now turn our attention to other wise provisions made with a view to maintaining the prosperity and virtue of the commonwealth. For that is the primary purpose of all civil society towards which the state should help men, partly by its institutions, partly by its laws. Now, first as to the education of free-born citizens. This is a problem on which the Greeks have wasted much endeavour: but our institutions are opposed to any detailed universal system of public education, obligatory by law. In fact my guest, Polybius, maintains that this is the one point on which our institutions can be accused of negligence.[20]

The education of the Roman child was never, in its best days, standardised. There was no prescribed curriculum, no impending examinations, and no state interference in any way.[21] And that was so precisely because the child was not educated in a school, but in the family. Plutarch was astonished at the lateness of what might be called technical Roman education. He writes in the *Roman Questions:*

> The Romans were late in beginning to teach for payment, as the first of them to open a school of letters was Spurius Carvilius,

[19] A. Gwynn: *Roman Education from Cicero to Quintilian*, pp. 14, 15.

[20] Cicero: *De Rep.* 4. 3. Translation as in A. Gwynn: *Roman Education from Cicero to Quintilian*, p. 11.

[21] A. S. Wilkins: *Roman Education*, p. 55.

> a freedman of that Carvilius who was the first to divorce his wife.[22]

The date of Carvilius is about 230 B.C. Plutarch's information is oddly definite and detailed; and must go back to something which is factual. There must have been some kind of schools in Rome. It may well be that his meaning goes back to a curious Roman custom. In Rome legal advice was given free by the most famous lawyers to all who cared to consult them; and a Roman advocate was in fact forbidden to charge his client any fee. The lawyer and the advocate were both dependent on the free-will gifts of their clients.[23] It may well be that up to the time of Spurius Carvilius Roman schools met, as it were, privately in the house of the teacher, and that he was the first fully professional teacher, who charged fees instead of being dependent on free gifts. In any event it is clear that Roman education was not a function for which the state was responsible; it was a function of the home. For that reason we can best see what early Roman education was like by following the progress within the home of a Roman child in the early days.

When a Roman child was born, he was laid before his father's feet. If the father lifted him, that meant that he acknowledged him, and accepted responsibility for him; if he turned away, it meant that he refused to acknowledge the child, and the child would be exposed.[24] If the child was acknowledged by his father, certain ceremonies followed. On the ninth day after birth for boys, and on the eighth day for girls came the *nundinæ*, or the *dies lustricus*, the day of purification. On that day, either in the home or in the temple, a sacrifice was offered for the purification of the child, and the child then received his or her name. On that day little gifts were given

[22] Plutarch: *Roman Questions* 50.

[23] Cp. A. Gwynn: *Roman Education from Cicero to Quintilian*, pp. 30, 31; A. S. Wilkins: *Roman Education*, pp. 23, 24.

[24] The word for lifting the child was *suscipere*; it came to all intents and purposes to mean "to acknowledge as legitimate," or even "to survive." In one of his periods of depression Cicero writes to Atticus: *Utinam susceptus non essem* (Cicero; *Ad Att.* 11. 9) which means: "Would that I had never been lifted up," i.e., "Would that I had never survived." Suetonius tells us of Gnipho, the famous grammarian, that he had been free-born, but that he had been *expositus* (*On Grammarians* 7).

to the child by the parents, relations, and friends, and even by the family slaves. In Plautus we read of a child being given a little gold sword (*ensiculus*) engraved with the father's name, or a little gold crescent or ring.[25] For the most part, Roman mothers nursed their own children. If a nurse was used, she must be carefully chosen. Quintilian sets the standard very high. According to him the child's nurse should be a philosopher! But failing that, it is most important that she should speak correctly, for it is the speech of the nurse which the child will first hear, and which he will naturally imitate. The Quintilian passage is worth quoting in full in order to see the care which the great teachers were prepared to expend on every detail of the child's education.

> Above all see that the child's nurse speaks correctly. The ideal, according to Chrysippus, would be that she should be a philosopher: failing that, he desired that the best should be chosen, as far as possible. No doubt the most important point is that they should be of good character: but they should speak correctly as well. It is the nurse that the child first hears, and her words that he will first attempt to imitate. And we are by nature most tenacious of childish impressions, just as the flavour first absorbed by vessels when new persists, and the colour imparted by dyes to the primitive whiteness of wool is indelible. Further, it is the worst impressions that are most durable. For, while what is good readily deteriorates, you will never turn vice into virtue. Do not then allow the boy to become accustomed even in infancy to a style of speech which he will subsequently have to unlearn.[26]

But in those early days it was the mother who was important, and Roman literature has many a tribute to the noble mothers of the great days. There was Cornelia, the mother of the Gracchi, who on her husband's death took upon herself all the care of the

[25] Plautus: *Rudens* 4. 4. 112; These little gold ornaments were commonly worn strung on a chain round the neck, as is nowadays perhaps more common with bracelets for the wrist. They tinkled as the child moved; hence their name, *crepundia*.

[26] Quintilian: *Instit. Or.* 1. 1. 4.

household and the education of her children and brought them up with such care "that though they were without dispute in natural endowments and dispositions the first among the Romans of their time, yet they seemed to owe their virtues even more to their education than to their birth." [27] There was the mother of Agricola, Julia Procilla, who was, as Tacitus said, "a woman of rare virtue," and "from whose fond bosom Agricola imbibed his education." [28] In the *Dialogue on Oratory* Tacitus praises the mothers and the noble women of the early days:

> In the good old days, every man's son, born in wedlock, was brought up, not in the chamber of some hireling nurse, but in his mother's lap and at her knee. And that mother could have no higher praise than that she managed the house and gave herself to her children. Again, some elderly relative would be selected in order that to her, as a person who had been tried and never found wanting, might be entrusted the care of all the youthful scions of the same house; in the presence of such an one no base word could be uttered without grave offence, and no wrong deed done. Religiously and with the utmost delicacy she regulated not only the serious tasks of her youthful charges, but their recreations also and their games. It was in this spirit, we are told, that Cornelia, the mother of the Gracchi, directed their upbringing, Aurelia that of Cæsar, Atia that of Augustus; thus it was that these mothers trained their princely children.[29]

The story of Coriolanus [30] may be historically legendary, but it is symbolically true. It tells how Coriolanus withdrew from Rome, and joined the Volscians. He led a Volscian army against Rome and would have taken it had he not been restrained by his mother Veturia, although he well knew that the Volscians would execute him for turning back. In those days when the family was the centre of the life of every Roman, the Roman mother was the queen of every home.

[27] Plutarch: *Tiberius Gracchus* 1; Cicero: *Brutus* 104; Quintilian *Inst. Or.* 1. 1. 6.

[28] Tacitus: *Agricola* 4.

[29] Tacitus: *A Dialogue on Oratory* 28.

[30] Livy: 2. 40. 3–10.

During his days of youth the Roman boy wore two distinguishing articles. He wore the *toga prætexta*, the toga with the purple band on it. Warde Fowler has an interesting suggestion about that toga. Roman sons and daughters were brought up to assist in the religious duties of the household as acolytes (*camillus*, *camilla*). The toga with the purple band on it was actually the same toga as Roman magistrates and priests at sacrifice wore; and it may be that it indicated the priestly character of the youth.[31] It is in fact worth noting how the home of the early Roman family was enveloped in religion and surrounded by its own gods. "No nation ever created so many deities to protect the home."[32] There was the goddess Levana, who presided over the lifting of children by the father.[33] There was Vaticanus or Vagitanus, who presided over the beginnings of human speech.[34] There was Cunina, who presided over the cradles (*cunæ*) of babies.[35] There were Edulia, Potica or Potina, and Cuba, who presided over eating and drinking and the bed, and to whom sacrifices were made as soon as the child was weaned from the breast to solid food, and left the cradle for a bed.[36] It was in fact much later the complaint of Prudentius that the Roman child could never get away from these encircling pagan gods and goddesses:

> The young heir bowed shuddering before anything which his hoary ancestors had designated as worshipful in their eyes. Children in their infancy drank in error with their first milk.

[31] W. Warde Fowler: *Social Life at Rome in the Age of Cicero*, p. 178.

[32] Quoted A. S. Wilkins: *Roman Education*, p. 11.

[33] Augustine: *De Civ. Dei* 4. 11—*levat infantes de terra.*

[34] Aulus Gellius: *Attic Nights* 16. 17. 2, quoting Marcus Varro's lost *Antiquities of the Gods*: "Just as Aius was called a god, and the altar was erected in his honour, which stands at the bottom of the Nova Via, because in that place a voice from heaven was heard, so that god was called *Vaticanus* who controls the beginnings of human speech, since children, as soon as they are born, first utter the sound which forms the first syllable of *Vaticanus*; hence the word *vagire* which represents the sound of a newborn infant's voice."

[35] Augustine: *De Civ. Dei* 4. 11—*cunas administrat.*

[36] Donatus on Terence: *Phormio* 1. 1. 15. Information on these various divinities is to be found in W. A. Becker: *Gallus*; English translation by F. Metcalfe, pp. 182, 183.

> While still at the crying stage, they had tasted of the sacrificial meal, and had seen mere stones quoted with wax, and the grimy gods of the house dripping with unguent. The little one had looked on a figure in the shape of fortune, with his wealthy horn, standing in the house, a hallowed stone, and watched his mother palefaced in prayer before it. Then raised on his nurse's shoulder he too pressed his lips to the flint, and rubbed it with them, pouring out his childish petitions, asking for riches from a sightless stone, and convinced that all one's wishes must be sought from thence.[37]

The atmosphere of the home was an atmosphere of religion, and it is not impossible that the *toga prætexta* was itself connected with that.

The second article worn by the lad was the *bulla*. The *bulla* was a round, flattish, hollow disk worn round the neck like a locket. It had originally been made of silver and of gold, and had been the mark of children of patricians and of senators; but in later times it came to be worn by all children, and was made of leather when nothing more expensive could be afforded. It was regarded as a charm and amulet to ward off *fascinatio*, the influence of the evil eye.[38]

For the first seven years the main influence on the child was his mother, but thereafter there came into the child's life a deliberate association with his father, which at its best and its highest must have been a very wonderful and a very lovely thing. From then on the child was attached to his father in such a way that his father was his one constant companion, and his only teacher. Roman literature has many a noble reference to this association between father and son.

Of this father-son relationship Gwynn says: "Once the first years of childhood were past, the mother's place in the boy's education was taken by her husband, and a companionship began between

[37] Prudentius: *C. Symm.* I. 199 ff. Prudentius describes the child "clinging with credulous faith to his witless tradition." When he goes outside the home, he sees in the city the statues of the gods, and the religious ceremonies and processions, and cannot but believe that "what is done by authority of the senate is genuine."

[38] For the *bulla* see Appendix C.

father and son for which it is hard to find a parallel outside Roman society. . . . Frequently the father took over in person the responsibility of giving his son whatever little book-learning was required for ordinary Roman life. . . . But these elementary lessons were the least part of the boy's education. Constantly at his father's side and with few other companions, he learnt to see in his parent the living representative of Roman tradition, the personification of Roman authority. At home he worked with his father on the farm. . . . On festival days he acted as acolyte to his father in all the religious ceremonies which centred round the Roman hearth; or accompanied him as guest at the house of friends, serving his elders at table and singing with others of his own age ballads of early Roman literature. When there was a meeting or assembly in the forum, he was there to listen to the public debates; and, if his father was a senator, he was allowed by special privilege—at least in the early days of the Republic—to go with him to the senate-house." [39] "The father of every youth served as his instructor," said Pliny.[40] Even when Horace came from Venusia to Rome for better schooling, he tells us of his father: "He himself, a guardian true and tried, went with me among all my teachers." [41] Even Augustus in later days, among all the cares of state, still personally attended to the education of the grandsons, Gaius and Lucius, whom he had adopted as his own sons. "He taught his grandsons reading, swimming, and the other elements of education, for the most part himself, taking special pains to train them to imitate his own handwriting; and he never dined in their company unless they sat beside him on the lowest couch, or made a journey unless they preceded his carriage, or rode close by it on either side." [42] The great ideal of Roman fatherhood never became completely lost. Even in the days of the Empire it was there before men's minds. The supreme instance of a Roman father was Cato. Plutarch in the twentieth chapter of his life of Cato sets out Cato's educational ideals. Long as it is, it must be quoted in full, for nowhere is there better expressed the ancient Roman ideal of education through fatherhood, and training in the home:

[39] A. Gwynn: *Roman Education from Cicero to Quintilian*, pp. 15, 16.

[40] Pliny: *Letters* 8. 14. 6: *Suus cuique parens pro magistro.*

[41] Horace: *Satires* 1. 6. 72.

[42] Suetonius: *Augustus* 64.

Cato was a good father and an honourable husband. In the management of his household he showed unusual ability, and was far from treating such questions as of little or secondary importance; so that I think it worth while to give some details of his success in these matters. He married a wife of good family rather than of great fortune, judging that, whilst both good birth and wealth make for pride and seriousness, women of noble family, owing to their dread of shame, are more obedient to their husbands in all questions of good conduct. He used to say that a man who struck his wife or his child was laying hands on the most holy of sacred things; that it was a greater honour to be a good husband than a distinguished senator; and that nothing was more admirable in old Socrates than that he lived in peace and quiet with a difficult wife and half-witted children. When his son was born, no duty (save perhaps some public function) was so pressing as to prevent him from being present when his wife bathed the child and wrapped it in its swaddling clothes. His wife suckled the child with her own milk, and would often give her breast to the children of the slaves, so as to gain their affection for her son by treating them as his brothers.

As soon as the boy was able to learn, Cato took him personally in charge and taught him his letters, although he owned an accomplished slave, named Chilon, who was a schoolmaster and gave lessons to many boys. But Cato, to use his own words, would not have his slave abuse his son, nor perhaps pull his ears for being slow at lessons; nor would he have his boy owe a slave so precious a gift as learning. So he made himself the boy's schoolmaster, just as he taught him the laws of Rome and bodily exercises; not merely to throw the javelin, to fight in armour or to ride, but also to use his fists in boxing, to bear heat and cold, and to swim against the currents and eddies of a river. And he tells us himself that he wrote books of history with his own hand and in large characters, so that his son might be able even at home to become acquainted with his country's past; that he was as careful to avoid all indecent conversation in his son's presence as he would have been in the presence of Vestal virgins; and that he never bathed with him. This last point seems to have been a Roman custom, for even fathers-in-law were careful not to bathe with their sons-in-law to avoid the necessity of stripping naked before them; but later, when the Romans had learned from the Greeks the custom of appearing naked, they actually taught the Greeks to do so before women.

When Cato had thus taken every pains to fashion his son, like an excellent work, to virtue, finding that his goodwill was beyond reproach and that he was naturally docile and obedient, but that his body was too delicate for hardship, he relaxed the excessive rigour and austerity of this régime. And in spite of weak health the lad proved himself a true man in the field, winning great distinction in the battle which Æmilius Paulus fought against Perseus. It was here that he lost his sword, which was struck from his grasp by a blow, or simply slipped owing to the moisture of his hand. Grieved at this loss the boy turned to some of his comrades who were about him, took them with him, and again charged the enemy. Much hard fighting was needed to clear the spot, but at last he found his sword amid a heap of arms and dead bodies, friend and foe piled up together. His general Paulus was delighted with the boy when he heard of the deed, and Cato himself wrote his son a letter which is still extant, giving him high praise for the honourable zeal he had shown in thus winning back his sword. Later the young man married Tertia, the daughter of Paulus, and Scipio's sister, and his admission to this noble family was due as much to his own merits as to the merits of his father. So that Cato's care for his son had its fitting reward.[43]

However narrow this training may have been, the moral earnestness of it, and the determination of the father to do his duty by his son, compel admiration.

Of Æmilius Paulus, the great general and statesman, Plutarch writes:

Afterwards he frequently intimated his desire of being a second time consul, and was once candidate; but meeting with a repulse, and being passed by, he gave up all thought of it, and devoted himself to his duties as augur, and to the education of

[43] Plutarch: *Cato Major* 20.

> his children, whom he not only brought up, as he himself had been in the Roman and ancient discipline, but also with unusual zeal in that of Greece. To this purpose he not only procured masters to teach them grammar, logic, and rhetoric, but had for them also preceptors in modelling and drawing, managers of horses and dogs, and instructors in field sports, all from Greece. And, if he was not hindered by public affairs, he himself would be with them at their studies, and see them perform their exercises, being the most affectionate father in Rome.[44]

Here is the picture of a wider culture; but once again it is the picture of a father whose aim was to make the education of his sons his life-work.

It is easy to see that this is not the kind of education which consists in amassing facts, or acquiring certificates, or obtaining degrees. It was initiation into a way of life. It was then that the boy learned by heart the Twelve Tables, as Scots boys used to learn the catechism. Cicero writes: "Though all the world exclaim against me, I will say what I think; that single little book of the Twelve Tables, if anyone look to the fountains and the sources of laws, seems to me, assuredly, to surpass the libraries of all the philosophers both in weight of authority, and plenitude of utility."[45] It was then that the Roman lad was initiated into the old, simple way of life. Varro tells us of his own boyhood. He had only one tunic and toga, wore sandals without any covering for his legs, rode his horse bare-backed, was seldom allowed a bath, and even less frequently a good dinner.[46] Things in Rome were to change; luxury was to take the place of frugality, and elaboration of simplicity; and yet the fact remains that in the Roman mind the ancient ideal was never completely forgotten, but remained always as a haunting and nostalgic memory.

But we must proceed to the next stage in the boy's training. Until the age of seven his mother was the greatest influence on his life; from seven he was in the constant care and charge of his father, who was often his only instructor. The next great day was when

[44] Plutarch: *Æmilius Paulus* 6. [45] Cicero: *De Oratore* 1. 44.

[46] Varro: *Apud Non.* 108. 24: A. Gwynn: *Roman Education from Cicero Quintilian*, p. 18.

the boy put away childish things. We can hardly call it coming of age, for it happened at no fixed age; but some time between the age of fourteen and seventeen, probably most often at sixteen, the day came when the boy was considered to have grown up. The ceremonies connected with this event generally took place on the Festival of the Liberalia which fell in the middle of March. The boy took off his *toga prætexta*, with its stripe of colour, and put on the pure white *toga virilis*, the clothing of a full-grown man. He removed his *bulla* from around his neck; and his *toga* and the *bulla* were offered to the Lares, the household gods. He was led in procession to the Forum, and to the Capitol that sacrifice might be offered; and then his name was inscribed in the list of full citizens in the *tabularium*. It would be a day that the boy would not readily forget.

But the boy's education was not finished yet. There followed what was called the *tirocinium fori*. This was a custom whereby a young man was put under the charge of some distinguished friend who was rich in years, in experience, and in honour. For a year, and sometimes for much longer, the young man lived and moved in the society of his distinguished mentor and pattern, that he might learn at first hand how to live and how to serve the state. So Cicero was put by his father under the care of Quintus Mucius Scævola, the augur. "I was taken by my father to Scævola, and bidden as far as possible never to leave his side."[47] Young men, he said, "must attach themselves to men who are wise and renowned, men who are famous for their patriotism, if possible men of consular rank, men who have played and are playing their part in public affairs."[48] So then the education of the Roman youth was completed by this close association with a man who was the kind of man that he himself was aiming to be. This association went on for at least a year, and often for much longer, until at last the young Roman was fit, able, and equipped to launch out on the service of the state for himself.

This may be taken to be the general pattern of Roman education down to 240 B.C., down to the days of the Punic Wars. Many parts of it, and its whole spirit, lasted until long after that; but it was after that time that changes began to be made.

[47] Cicero: *De Amicitia* 1. [48] Cicero: *De Officiis* 2. 46.

In this early system of Roman education there was hardly anything which could be called technical education at all. It was not the transmission of knowledge; it was the transmission of tradition. It did not teach either philosophies or techniques; it taught a certain kind of life. The tragedy of it was that in the nature of things it was doomed to extinction. And the sting of the tragedy lies in the fact that it was the increasing greatness of the Roman Empire which killed the ancient greatness of Roman education. By its very nature this early Roman education was only possible in a comparatively small and limited society. It depended on the father. But when Rome became an empire, the father was claimed for foreign service in the Roman armies and might not see his family for years; he was claimed for public service of the state, and could become so involved in it that he could not give the time to that unique friendship with his son which had been the distinguishing mark of that early education. When the scope and the tempo of life changed, when the essentially peasant education had to deal with an urban civilisation, when the home on the farm became the home in a great tenement in a crowded city, change was bound to take place. A school system was bound to arise. And so it did arise.

There are very early references to schools in Roman literature. Plutarch says that Romulus and Remus went to school at Gabii.[49] According to the old story, it was when Virginia was coming into the forum, where the schools of the teachers of letters were, that she was assaulted by the agent of Appius Claudius, the lustful decemvir.[50] Again according to Livy, when Camillus entered Tusculum, he found, among other signs of profound peace "the schools resounding with the voice of scholars."[51] And yet we have also seen that Plutarch tells us that Spurius Carvilius was the first Roman to teach for pay.[52] In the nature of things there can hardly ever have been a time when children did not learn in company, but we may take the beginning of what we might call organised schooling to date from the middle of the third century B.C.

That schooling had three stages. Apuleius outlines them in metaphorical language:

[49] Plutarch: *Romulus* 6. 2.

[50] Livy 3. 44. Dionysius of Halicarnassus: *Roman Antiquities* 11. 28.

[51] Livy 5. 25. [52] Plutarch: *Roman Questions* 59.

> At a banquet the first cup is for thirst, the second for joy, the third for sensual delight, and the fourth for folly. At the feasts of the Muses on the other hand, the more we are given to drink, the more our soul gains in wisdom and in reason. The first cup is poured for us by the *litterator*, who begins to polish the roughness of our mind. Then comes the *grammaticus* who adorns us with varied knowledge. Finally it is the *rhetor's* turn who puts into our hands the weapon of eloquence.[53]

So then in Roman education there were three stages, presided over by the *litterator*, the *grammaticus*, and the *rhetor* respectively. Let us take them one by one.

The *litterator* taught the elements of knowledge, the three R's, reading, writing and arithmetic. Although Quintilian was to leave as fine an outline of primary education as any man ever produced,[54] it is probably true to say that never at any time in the history of education was primary education worse done than it was in Rome. Carcopino condemns the whole system and its results: " On the whole we are compelled to admit that at the most glorious period of the Empire the schools entirely failed to fulfil the duties which we expect of our schools to-day. They undermined instead of strengthened the children's morals; they mishandled the children's bodies instead of developing them; and, if they succeeded in furnishing their minds with a certain amount of information, they were not calculated to perform any loftier or nobler task. The pupils left school with the heavy luggage of a few practical and commonplace notions laboriously acquired and of so little value that in the fourth century Vegetius could not take for granted that new recruits for the army would be literate enough to keep the books for their corps (*De Re Militari* 2. 19). Instead of happy memories, serious and fruitful ideas, any sort of intellectual curiosity vital to later life, school children carried away the gloomy recollection of years wasted in senseless, stumbling repetitions punctuated by savage punishments. Popular education then in Rome was a

[53] Apuleius: *Florida* 20: translation as in J. Carcopino: *Daily Life in Ancient Rome*: English translation by H. T. Towell.

[54] Quintilian: *Instit. Or.* Book I.

failure."[55] Let us then see what justification there is for these strong words.

The child began primary school at the age of seven and remained in it until he was twelve. Quintilian attributes this view of the age at which study should begin to Hesiod and Eratosthenes, but he does not agree with it. It is his view that education cannot begin too young. A child must be kept occupied somehow or another. Why not profitably? He recognises that very little can be done, and he insists that " we must take care that the child, who is not yet old enough to love his studies, does not come to hate them and to dread the bitterness which he has once tasted, even when the years of infancy are left behind."[56] But in practice seven was the age when the child began in the primary school. These schools were private; the state had nothing to do with education. There were therefore no control, no curriculum and no standards.[57] They therefore varied widely. Horace was brought from Venusia to Rome by his father for better schooling. He writes:

> I owe this to my father, who, though poor, with a starveling farm, would not send me to the school of Flavius, to which grand boys used to go, sons of grand centurions, with slate and satchel slung over the left arm, each carrying his eightpence on the Ides. Nay, he boldly took his boy off to Rome, to be taught those studies that any knight or senator would have his own offspring taught. . . . He himself, a guardian true and tried, went with me among all my teachers.[58]

Horace has a horror of these inefficient country schools. " This fate too awaits you," he said, " that stammering age will come upon you, as you teach boys that A B C in their city's outskirts."[59] But it was by no means every father who would go to the trouble and expense to seek out the best school for his son.

The Roman schools met in almost impossible conditions. They met in the *tabernæ* or the *pergulæ*. They were simply like open

[55] J. Carcopino: *Daily Life in Ancient Rome*, pp. 106, 107.
[56] Quintilian: *Instit. Or.* I. I. 17–20.
[57] Cp. A. S. Wilkins: *Roman Education*, p. 55.
[58] Horace: *Satires* I. 6. 72. [59] Horace: *Epistles* I. 20. 17.

shops opening on to the street, sometimes not even separated from the street at all, sometimes separated by a canvas curtain. They were badly equipped. In the ordinary schools there would be nothing more than the chair for the master, the simplest benches and forms for the pupils, some wax writing-tablets, and some counting-boards (*abaci*). It is true that in the better furnished schools they had the glimmerings of visual aids. There were busts of famous authors; there was a famous set of cartoons illustrating the story of the *Iliad*, which may have been used to educate no less a person than the boy who was to become Augustus; there appear to have been maps, for Propertius tells how he was compelled to learn the worlds from painted pictures, and Varro speaks of a painted Italy (*picta Italia*) on the wall of a temple.[60] Eumenius, speaking of the situation in Gaul as late as the fourth century says: "Let the boys also see in these cloisters, and daily have before their eyes, all the lands and seas, all the towns and nations and tribes, which our victorious emperors subdue." Thus, he says, things may be grasped with the eyes which would otherwise be more difficult to understand.[61] Quintilian suggests stimulating the children by giving them ivory letters to play with.[62] Herodes Atticus—but this was in Athens—had a brilliant idea to help his son who could not learn the alphabet. "He brought with him twenty-four boys of the same age named after the letters of the alphabet, so that he would be obliged to learn his letters at the same time as the names of the boys."[63] But all this was quite exceptional, and quite beyond the orbit of the ordinary elementary schoolmaster.

The schoolmaster himself was a badly paid drudge. The eightpence which the centurions' sons of Venusia were carrying to the school on the Ides was their contribution to the teacher's salary.[64] The teacher largely depended on the free-will gifts which the pupils brought on the festival days; and Orbilius, the teacher of Horace, wrote a book called the *Perialgos* on "the wrongs which teachers

[60] Propertius 5. 3. 37; Varro: *De Re Rust.* 1. 2. 1.

[61] Eumenius: *De Restaur. Schol.* 120. See A. S. Wilkins: *Roman Education*, pp. 45, 46.

[62] Quintilian: *Instit. Or.* 1. 1. 26.

[63] Philostratus: *Lives of the Sophists* 2. 1. 10 (558).

[64] Horace: *Satires* 1. 6. 76.

suffered from the indifference or selfishness of parents."[65] Frequently the schoolmaster was obliged to augment his scanty emoluments by clerking for the community, and by drawing up wills and the like. It was in the last degree unlikely that the drudgery and the poverty of a schoolmaster's life would attract anyone into such a profession.

Schools began very early in the morning. Juvenal tells that one of the trials of the teacher's life is that he has "snuffed up the odour of as many lamps as you had scholars in your class thumbing a discoloured Horace or a soot-begrimed Virgil."[66] In that case the school must have begun before dawn. Martial writes bitterly of the notorious noise of Rome, and says that there is no place for thought or quiet: "Schoolmasters in the morning do not let you live."[67] He talks about the schoolmaster who has begun his shouting and his punishing although "not yet have the crested cocks broken the hush of the night.[68] "Get up," he urges, "already the baker is selling to boys their breakfast, and the crested fowls of dawn are crowing on all sides."[69] Apparently the Roman boy had to creep to his comfortless school before the dawn broke.

The elementary schoolmasters of Rome were notoriously savage in their punishments to their pupils. The legend was that Achilles was taught the lyre by the centaur Chiron; and Juvenal writes: "Achilles trembled for fear of the rod when already of full age, singing songs in his native hills; nor would he then have dared to laugh at the tail of his musical instructor."[70] Martial complains against the din of punishment and teaching combined:

> What have you to do with us, accursed pedagogue, a fellow odious to boys and girls? Not yet have the crested cocks broken the hush of the night, already with menacing voice and with thwacks you raise an uproar. So heavily re-echoes brass on smitten anvils, when a smith is fitting a pleader's statue astride a steed. Milder in the huge amphitheatre riots the shout when its own faction acclaims the small shield. We neighbours don't ask for sleep all the night; for some wakefulness is a trifle, but to wake all night is no joke. Dismiss your pupils. Are you willing,

[65] Suetonius: *On Grammarians* 9. [66] Juvenal 7. 222.
[67] Martial 12. 57. [68] Martial 9. 68.
[69] Martial 14. 223. [70] Juvenal 7. 210.

> you blatant fellow, to accept for holding your tongue as much as you accept for bawling?[71]

The clamorous schoolmaster is a byword. "Now the boy," writes Martial, "sad to desert his huts is recalled to school by his clamorous master." He writes an address to a schoolmaster:

> Schoolmaster, spare your simple flock; so in crowds may curly-headed boys listen to you, and a dainty bevy round your table be fond of you, and no arithmetic master or rapid shorthand teacher be ringed with a larger circle. The glaring days glow beneath flaming Leo, and blazing July ripens the parched grain. Let the Scythian's hide, thonged with bristling lashes, with which Marsius of Celænæ was scourged, and the alarming ferules, sceptres of schoolmasters, rest and sleep till October's Ides. In summer, if boys are well, they learn enough.[72]

He speaks of "ferules, hated much by boys and welcome to schoolmasters."[73] Ovid upbraids Aurora "who cheats boys of their slumber, and hands them over to the master, that their tender hands may yield to the cruel stroke."[74] Horace sent his master down to history notorious for ever as "the flogger" (*plagosus Orbilius*).[75]

This savagery of the Roman elementary teachers had become proverbial. Seneca speaks of the teacher in a passion teaching that no one must ever get into a passion.[76] Menander said: "The man who has not been flogged has not been trained."[77] Cicero justifies the teacher's temper. "The more ingenious and clever a man is," he says, "the more teaching is vexatious and difficult for him. When he sees something which he himself grasps quickly being but tardily perceived, it is torture for him."[78]

Normally punishment was on the hand with the rod (*ferula*). "I too," said Juvenal, "have drawn my hand away from the rod."[79] Plutarch describes the festival of the *Lupercalia* when magistrates

[71] Martial 9. 68. [72] Martial 10. 62. [73] Martial 14. 80.
[74] Ovid: *Am.* 1. 13. 17. [75] Horace: *Epistles* 2. 1. 70.
[76] Seneca: *Ep.* 94. 9. [77] Menander: *Sententiæ* 422.
[78] Cicero: *Pro. Rosc. Am.* 11. 31. [79] Juvenal: *Satires* 1.15.

and youths ran through the streets naked. To be struck by one of them meant an easy delivery in childbirth, or the ability to conceive a child. So the matrons met them and "like children at school present their hand to be struck."[80] But sometimes the more savage *scutica*, the lash, was used. That too was a weapon of the notorious Orbilius, and Domitius Marsus, the poet, spoke of him "thrashing with the rod or the whiplash of leather."[81] And from a fresco at Herculaneum we see that it was even possible for a boy to be stripped, held down by his comrades, and horse-whipped by the master.

Just occasionally there must have been rewards. Horace justifies driving a lesson home with a smile. "What is to prevent one telling truth as he laughs—even as teachers sometimes give cookies to children to coax them into learning the A B C?"[82]

Only Quintilian is a lonely voice against this policy of the lash. He insists of the child: "His studies must be made an amusement: he must be questioned and praised and taught to rejoice when he has done well; sometimes too, when he refuses instruction, it should be given to some other to excite his envy; at times also he must be engaged in competition and should be allowed to believe himself successful more often than not, while he should be encouraged to do his best by such rewards as may appeal to his tender years."[83] He emphatically disapproves of flogging. It is a punishment fit only for slaves and an insult. If the boy will not learn, flogging will in the end only harden him, until he becomes more and more insensitive. A good disciplinarian should never have any need to flog a pupil. You may flog a child, but what will you do with him when he becomes a young man, if that is your only method of controlling him? The result may well be to unnerve and to depress the mind and to make the child shun and loathe the light. The ultimate effects of flogging may be evil, and even tragic. Quintilian finishes his castigation of a policy of flogging with a strangely penetrating observation: "I will content myself with saying that children are helpless and easily victimised, and that therefore no one should be given unlimited power over them."[84] But it must be remembered that Quintilian was one of the most

[80] Plutarch: *Cæsar* 61. 1.
[81] Suetonius: *Grammarians* 9.
[82] Horace: *Satires* 1. 1. 25.
[83] Quintilian: *Instit. Or.* 1. 1. 20.
[84] Quintilian: *Instit. Or.* 1. 3. 14–17.

enlightened educationalists of all time, and his protest against this savage punishment so prevalent in Roman schools was a voice crying in the wilderness. One thing is clear—it can have been very seldom that a Roman elementary school was a place to which a child looked forward with anything but boredom and fear.

It was little enough that the boy would learn at the elementary school; and what little he did learn would be thrashed into him. It might be that what the school could teach him would be supplemented by the work of a private tutor; but the private tutor would be a Greekling, a slave and a man of no morals, whose effect on the boy would ultimately be harmful, and not good.[85]

The boy would learn to read, first learning the letters, then the syllables, then the words. By the time of Cicero there would be no lack of books, if the boy would read them, and books at very reasonable prices. Cicero's friend Atticus was also his publisher.[86] By the time of Augustus the retail bookshops were a feature of the centre of the town, with advertisement of new books, and the books themselves, on display upon their pillars, and each with its coterie of literary devotees. Slave labour was employed, and hundreds of scribes acted like a modern printing press. To take an example—Friedländer estimates that, since two hours were enough to take down Martial's second book of epigrams, a complete edition of his epigrams could be turned out in about seventeen hours by hand. That is to say—a publisher with fifty slave-copyists in his factory could easily produce an edition of a thousand copies in a month. Prices were not dear. The price of the first book of Martial's epigrams—118 epigrams, about 700 lines—in an elegantly produced edition was 5 denarii (about 4/–), and there were editions as cheap

[85] Cicero has a very revealing remark about the Greeks. He says that he concedes that they have all kinds of literary and rhetorical skill, but that, as a race, the Greeks never understood or cared for the sacred binding force of testimony given in a court of law (*Pro Flacc.* 4. 8). The Greek tutor would have culture, but he would not have character.

[86] Cicero: *Ad. Att.* 13. 12: "You have given my speech for Ligarius a magnificent start. Henceforth when I write anything, I shall leave it to you to advertise it." 13. 22: "There are no hands in which I would rather have my writings than in yours . . . I acquit your copyists of fault."

as 1/2d. His *Xenia*—274 lines—was produced and published by Tryphon, the book-seller, for 4 sesterces (about 10d.).[87] Julius Cæsar had planned to open public libraries in Rome, but died before the plan was carried out. Asinius Pollio was the first to open a library. Augustus added two more; and the number steadily increased until by the fourth century Rome possessed no fewer than twenty-eight libraries. The material was there to read.

The boy would learn to write. Sometimes the boy learned to write on wax tablets on which the faint outline of the letters had been traced, and his hand was guided over the outline by his teacher. Later he would go on independently to copy a copyhead copper-plate line of writing. Seneca uses this method as an illustration of how the growing personality of the young man should be taught and guided and controlled: "Boys study according to direction. Their fingers are held and guided by others so that they may follow the outline of the letters; next they are ordered to imitate a copy, and base thereon a style of penmanship."[88] Quintilian speaks of children tracing the letters of the alphabet which others have written first; and he also describes a system by which the lad was taught to write apparently by the use of little stencils of the letters.[89] Papyrus and parchment were not cheap, and wax tablets were the usual writing material. They were like shallow boxes with the bottom filled with a layer of wax, which could be written on with a stylus, and then smoothed over to be used again. Sometimes the boys used already used parchment or papyrus, and wrote their exercises on the back of it. That was the lowest use to which an author's books could come, when they would not sell in the shops, and were disposed of as scrap paper for schoolboys to scribble on. That is the fate that Martial feared for his book, unless it pleased the critics: "If you would be approved by Attic ears," he writes to it, "I exhort and warn you, little book, to please the cultured Apollinaris. . . . If he hold you in his heart, if on his lips, you will neither fear the loud sneers of envy, nor supply dolorous wrappers for

[87] See L. Friedländer: *Roman Life and Manners;* English translation by J. H. Freese; vol. 3, pp. 36–8.

[88] Seneca: *Ep. Mor.* 94. 51.

[89] Quintilian: *Instit. Or.* 5. 14. 31; 1. 1. 27.

mackerel. If he shall condemn you, you must fly at once to the drawers of the salt-fish sellers, fit only to have your back ploughed by schoolboys' pens."[90]

The boy would learn arithmetic. He would learn it by chanting the tables. " One and one are two, two and two are four was a hateful chant to me," says Augustine.[91] Then he would learn to use the *abacus* which was a board, marked out in lines, with pebbles placed on them. There was a line for units, fives, tens, fifties, hundreds, five hundreds, and thousands, each marked with the Roman letter which stood for the number—I V X L C D M; and when the pebbles were moved about quite large calculations could be made; but the Roman was never interested in mathematics as such. He only desired enough arithmetic to balance his accounts, and enough geometry to settle arguments about the boundaries of his estate.

The boy would learn to write much to dictation. He would be compelled to memorise a large number of *sententiæ*, short, pithy, worldly-wise sayings. Of these there was a collection of more than seven hundred from the works of Publilius Syrus, a Syrian slave who had made his way to Rome, who had somehow won his freedom, and who was well known for his plays and mimes with these sententious lines in them. Here are some typical specimens of his sayings:

> The miser is the cause of his own wretchedness.
> Courage increases by daring, fear by delaying.
> You will find fortune more easily than you will retain her.
> The anger of a good man is a very serious thing.
> Man's life is lent, not given, to him.
> That plan is bad which is incapable of being altered.
> You will make fewer mistakes, if you know what you do not know.
> He who uses mercy is a perpetual conqueror.
> When old age sins, youth learns to sin.[92]

So into the boy's mind there was instilled a kind of proverbial

[90] Martial 4. 86. 11. [91] Augustine: *Confessions* 1. 13.

[92] W. Warde Fowler: *Social Life at Rome in the Age of Cicero*, p. 185.

wisdom; but all he learned was of little use, if it was belied by the prevailing immorality which existed on every side.

In truth this is a meagre enough curriculum, and it took no less than five years to work it out, for the boy did not leave the elementary school until he was twelve. The weary, cynical drudge of a schoolmaster did not need to hurry; he had no standards, no controls, no one to whom he was answerable other than the parents of the children; he had all the time in the world to thrash a bare knowledge of the educational minimum into the pupils by constant repetition, and to bore them for ever with the labour of learning.

But in fairness it must be remembered that there is another side to all this. Since so much depended on the individual teacher, and since there was no kind of official control, there must have been the widest possible variation in Roman schools. There must have been many teachers who were weary, cynical, disillusioned, ill-paid drudges; but there must have been at least a few who were dedicated to their profession. And, since it is ideals about which we are thinking, it would be quite unjust to say nothing of the Roman ideal. The Roman educational ideal is to be found in the *Institutio Oratoria* of Quintilian, which is one of the most illuminating and useful handbooks of education which has ever been written. It is true that it deals with the making of an orator, and that therefore much of it deals with higher education, and therefore does not concern us here; but Quintilian begins at the beginning with primary education.

Marcus Fabius Quintilianus was a Spaniard from Calgurris on the Ebro. He was born in A.D. 35; and he was probably the son of a teacher of oratory. It may well be that he was educated in Spain, for in those days Spain was one of the cultural centres of the world. Sometime in the fifties of the first century he was in Rome assisting Domitius Afer, the greatest advocate of his day, and meeting all the famous ones of Rome. On the death of Domitius, about A.D. 58, Quintilian returned to Spain. He was brought back to Rome by Galba, and a few years later he was appointed by Vespasian to the professorship of Greek and Latin rhetoric at Rome. That chair he occupied for twenty years until A.D. 90, when he became tutor to the sons of Flavius Clemens, the grandnephews of Domitian, and marked out as heirs to the imperial power. Quintilian was easily the most famous teacher of rhetoric in Rome; and not only was he a teacher and a theorist; in practice he was a famous advocate at the bar. Juvenal quotes him as an example of wealth and of success among the less fortunate rhetoricians.[93] Martial, in an epigram, calls him "the highest guide of wandering youth, and the glory of the Roman bar."[94]

But there is a certain pathos in the *Institutio Oratoria.* It is the fruits of twenty years of teaching; but it was also written out of a broken heart. In his old age he married a girl who cannot have been more than seventeen, and it was an ideally happy marriage; she died in her nineteenth year. She had every virtue that it is given to a woman to possess, and she left Quintilian a grief which nothing could soothe, a loneliness in which no gift of fortune—and fortune was kind to him—could ever bring him happiness again.[95] Quintilian's sorrows were not at an end. His girl wife had left him two little sons. First the younger died at the age of five. Even in his childhood the little boy had loved his father even more than the nurses and the grandmother who brought him up. "How can I forget the charm of his face, the sweetness of his speech, his first flashes of promise, and his actual possession of a calm and—incredible as it may seem—a powerful mind?"[96] But even yet fortune was not done with Quintilian. At least in part he wrote the *Institutio* as an inheritance for his surviving son, a boy "whose ability was so remarkable that it called for the most anxious cultivation on the part of the father." But, even as Quintilian was writing the *Institutio* this boy too died, at the age of nine. "I have lost him of whom I had formed the highest expectations, and in whom I reposed all the hopes that should solace my old age." And in his grief Quintilian asks poignantly: "What is there left for me to do?"[97] The *Institutio* emerged from a background of tears. Let us then see Quintilian's ideal, and his practical advice.

His aim is to produce in the end the perfect orator, but "the first essential for such an one is that he should be a good man."

[93] Juvenal: *Satires* 7. 186–90.

[94] Martial 2. 90. 1, 2:

Quintiliane, vagæ moderator summe iuventæ,
Gloria Romanæ, Quintiliane, togæ.

[95] *Instit. Or.* 6. preface, 4, 5.

[96] *Instit. Or.* 6. preface, 7, 8.

[97] *Instit. Or.* 6. preface, 1, 2.

Not only must he have gifts of speech; he must have excellence of character; and so Quintilian must often be compelled to speak of such virtues as courage, justice, self-control, for there is no such thing as a case in which at least one of these will not emerge.[98] But this aim must have a subsidiary aim, for to attain it the study of literature is necessary, and " the study of literature is a necessity for boys and the delight of old age, the sweet companion of our privacy, and the sole branch of study which has more solid substance than display." [99]

We will not then be surprised to find that Quintilian demands the highest qualities in his teacher. He must have a stainless character which will keep his pupils from harm, and a weight of authority which will guard them from excess. He must himself be a man of rigid self-control, and he must be a disciplinarian to the scholars who gather around him. He must be a father to his students, and he must ever remember that he is taking the place of the parents who entrusted them to him. He must have no vice himself, and tolerate no vice in those whom he teaches. He must be " stern but not melancholy, friendly but not familiar, lest in the one case he incur dislike and in the other contempt." He must never lose his temper, and yet he must correct what needs correcting. He must be ready to answer all questions, and to put questions to those who do not readily ask them. He must not be so niggardly in praise as to raise a distaste for work in his scholars; neither must he be so extravagant in praise as to make them self-complacent. He must never be harsh and abusive when he has faults to find; for many are driven away from study by teachers who find fault as if they hated the offender. Every day he must recite something which the pupils can take away with them. True, they have their books, but the living voice gives richer nourishment, especially if it be the voice of a teacher whom the pupils respect and love.[100] He will never seek to avoid the toil of teaching the elementary things. There are some who think that the great master of eloquence cannot condescend to teach elementary truths; but if a teacher avoids this elementary teaching it is either because he dislikes drudgery or because he cannot teach. The greater the teacher the more ready he will be to teach the simple

[98] *Instit. Or.* 1. preface, 9–12.

[99] *Instit. Or.* 1. 4. 5. [100] *Instit. Or.* 2. 2. 3–8.

things. Certainly he must know how to teach. He must come down to the level of his pupils "as a swift walker, if he happens to be walking with a child, gives him his hand and shortens his stride, and does not go too fast for his small companion." The first virtue of eloquence is clearness, and the more truly learned a man is the more lucid his instruction will be, and the easier to understand. He must be outstanding alike in eloquence and in moral character, for he must teach his pupils both how to teach and act.[101]

Teaching can do much, but natural gifts are essential. "The student who is devoid of talent will derive no more profit from this work than barren soil from a treatise on agriculture." "Without natural gifts technical rules are useless." [102]

But for all that Quintilian sets out with the highest possible belief in the child. A father must conceive the highest hopes for his child from the moment of his birth. Most children are quick to reason and ready to learn. "Reasoning comes as naturally to man as flying to birds, speed to horses and ferocity to beasts of prey." Those who are dull and unteachable are as abnormal as prodigious births and monstrosities. When promise is not fulfilled the fault lies not in the failure of natural gifts, but in the lack of the requisite care.[103] "That there are any," says Quintilian, "who gain nothing from education, I absolutely deny." [104]

Early influences are all important. The child's nurse ideally should be a philosopher; she must be of good character; and she must speak correctly; for the boy will imitate her, and it is almost impossible to unlearn first impressions.[105] The boy's *pædagogus* must be carefully chosen. He must have a thorough education, or, if he has not, he must be aware of the fact. There is no man more dangerous than the man who, the moment he has progressed beyond the alphabet, thinks himself the possessor of real knowledge, and who becomes imperious and brutal in instilling into others that which is nothing other than a dose of his own folly.[106] It would be well if parents, mothers as well as fathers, were themselves well educated; and, if they are not, that should be to them a reason for taking more, and not less, care that their children are given the

[101] *Instit. Or.* 2. 3. 3–12. [102] *Instit. Or.* 1. preface, 26.
[103] *Instit. Or.* 1. 1. 1, 2. [104] *Instit. Or.* 1. 1. 3.
[105] *Instit. Or.* 1. 1. 4–6. [106] *Instit. Or.* 1. 1. 8.

education which they themselves do not possess.[107] Education cannot begin too young, and should not be put off till the age of seven. The child's mind should never be allowed to lie fallow. As soon as the child is capable of receiving moral education, he is capable of receiving literary education. The early years must not be wasted. A child must be doing something; he might as well be learning; and his memory is never as retentive as it is in his earliest years.[108]

But that does not mean that the child is to be forced. Care must be taken to see that when the child is not old enough to love his studies he is not so forced as to begin to hate them. His studies must become his amusement; and he must be praised and coaxed into learning with willingness and joy.[109]

Only the very best of teachers is good enough for the boy.[110] Philip procured no less a teacher than Aristotle for Alexander his son.[111] And Timotheos, the great teacher, used to charge double fees when a boy had been at another teacher before he came to him, for he had to begin by undoing the harm that the inferior teacher had done.[112] Some people advocate that teaching should begin with lesser authors, because they are easier to understand; but Quintilian believed that teaching should begin with the best from the very first, and especially with Cicero, who, he says, is not only a useful model, but can also be loved.[113] That which is given for memorisation should always be the best, for it gives an unconscious standard to imitate, and in the end it will reproduce itself in the style of the scholar who has memorised it.[114]

Quintilian was not only an educational theorist, he was also a practical teacher; and he has certain practical rules to lay down. He insists that the boy should begin by learning Greek; Latin will look after itself, because day by day he will be soaking it in. But the study of Latin must not be long delayed lest the boy learn to speak in a Greek accent and in Greek idioms, and very soon Latin and Greek should be proceeding side by side.[115]

Quintilian has strong views about the teaching of the alphabet. The common educational practice in his day was to begin by

[107] *Instit. Or.* 1. 1. 6, 7. [108] *Instit. Or.* 1. 1. 17–19.
[109] *Instit. Or.* 1. 1. 20. [110] *Instit. Or.* 1. 1. 11. [111] *Instit. Or.* 1. 1. 23.
[112] *Instit. Or.* 2. 3. 3. [113] *Instit. Or.* 2. 5. 18–20.
[114] *Instit. Or.* 2. 7. 2, 3. [115] *Instit. Or.* 1. 1. 12, 14.

teaching boys the names of the letters before the shapes of the letters were known, so that a boy could rhyme off the names of the letters before he was able to recognise them. Quintilian advocates that boys should be taught to know letters in the same way as they are taught to know people, that the name of the letters and the appearance of the letter should be learned at the same time. To encourage them to learn letters children should be given little ivory letters to play with, " the handling and naming of which is a pleasure." [116] The learning of letters is followed by the learning of syllables, and then of words. Then comes reading. Here Quintilian advocates a policy of slowness and gradualness. " You will hardly believe," he says, " how much reading is hindered by undue haste. If the child attempts more than his powers allow, the inevitable result is hesitation, interruption and repetition, and the mistakes which he makes merely lead him to lose confidence in what he already knows." Reading is a difficult physical act, for it involves looking to the right and looking ahead at the same time. It must therefore be kept slow for a considerable time, until practice brings speed unaccompanied by error.[117]

Quintilian has much to say about writing. " The art of writing well and quickly is not unimportant for our purpose, though it is generally disregarded by persons of quality. . . . A sluggish pen delays our thoughts, while an unformed and illiterate hand cannot be deciphered. . . . We shall therefore at all times and in all places, and above all when we are writing letters to our friends, find a gratification in the thought that we have not neglected even this accomplishment." [118] Quintilian rightly believed that to be able to write quickly was a very valuable scholastic asset, but to insist on writing legibly was an essential part of good manners and of courtesy.

The time will soon come when the boy must practise this writing. If he is copying out words, let him not waste his time in copying common words, the meaning of which he knows already. If he is copying sentences, let them be sentences which are worth copying, full of moral value, aphorisms which will still be printed in his memory when he is an old man. Let them be the sayings of

[116] *Instit. Or.* I. I. 24–7.

[117] *Instit. Or.* I. I. 31–4.

[118] *Instit. Or.* I. I. 28, 29.

famous men, and, above all, let there be much from the poets, " for poetry is more attractive to children." It is at this age, when originality is impossible, that " memory is almost the only faculty which can be developed by the teacher," and it is a duty to store it, not with trivial things, but with that which is worth remembering.[119]

Quintilian discusses the question of whether it is better for a boy to be educated at home or at school; and he comes down emphatically on the side of a school education. It is urged that school may bring bad influences and may corrupt the boy's character. It is Quintilian's view that, as things were in Rome at that time, the boy had every bit as good a chance of being corrupted in his own home. He writes in a famous passage: " Would that we did not too often ruin our children's character ourselves! We spoil them from the cradle. That soft upbringing, which we call kindness, saps all the sinews both of mind and body. If the child crawls on purple, what will he not desire when he comes to manhood? Before he can talk he can distinguish scarlet and cries for the very best brand of purple. We train their palates before we teach their lips to speak. They grow up carried in litters; if they set foot on earth, they are supported by the hands of attendants on either side. We rejoice if they say something over-free, and words which we should not tolerate from the lips of even an Alexandrian page are greeted with laughter and a kiss. We have no right to be surprised. It was we who taught them; they hear us use such words, they see our mistresses and our minions; every dinner party is loud with foul songs, and things are presented to their eyes of which we should blush to speak. Hence springs habit, and habit in time becomes second nature. The wretched children learn these things before they know them to be wrong. They become luxurious and effeminate, and far from acquiring such vices at schools, introduce them themselves." [120]

It is further objected that the teacher of a class cannot give the attention to each boy that a tutor can give to one boy. But, after all, no boy can be worked all out all day. By far the greater part of a boy's study should be private study for himself, and, Quintilian finely says, the purpose of the teacher is to give " purpose and direction " to the day's work, and then to encourage the boy to do it for himself. When a teacher lectures, all the pupils receive the

[119] *Instit. Or.* I. I. 34–6. [120] *Instit. Or.* I. 2. 6–8 and see Appendix D.

same value. "The voice of a lecturer is not like a dinner which will only suffice for a limited number; it is like the sun which distributes the same quantity of light and heat to all of us." In the class of a good teacher the one boy will never be swamped in the many. A good teacher will never take more pupils than he can teach well, and it will be his first aim to make himself on friendly and intimate terms with all of them, and to make his teaching "not a duty but a labour of love."

Having dealt with the objections to school education, Quintilian goes on to point out its positive advantages. It is not the teacher's aim to produce the "pale student, the solitary and the recluse," but one who can move graciously and charmingly in any society; and the society of a school is an excellent training for the society of men in after days. Friendship is one of the world's supreme values, and a school supplies friendships which are never open to the boy with a private tutor. In a school the boy learns not only what he is taught, but what others are taught as well. In a school he has the incentive of competition which individual teaching cannot bring. In a school he has those who are only a little older than himself to copy and to imitate, and is not presented with only the hopeless task of copying the teacher. Nor must the effect on the teacher himself be forgotten. The teacher cannot develop the same energy and intelligence before an audience of one, that the presence of a numerous audience would kindle. The teacher cannot expend eloquence on an audience of one, but is bound to speak in a conversational tone. "There would be no such thing as eloquence, if we spoke to only one person at a time."[121] Quintilian would have agreed with the dictum that any preacher kindles at the sight of men. It was the conviction of Quintilian that both from the point of view of scholar and of teacher education in a school was always to be preferred to education by a private tutor.

Even if teaching be in a class, the good teacher will make certain that he knows the ability and character of every individual boy. Quintilian believed that the surest test of a boy lies in his memory; any mind which is quick to receive impressions and faithful to retain them is a good mind. The second distinguishing character-

[121] *Instit. Or.* I. 2. 1–31. This is one of the fullest and most interesting discussions in the *Institutio*.

istic of the boy is the power of imitation, not imitation to raise a laugh, but imitation of that which he is taught. As the teacher discovers the individual character and ability of each boy, he will match his treatment to the boy's needs. "There are some boys who are slack unless pressed on; others again are impatient of control; some are amenable to fear, while others are paralysed by it; in some cases the mind requires continued application to form it, in others this result is best attained by rapid concentration. Give me the boy who is spurred on by praise, delighted by success, and ready to weep over failure. Such a one must be encouraged by appeals to his ambition; rebuke will bite him to the quick; honour will be a spur, and there is no fear of his proving indolent." [122]

But even amidst effort relaxation is necessary for the mind, as it is for everything else. "I approve of play in the young," Quintilian writes. "It is the sign of a lively disposition, nor will you ever lead me to believe that a boy who is gloomy, and in a continual state of depression, is ever likely to show alertness of mind." And Quintilian was sure that there is nothing like games for revealing character, for in them there is instinctively revealed the sense of right and wrong.[123]

As we have seen, Quintilian emphatically disapproved of flogging, as being in itself useless to make a boy learn, and ultimately injurious to his whole personality.[124]

Here indeed is an educational ideal. Its aim is in the end, and in the years to come, to produce the ideal orator, who is defined in Cato's words, as "a good man skilled in speaking." [125] Oratory without character seemed to Quintilian a hateful thing, for then fluency of speech would be "the accomplice of crime, the betrayer of innocence, the enemy of truth." [126] No one can be an orator unless he is a good man.

There were minds in Rome which were building up an ideal of elementary education which was second to none; but it was seldom, or almost never, that that ideal was put into practice. It is clear that even Quintilian's ideal, with its philosophic nurse and its ivory letters to play with, was an ideal which only the well-to-do

[122] *Instit. Or.* 1. 3. 1, 6, 7. [123] *Instit. Or.* 1. 3. 9, 10, 12.

[124] *Instit. Or.* 1. 13, 15, 17, 18.

[125] *Instit. Or.* 1. 12. 1. [126] *Instit. Or.* 1. 12. 2.

could ever realise for their children. For by far the most part Roman elementary education consisted of knowledge driven into a boy by almost sadistic flogging and by wearisome repetition, which made of it a kind of nightmare compounded of boredom and of fear.

By far the larger number of Roman boys would never proceed beyond the school of the *litterator*, and the stage of elementary education. If they did, they would meet two further teachers, first the *grammaticus*; and then the *rhetor*. With the *rhetor*, the teacher of rhetoric proper, we are not at this point concerned; but we must now go on to look at the *grammaticus*. The *grammaticus* was the teacher of literature.

The *grammaticus* and his curriculum were later in emerging than the *litterator* and the elementary school. The reason was quite simply that in the early days Rome had no literature of her own; but then Greek began its penetration. The coming of Greek was inevitable. Greek was in any event the language of the civilised world, and no man could move in the wider world without it. When Rome began to possess slaves, many of these slaves were Greeks, and brought their language and their culture with them. When, in the first half of the second century Rome conquered Greece, many a Greek hostage was brought to Rome. Among them there were men of the stature of Polybius, and these men brought an incalculable contribution to the land whose captives they were. There were Romans, and those among the greatest, who found in Greek culture and beauty that which had been missing from their lives, and who welcomed the best of it. Notable among them was Cornelia, the mother of the Gracchi, who, as Cicero tells us, educated her sons diligently in Greek from their boyhood days, and engaged for them the most carefully chosen Greek tutors.[127] There was Æmilius Paulus who trained his sons, as Plutarch tells, not only in the ancient Roman discipline, but also in that of Greece. He procured masters to teach them grammar, logic, rhetoric, preceptors to teach them modelling and drawing, managers of horses and dogs, and instructors in field sports, and all from Greece.[128] It was this Æmilius Paulus who finally shattered the power of Macedonia at the battle of Pydna. He would take none of the spoils for himself, but handed

[127] Cicero: *Brutus* 104. [128] Plutarch: *Æmilius Paulus* 6.

them all over to the public treasury. "He only permitted his sons who were great lovers of learning to take the king's books." [129]

It was the sons of Æmilius Paulus, Fabius and Scipio, the elder twenty years old, the younger in his nineteenth year, who were so intimate with Polybius, the great historian, who was one of the hostages brought from Achæa in 167 B.C. Polybius himself tells, in one of the most charming passages in Greek literature, of the young Scipio's devotion to himself:

> The beginning of my companionship with the two boys was due to the loan of books, and to conversation on that subject. Our friendship soon became closer, and when the hostages were sent to the Italian cities, Fabius and Scipio begged their father to allow me to remain in Rome. This was granted and our intimacy was already far advanced when the following incident occurred. One day, after we had left the house of Fabius together, Fabius turned down towards the forum, whilst Scipio went with me in another direction. After a while Publius said to me, blushing and in a low quiet tone: "Tell me, Polybius, why is it that, though there are two of us, you always address your conversation to my brother, putting him your questions, and giving him your replies, while you leave me alone? I suppose you share the opinion of my fellow-citizens. They all believe, so I am told, that I am too easy-going and lazy, the very opposite to a Roman in my way of life, because I do not care to plead in the courts. They say too—and this is what pains me most—that the family to which I belong needs a very different man at its head from what I am likely to be." I was puzzled at the boy's way of opening the conversation (for he was then not more than eighteen years old) and answered: "Scipio, I beg of you, do not say such things; do not even think them. It was neither through contempt nor through any low opinion of your character that I acted as you describe; far from it. But your brother is the older, and that is why I always begin and end the conversation with him, addressing my answers and words of advice to him, and supposing that you share his opinion. But now I am glad to hear from you how pained you are at the idea

[129] Plutarch: *Æmilius Paulus* 28.

> of being less active than becomes one of your family. That shows your noble spirit, and I would gladly help you to say and do something worthy of your ancestors. You will have no lack of helpers, you and your brother, in the studies which are now, I see, absorbing most of your energies and ambitions: for I have noticed this tribe of teachers flocking over just now from Greece to Rome. But as for the problem which you tell me is now troubling you, I think you will find no one better suited than I to help you in your work." As I was still speaking, he caught my right hand in both his, and pressing it warmly said: "Would that I could see the day when you would lay all other interests aside to live with me, and give me the whole of your attention! From that day I feel sure that I would soon prove worthy of my family and ancestors." I was overjoyed at the lad's eagerness to accept my proposal. But when I thought of the greatness of his family and the success of so many of its members, I began to hesitate. However, once the conversation had taken place, the boy was never out of my company, and seemed to care for nothing so much as his intimacy with me.[130]

It is easy to see in that passage the thrill which this new knowledge brought when the best of the Romans came into living contact with the finest of the Greeks. Naturally there were those who were against all this new culture, although even Cato was to capitulate in the end. But culture and Greek became synonymous in Roman education.

It is of interest to note the spread of the tide of Greek through Rome.[131] As far back as 282 B.C. the Roman envoy Postumius had made a speech in Greek at Tarentum, even if the Greek was far from perfect. When Cineas the envoy of Pyrrhus addressed the Roman senate, all the probability is that he did so in Greek, for Greeks did not learn any language but their own. Sempronius Gracchus, the father of the Gracchi, consul both in 177 and in 163 B.C., addressed the Rhodians in polished and in excellent Greek. In 131 B.C. Licinius Crassus, the proconsul of Asia, was to show his complete proficiency in no fewer than five Greek dialects. The earliest Roman historians, Fabius Pictor and Cincius Alimentus,

[130] Polybius 31. 23. [131] J. W. Duff: *E.R.E.* 5. 210.

wrote their histories in Greek. The day was to come when Paul was to address the Roman Church, Hadrian was to write his epigrams, and Marcus Aurelius his *Meditations*, all in Greek. Quintilian was to recommend that the Roman schoolboy should begin his studies with Greek even before he began Latin.[132] Juvenal was to tell in his satires and Martial in his epigrams how even the ladies of love did their love-making in Greek.[133] Greek had conquered every walk of life. A. S. Wilkins makes the interesting comment: " The Romans came to be the first nation to base their culture on the study of a literature in a foreign language, and so marked out the lines on which the higher education of all civilised nations was to move down to the present time." [134]

Everything must have a beginning, and the beginning of the Roman study of Greek literature happened about 270 B.C. About that time Livius Andronicus came from Tarentum to Rome. He was originally a slave, and he was set to teaching the children of certain of the great families in Rome. He knew Greek literature and he felt acutely the need of something more than the Twelve Tables to be the literature of Roman education; so he translated the *Odyssey* into Latin for his scholars, and his book remained an educational standard text-book for nigh on three centuries. He went on to translate certain of the Greek plays also. At the same time Ennius was helping on the process. So far, as Suetonius says, " the beginnings of the subject were very humble." [135] Slowly this teaching developed, and then a hundred years later in 168 B.C. there

[132] Quintilian: *Instit. Or.* 1. 1. 12.

[133] Juvenal: *Satires* 6. 186 ff: " What can be more offensive than this, that no woman believes in her own beauty unless she has converted herself from a Tuscan into a Greekling, or from a maid of Sulmo into a true maid of Athens? They talk nothing but Greek. . . . Their fears, their wraths, their joys, and their troubles—all the secrets of their soul—are poured forth in Greek; their very loves are carried on in Greek fashion." Martial 10. 68: " Although your home is not Ephesus or Rhodes nor Mitylene, but a house, Lælia, in Patrician Street, and though your mother was one of the sunburned Etruscans, and never rouged, your sturdy father one from the district of Aricia, you are continually heaping on me in Greek, 'My lord,' 'My honey,' 'My soul.' Shameful! Although you are a fellow-citizen of Hersilia and Egeria . . . you may learn by heart and produce all the ways of Corinth, yet nohow, Lælia, will you ever be a Lais! "

[134] A. S. Wilkins: *Roman Education*, p. 20.

[135] Suetonius: *Grammarians* 1.

happened one of these odd accidents, which have a quite disproportionate effect on life. In that year King Attalus sent Crates of Mallos on an embassy to Rome. Crates was one of the great scholars and teachers of his day; he was the head of the famous library at Pergamum, and himself "a living library."[136] Let Suetonius tell the story in his spare account:

> In my opinion, then, the first to introduce the study of grammar into our city was Crates of Mallos. . . . He was sent to the senate by King Attalus between the second and third Punic Wars, at about the time when Ennius died; and, having fallen into the opening of a sewer in the Palatine quarter and broken his leg, he held numerous and frequent conferences, at which he constantly gave instruction, and thus set an example for our countrymen to imitate.[137]

The majority of the Romans had never heard a scholar or lecturer like Crates before, and so education in literature was born in Rome because a Greek librarian slipped in the opening of a sewer!

It was of course with Homer that everything began. As Horace wrote, describing his schooldays: "At Rome I had the luck to be bred, and taught how much Achilles' wrath had harmed the Greeks."[138] Æsop, too, was useful for teaching boys, for they could learn to paraphrase his fables.[139] Cicero desired the son of his friend Lepta to know Hesiod with his ripe wisdom.[140] Quintilian approves of the Greek tragedies; the comedies have their uses; the lyric poets may be read, provided the poet and the passage is carefully chosen; the erotic elegiacs and the hendecasyllables must be banished as unfit for the consumption of youth, or at least kept for the very senior classes.[141] It is to be noted that everything is centred on poetry. Sergius the grammarian defines the art of the *grammaticus* by saying that it consists mainly in the understanding of the poets; while Cicero, speaking of the works of the Greek poets,

[136] A. S. Wilkins: *Roman Education*, p. 22. [137] Suetonius: *Grammarians* 2.

[138] Horace: *Epistles* 2. 2. 42. For the place of Homer cp. Quintilian: *Instit. Or.* 1. 8. 5.

[139] Quintilian: *Instit. Or.* 1. 9. 5.

[140] Cicero: *Ep.* 6. 18. 5. [141] Quintilian: *Instit. Or.* 1. 8. 5–7.

says: "These we read and learn from our boyhood; these we believe to be liberal knowledge and teaching."[142]

Meanwhile Rome was building up a literature of her own, which, sooner or later, must find an entry into the curriculum. The first man to lecture in Latin on Latin authors was Quintus Cæcilius Epirota, who opened his school about 25 B.C.[143] It was inevitable that the first of the Roman writers to be included in the curriculum was Virgil. Then one by one they came in. Of the ancients, the *Annals* of Ennius had first place. Of the dramatists Pacuvius, Accius, Plautus, Cæcilius and Terence were received. The *Epistles* of Horace, the *Fasti* of Ovid, the *Pharsalia* of Lucan, the *Thebais* of Statius, the prose treatises of Seneca came each in their day into the curriculum. But to the end of the day it was Homer and Menander who remained the most basic of all.

We must now look at the actual curriculum which the *grammaticus* taught, and at the methods he used. Fortunately for this we have the full description of Quintilian in chapters 5 to 12 of the first book of the *Institutio*.

Broadly speaking the work of the *grammaticus* fell into two parts.

First of all, he taught *recte loquendi scientia*, the knowledge of right speaking. Quintilian would have this done with the greatest of thoroughness. The scholar must be taught the value and the history of the letters and of the vowels. Is there somewhere, for instance, a missing vowel, since the correct pronunciation is somewhere between *optime* and *optume*?[144] Changes in words by inflection must be studied, and it must be understood, for instance, why *cado* becomes *cecidi* in the perfect tense. Historical changes in words must be examined. How did *clamos* became *clamor*, and *duellum*, *bellum*?[145] The parts of speech must be studied, verbs, nouns and conjunctions.[146] The inflexions of nouns and verbs must be examined; and such questions must be studied as why *Murena* is feminine in form and yet a masculine name; and why *Glycerium* is neuter in form and yet feminine as a name.[147] This section in

[142] Sergius 4. p. 186, ed. Keil; Cicero: *Tusc. Disp.* 2. 11. 27; quoted A. S. Wilkins: *Roman Education*, p. 57.

[143] Suetonius: *Grammarians* 16.

[144] *Instit. Or.* 1. 4. 6 ff.

[145] *Instit. Or.* 1. 4. 13 ff.

[146] *Instit. Or.* 1. 4. 17 ff.

[147] *Instit. Or.* 1. 4. 22.

Quintilian is of considerable length and detail. Certainly the boy was going to understand the language which he was going to read and speak.

Next *diction* is discussed, and it is laid down as a foundation that diction must be correct, clear and elegant.[148] *Barbarisms*—that is, faulty use of individual words—and *solecisms*—that is, incorrect combinations of words—must be examined and avoided. False quantities and mistakes in accents must be eradicated so that *orthoepeia*, right speaking, may result. All this is discussed with a wealth of illustration in Quintilian.[149]

What is it then that authorises diction? What are the standards which entitle us to adopt a word? Four standards are laid down. (i) There is *ratio*, which may be called "theory." It works mainly by analogy; that which is uncertain is established by analogy with that which is certain. (ii) There is *vetustas*, "age." A word which has a long pedigree of usage is a word with dignity; but the pedigree must be sought in the orators and historians, and not in the poets, whose use of words is subject to their metres; and a word must not be obsolete, for then it becomes unintelligible. (iii) There is *auctoritas*, "authority." Our right to use a word depends on a study of the authors who have already used it. (iv) Finally, there is the most important test of all; there is *consuetudo*, "custom" or "usage." Usage is *certissima loquendi magistra*, the fact which most certainly controls our speaking; but it must be noted that the usage in question is the usage of scholars, and not of the mob.[150]

There is a good deal here of what we would call in the narrower sense grammar. When the Roman *grammatici* began to teach there was no such thing as a Latin grammar. They borrowed and adapted the Greek grammar of Dionysius Thrax, which was a slim volume of no more than sixteen pages, and which yet remained a standard work for thirteen centuries. The first Latin grammar proper was composed by Quintus Remmius Palæmon, who may well have been Quintilian's own teacher, early in the reign of Vespasian.

The second part of the task of the *grammaticus* was called *poetarum enarratio*, the explanation of the poets. This must be preceded by *emendatio*, the ascertainment of the correct text, a very necessary

[148] *Instit. Or.* 1. 5. 1.

[149] *Instit. Or.* 1. 5. 5–31.

[150] *Instit. Or.* 1. 6. 1 ff.

task in days when manuscripts were produced by hand. First, there comes reading. To understand a passage is the golden rule for reading it well. Reading must be natural; it must never be intoned in a kind of sing-song. Quintilian quotes with relish a saying of the young Gaius Cæsar to one of these sing-song, intoning readers: "If you are singing, you sing badly; and if you are reading, you are singing."[151] It is well to start with Homer; the lad may not understand it all, but it will do him good to be soaked in its greatness.[152]

Then there follows the lecture of the *grammaticus* on the passage. The lecture should always be on such things as will enlarge the mind and provide the greatest nourishment for the intellect; life is long enough to leave aside for a while the study of subjects which interest no one but learned men.[153] Nor must the teacher try to deal with every possible detail and every possible word. Quintilian caustically remarks: "I shall count it a merit in a teacher of literature that there should be some things which he does not know."[154] It is obvious that at this point the lesson could become either completely fascinating or completely boring. The teacher had to give an account of the life of the author and the circumstances under which the book was written and published, or, in the case of a play, the conditions and date of its first production. He had to explain all the allusions in it, whether they were to mythology, to history, to astronomy or to anything else. He had to discuss the figures, and the arrangements of words, the dissonances and the assonances. He had to criticise the style, and nothing that was barbarous, or improper, or contrary to the laws of language must be allowed to escape.[155] At this point not even the greatest authors were allowed to escape without criticism, nor even the greatest men. Marcus Pomponius Marcellus criticised a word in a speech by Tiberius. Ateius Capito declared that, whatever the word had been before, it must be good Latin now that Cæsar had used it. "Cæsar can confer citizenship upon men," said Marcellus, "but not upon a word."[156] It was here that the lecture could deal with the most recondite questions and riddles; and it was here that the *grammaticus*

[151] *Instit. Or.* I. 8. 2, 3. [152] *Instit. Or.* I. 8. 5.
[153] *Instit. Or.* I. 8. 8. [154] *Instit. Or.* I. 8. 21.
[155] *Instit. Or.* I. 8. 15 ff. [156] Suetonius: *Grammarians* 22.

could propound the most abstruse questions, or indeed questions to which there was no answer at all. Juvenal tells how the *grammaticus* should be able to tell who was the nurse of Anchises, what was the name and birthplace of Anchemolus's stepmother (*Æneid* 10. 389), to what age Acestes lived, how many flagons of Sicilian wine he presented to the Trojans (*Æneid* 5. 73 ff.). It was Tiberius himself who used to propound to *grammatici* the famous questions, Who was Hecuba's mother? What was the name of Achilles among the maidens? What was the song the Sirens sang? [157]

It is clear from all this that the *grammaticus* must be a man equipped with a vast store of general and of detailed knowledge. Quintilian says of him: " Nor is it sufficient to have read the poets only; every kind of writer must be carefully studied, not merely for the subject matter, but for the vocabulary; for words often acquire their authority from their use by a particular author. Nor can such training be regarded as complete, if it stop short at music, for the teacher of literature has to speak of metre and rhythm; nor again if he be ignorant of astronomy, can he understand the poets; for they, to mention no further points, frequently give their indications of time by reference to the rising and setting of the stars. Ignorance of philosophy is an equal drawback, since there are numerous passages in almost every poem based on the most intricate questions of natural philosophy, while among the Greeks we have Empedocles, and among our own poets Varro and Lucretius, all of whom have expounded their philosophies in verse. No small powers of eloquence also are required to enable the teacher to speak appropriately and fluently on the various points which have just been mentioned. For this reason those who criticise the art of teaching literature as trivial and lacking in substance put themselves out of court." [158] If that be the standard, then indeed the *grammaticus* must be a man of encyclopædic knowledge.[159]

There still remain two further items which Quintilian declares should be in the curriculum of the *grammaticus*. There is music. It is the noblest of the arts; and the first of all the arts to be related to literature. Pythagoras, Plato, Socrates, and in the ancient days Orpheus, were both philosophers and musicians. Without a

[157] Suetonius: *Tiberius* 70. [158] *Instit. Or.* 1. 4. 4, 5.

[159] For the *grammatici* see Appendix E.

knowledge of music a man cannot be truly cultured. Cicero tells us that in Greece it was the custom to pass the lyre round the company after dinner. On one such occasion the lyre was passed to Themistocles, who confessed that he could not play it; and this was taken as a sign that his education was imperfect.[160] Music is the perfect solace; the galley slave finds comfort in it as he plies his oar to its rhythm; and even the solitary worker is cheered as he sings to himself his artless strain.[161] The Greeks were always impressed by the moral power of music; they regarded music as a power which actually moved a man to action either good or bad.

> We are told that Pythagoras on one occasion, when some young men were led astray by their passions to commit an outrage on a respectable family, calmed them by ordering the piper to change her strain to a spondaic measure, while Chrysippus selects a special tune to be used by nurses to entice their little charges to sleep. Further I may point out that among the fictitious themes employed in declamation is one, doing no little credit to the author's learning, in which it is assumed that a piper is accused of manslaughter because he had played a tune in the Phrygian mode as an accompaniment to a sacrifice, with the result that the person officiating went mad and flung himself over a precipice. . . . Music is a necessary element in the education of an orator.[162]

But Quintilian is clear about certain things in this teaching of music. The music taught must not be modern music:

> I think I ought to be more emphatic than I have been in stating that the music which I desire to see taught is not our modern music, which has been emasculated by the lascivious melodies of our effeminate stage, and has to no small extent destroyed such manly vigour as we still possessed. No, I refer to the music of old which was employed to sing the praises of brave men, and was sung by the brave themselves. I will have none of your psalteries and viols, that are unfit even for the use of a modest

[160] Cicero: *Tusc. Disp.* I. 2. 4; Quintilian: *Instit. Or.* I. 10. 9, 11, 19.

[161] *Instit. Or.* I. 10. 15, 16. [162] *Instit. Or.* I. 10. 33.

girl. Give me the knowledge of the principles of music, which have power to excite or to assuage the emotions of mankind.[163]

Quintilian is not in the least interested in music from the æsthetic point of view; he is interested in it only as a moral power.

Further, Quintilian's view of music as part of the curriculum of the *grammaticus* is unashamedly utilitarian. Music to the Greek always included dancing; therefore music deals with two things, with melody and with rhythm. Now to awaken the correct emotions in his audience a man must study the melodious intonations of his voice; and to make his speech doubly effective he must study the eurhythmics of gesture. It is solely for this purpose that music is to be studied. It is to be studied so that a man will speak melodiously and move eurhythmically.[164] To prove his point he quotes a curious story about the great orator Caius Gracchus. Caius Gracchus, when he was delivering a speech, always had a musician standing behind him, with a pitchpipe, or as the Greeks call it a *tonarion*; and it was the duty of this musician to give him the tones in which his voice was to be pitched. Even in his most turbulent speeches he was careful to observe this custom.[165]

Those who believe in music for music's sake, and for nothing beyond itself, will be moved to violent opposition by the insistence of Quintilian that music must be taught by the *grammaticus* because of its moral effect, and because of its technical rhetorical usefulness.

The second subject which Quintilian adds additionally to the curriculum of the *grammaticus* is geometry, by which he meant mathematics as a whole. Once again his view is completely utilitarian. The idea of pure mathematics, as, for instance, Plato saw it, had no relevance at all for the Roman mind. It is useful for a lad to learn mathematics for that study exercises his mind, sharpens his wits, and generates quickness of perception. The value of mathematics lies not in the knowledge gained but in the process of learning; it is not the knowledge gained, but the mental discipline undergone and mental habits formed, which are valuable.[166] To learn mathematics is a practical necessity. By mathematics we can learn and demonstrate the fixed order of the stars, and so lead on to

[163] *Instit. Or.* I. 10. 31. [164] *Instit. Or.* I. 10. 22–6.
[165] *Instit. Or.* I. 10. 27, 28. [166] *Instit. Or.* I. 10. 34.

the idea of a guiding and controlling destiny—a thought an orator will often have to use. Mathematics teaches us the logical development of thought; and what lesson can be more necessary for a pleader? And—and Quintilian set this first—linear geometry is necessary in every case which deals with limits and boundaries of land, questions with which an advocate has frequently to deal.[167] Once again Quintilian is quite unconscious of the detached delight of the subject he describes; all he is interested in is its practical use.

Quintilian touches more briefly on one further department of study—on gymnastics. Here again his view is exactly the same. It is as usual entirely utilitarian. He is quite willing to set aside a certain portion of time for gymnastics, but he has no time at all for those "who kill the mind by over-attention to the body." [168] The sole use of gymnastics is as an aid to correct delivery of an oration. Gymnastics must be used only to form gesture and motion so that the arms may be extended in the proper manner, the management of the hands free from all trace of rusticity and inelegance, the attitude becoming, the movements of the feet appropriate and the motions of the head and eyes in keeping with the poise of the body. [169] He agrees with Crassus as Cicero quotes him in the *De Oratore* that "the orator should learn to move his body in a bold and manly fashion, not derived from actors on the stage, but from martial and even gymnastic exercises." [170] Whatever the subject, be it music, be it mathematics, be it gymnastics, its only justification lies in its use for oratory in the days to come. Art for art's sake was not a principle which was on Quintilian's horizon.

Finally in our examination of the curriculum of the *grammaticus* we must look at the work which was demanded from the pupil himself.

It did not at this stage amount to very much. It began by setting the pupil to reproduce, either orally or in writing, a story which had been told to him, or which he had read. For that exercise the Fables of Æsop were the favourite material. It then went on to exercise the student in the art of paraphrase. This began simply by the restatement of poetry in prose; but it went on to

[167] *Instit. Or.* I. 10. 35–47.

[168] *Instit. Or.* I. 11. 15. [169] *Instit. Or.* I. 11. 16.

[170] *Instit. Or.* I. 11. 18; Cicero: *De Or.* 3. 59. 220.

develop until the thought of a passage could be freely paraphrased in the scholar's own words. In point of fact this was an exercise of which Cicero disapproved. His objection was that a great author will already have expressed what he has to say in the best possible words; and that therefore paraphrase means nothing more than putting worse words in place of better ones. A. S. Wilkins comments that there is a modern tendency to accept this and to hold that only second-rate literature should be set for paraphrase.[171] Oddly enough translation from one language to another did not form part of the work of the pupil under the *grammaticus*; this was considered to be preferable at a later and more developed stage.

Following that there came the treatment of *sententiæ*, that is, of moral maxims and aphorisms. That began at first by simple exercises in merely altering the form of the *sententia*. The saying has, so to speak, to be "declined." Carcopino takes as an example the statement: "Marcus Porcius Cato has said that the roots of science are bitter." That can be altered into: "This maxim of Marcus Porcius Cato which says that . . .," "It appeared to Marcus Porcius Cato that . . .," "The Marcus Porcius Catos have maintained that . . ." And so the changes could be rung indefinitely, even more so in Latin than in English. It does seem a trivial occupation, and yet it had its uses in giving the pupil a facility of expression. Then essays had to be written on the *sententia*, and expansions of it had to be made. The aim was that the scholar should acquire and retain in his memory a vast mass of common-places, all ready pigeon-holed, to be produced ready-made in any speech and at any moment. Finally, the student was set the task of writing stories founded on the materials which the poets gave.[172]

It can be seen that the whole system aimed at equipping the student with a fluent, if somewhat mechanical and stereotyped, gift of self-expression, if need be at a moment's notice.

Such then was the content and method of Roman education. In the ancient days it was founded on an ideal of the home and of parental duty than which none has ever been higher. The very circumstances of empire conspired to make that ideal impossible. So Rome produced a primary education which was founded on the

[171] Cicero: *De Or.* I. 154; A. S. Wilkins: *Roman Education*, p. 72.

[172] *Instit. Or.* I. 9. 2 ff.

drudgery of repetition and the incentive of corporal punishment; and she produced a secondary education which was dominated by the conviction that the power to speak in public was the only power worth having, and the career of the orator the only possible career. And yet it remains to be said that buried deep down in the Roman soul the ancient ideal never went totally lost, and that in the hands of a Quintilian even that meagre curriculum could become a liberal education. Somehow, even in the days of decadence, Roman education succeeded in producing at least a few men who had penetrated to the ideal which lay beyond and behind the practice, and by whom the ancient *gravitas* was not forgotten.

V. The Christian Attitude to Pagan Culture

THE CHRISTIAN attitude to pagan culture in the days of the Early Church is only one side of the general Christian attitude to the world. In the ancient days Abraham "sojourned in the land of promise, as in a strange country," and all the time he was looking "for a city which hath foundations, whose builder and maker is God."[1] It is to the "strangers" scattered throughout Asia Minor that Peter writes his letter, and it is as "strangers and pilgrims" that he appeals to them to abstain from fleshly lusts.[2] In two New Testament passages this specially emerges. It emerges when Paul is writing to the Corinthians, and when his advice is to abstain even from marriage, because "the time is short" and "the fashion of this world is passing away.[3]" And it occurs in *I Thessalonians* when the Thessalonians have become so impressed with the transitoriness of life that they have abandoned the ordinary activities of life, and have to be reminded to be at peace and to go on with their own business.[4]

The Christians were not without warrant for this attitude even in pagan literature itself. Philo had called all the wise men who are spoken of in the books of Moses "sojourners," "for their souls are sent down from heaven upon earth as to a colony . . . looking upon the heavenly country in which they have the rights of citizenship as their native land, and the earthly abode in which they dwell for a while as a foreign land."[5] "Your citizenship," wrote Paul to the Philippians, "is in heaven."[6] Marcus Aurelius, the Roman Emperor and Stoic saint, had said: "Life is a warfare and a sojourn in a foreign land."[7] Diogenes Lærtius tells of Anaxagoras, the

[1] *Hebrews* 11. 9, 10. [2] *I Peter* 1. 1; 2. 11.
[3] *I Corinthians* 7. 29–32. [4] *I Thessalonians* 4. 11.
[5] Philo: *De. Conf. Ling.* 77 f. [6] *Philippians* 3. 20.
[7] Marcus Aurelius: *Meditations* 2. 17.

philosopher. He gave away his patrimony; he went into retirement to devote himself to thought, and took no part in public affairs. He was asked: "Have you no concern for your native land?" "I am greatly concerned with my fatherland," he said, and pointed to the sky.[8] Epictetus draws his picture of life. Man is a traveller on the way to his own country. He stops at a pleasant inn, and the inn pleases him. "Man, you have forgotten your purpose! You were not travelling *to* this, but *through* this." The inn may be pleasant, and the meadow may be lovely—"yet simply for passing through."[9] "The world is merely a bridge," runs the unwritten saying of Jesus, "ye are to pass over it, and not to build your dwelling on it."[10] The Oxyrhynchus Logion runs: "Unless ye fast to the world, ye shall in no wise find the Kingdom of God."[11]

This attitude bit deep into Christian thought. Clement writes to the "Church of God which sojourns at Rome."[12] Polycarp's Letter to the Philippians is addressed to the "Church of God sojourning at Philippi."[13] The *Martyrdom of Polycarp* is sent "from the Church of God which sojourns at Smyrna, to the Church of God sojourning in Philomelium."[14] "This world and the next are two enemies," writes the author of the homily known as *Second Clement*. "The one urges to adultery and corruption, avarice and deceit; the other bids farewell to these things. We cannot therefore be the friends of both; and it behoves us, by renouncing the one, to make sure of the other. Let us reckon that it is better to hate things present, since they are trifling and transient and corruptible; and to love those which are to come, as being good and incorruptible."[15] In the Vision of Hermas, the golden part consists of those "who have fled from the world."[16] In the *Dialogue with Trypho* Justin quotes *Isaiah*: "Depart ye, depart ye, depart ye, go ye out from thence

[8] Diogenes Lærtius: *Lives of the Philosophers* 2. 3. 7.

[9] Epictetus: *Discourses* 2. 23. 36 ff.

[10] For the story of this saying, see David Smith: *Unwritten Sayings of our Lord*, pp. 71–82.

[11] Ox. Log. 2. [12] *I Clement* 1. 1.

[13] Polycarp: *The Letter to the Philippians*, The Address.

[14] *The Martyrdom of Polycarp*, The Address.

[15] *Second Clement* 6. 5. [16] Hermas: *Visions* 3. 3, 4.

and touch no unclean thing." [17] In the *Acts of Paul and Thecla* Paul says: "Happy are those who bid farewell to this world, for they will be well-pleasing to God." [18] Cyprian condemns those who have renounced the world in words only and not in deeds. He writes: "We had renounced the world when we were baptised." He condemns those who have returned to the world which they have renounced.[19] Pontius, in his life of Cyprian, says that banishment was no punishment to him, for "to the Christian the whole of this world is a single home. . . . Further than that, while he is honestly serving God, he is a stranger even in his own state." [20]

As might be expected this tendency is strongly marked in Tertullian. He says of the Christian Church: "She knows that her part is that of a foreigner upon earth, that amongst aliens she easily finds enemies, while she has her race, her home, her hope, her welcome and her honour in heaven." Again he writes: "We have no concern in this life except to depart from it as speedily as possible." [21] In the *De Spectaculis* he writes: "For what else is our prayer, but that of the apostle—to leave the world and to be at home with the Lord?" [22] In the *De Oratione*, commenting on the fourth clause of the Lord's Prayer—"Thy Kingdom come"—he writes: "If the manifestation of the Lord's Kingdom pertains unto the will of God, and unto our anxious expectations, how do some pray for the prolonging of this age, when the Kingdom of God, which we pray may arrive, tends to the consummation of this age? Our wish is that our reign may be hastened, not our servitude protracted." [23] In the *De Patientia* he urges that death is to be desired and the death of a loved one must never be a matter of grief: "Grief for death is needless. . . . Why should you grieve, if you believe that your loved one has not perished? . . . That which you think to be death is departure. He who goes before is not to be lamented, but his fate is to be desired. . . . We wound Christ

[17] Justin Martyr: *Dialogue with Trypho* 13. The quotation is from *Isaiah* 52. 11. The thrice repeated, *Depart ye*, is Justin's own version. It occurs only twice in the Hebrew and the LXX.

[18] *Acts of Paul and Thecla* 5. [19] Cyprian: *Epistles* 7. 1; 6. 5; 53. 3.

[20] Pontius: *Life of Cyprian* 11. [21] Tertullian: *Apology* 41.

[22] Tertullian: *De Spectaculis* 28. [23] Tertullian: *De Oratione* 5.

when we accept not with equanimity the summoning out of the world of any by Him, as if they were to be pitied."[24]

Pionius, in the *Life of Polycarp*, writes: "He knew that to the servant of God the whole world is his city; but that his fatherland is the heavenly Jerusalem. We have been enjoined as strangers and sojourners to sojourn here but not to dwell here."[25]

We may add two further quotations. In *De Doctrina Christiana* Augustine writes: "We are sojourners, unable to live happily exiled from our fatherland. We seek for a way to help us to end our sorrows and to return to our native country."[26] And in the *De Mortalitate* Cyprian writes: "We should consider, dearly beloved brethren, we should ever and anon reflect that we have renounced the world, and in the meantime are living here as strangers and guests. Let us greet the day which assigns each of us to our own home, which snatches us hence, which lifts us from the snares of the world, and restores us to paradise and to the Kingdom. Who that has been placed in foreign lands would not hasten to return to his own country? Who that is hastening to return to his friends would not desire a prosperous gale, that he might the sooner embrace those dear to him? We regard Paradise as our country."[27]

The idea of the Christian as a stranger and a pilgrim is widely diffused; and it would be bound to have its reaction on the whole Christian idea of education in the early Church. But before we can see the situation aright, we must remember that mixed with this there is another strain. We must remember that, although the Christian felt himself a stranger in the world, he did not ordinarily withdraw from the world. The writer of the *Letter to Diognetus* can say: "The soul, though immortal, dwells in a mortal tabernacle; and Christians sojourn among corruptible things, awaiting the incorruptibility which is in heaven."[28] It is this very same writer who can write the noblest of all descriptions of the Christian in the world:

For Christians are distinguished from the rest of men neither

[24] Tertullian: *De Patientia* 9. [25] Pionius: *Life of Polycarp* 6.
[26] Augustine: *De Doctrina Christiana* 2. 4.
[27] Cyprian: *De Mortalitate* 26. [28] *The Letter to Diognetus* 6. 8.

> by country, nor by language, nor by customs. For nowhere do they dwell in cities of their own; they do not use any strange forms of speech or practise a singular mode of life. . . . But while they dwell both in Greek and barbarian cities, each as his lot was cast, and follow the customs of the land in dress and food and other matters of living, they show the remarkable and admittedly strange order of their own citizenship. They live in fatherlands of their own, but as aliens. They share all things as citizens, and suffer all things as strangers. Every foreign land is their fatherland, and every fatherland a foreign land. . . . They pass their days on earth, but they have their citizenship in heaven.[29]

In the *Dialogue with Trypho* the Jew is amazed at the Christian in the world: "This is what we are most at a loss about; that you, professing to be pious, and supposing yourselves better than others, are not in any particular separated from them, and do not alter your mode of living from the nations."[30] It is in fact the claim of Justin that Christianity brought Christians nearer to their fellowmen: "We who hated and destroyed one another, and on account of their different manners would not use the same hearth as men of a different tribe, now, since the coming of Christ, live familiarly with them."[31] Tertullian faces the charge that Christians are unprofitable in business matters. He willingly agrees that the Christian has nothing to do with the worship of the gods, and the luxuries of the pagan, but at the same time he demands:

> How can this be true of men who live with you, enjoy the same food, have the same manner of life, and dress, the same requirements for life? For we are neither Brahmins nor Indian gymnosophists, dwellers in the forests, and exiles from ordinary life. We remember the gratitude we owe to God, our Lord and Creator; we reject no fruit of his works; though it is true we refrain from excessive and wrong use of them. Consequently we cannot dwell together in the world without the market-place, without the shambles, without your baths, shops, factories,

[29] *The Letter to Diognetus* 5. [30] Justin Martyr: *Dialogue with Trypho* 10.
[31] Justin Martyr: *Apology* 1. 14. 3.

taverns, fairs, and other places of resort. We also sail with you and serve in the army, and we till the ground and engage in trade as you do, we join our crafts, we lend our services to the public for your profit. How we can seem unprofitable to your business affairs, when we live with you and by you, I cannot tell.[32]

Lactantius is clear that no man ought to withdraw from human society: "If a man dissociates himself and separates himself from the body, that man must be said to live not in the custom of a human being, but in the manner of wild beasts. But if this is not allowable, the bond of human society must be in every way retained, because life is impossible for man without man. The retention of society is community, which means to give help to others, that we may be able to receive it ourselves." [33]

It is true to say, however, that although this was so, and although Christians were to be found in every walk of life, there was a strong feeling that Christians should not take part in public life, and accept public office. Lactantius himself warns his young friend Demetrianus to be careful that the duties of such office do not divert his mind from justice and truth.[34] The Synod of Illiberis ordained that a Christian municipal magistrate must absent himself from Church during his year of office, and the Synod of Arelate declares that if a Christian magistrate acts contrary to Church discipline, he must be excluded from communion; "and similarly with those who wish to take up political life." [35]

So then it is generally true that, although the Christian accepted the duties of the society in which he lived, he never felt himself to be fully a member of it, and it was only infrequently that he took anything to do with the administration of it. And such an attitude was bound to react on his view of the education that the world had to offer.

Another factor has to be added to any study of the Christian attitude to pagan culture in the days of the Early Church. There

[32] Tertullian: *Apology* 42. [33] Lactantius: *Instit.* 6. 10. 25.

[34] Lactantius: *Opif. Dei* 1. 4.

[35] These examples are quoted from C. J. Cadoux: *The Early Church and the World*, pp. 536–7.

was in the Early Church what one might call a strain of deliberate non-intellectualism. There was a deliberate stressing of, and even glorying in, the fact that so many of the Christians were humble and unlettered people. The Early Church did not easily grow tired of quoting *I Corinthians*: "It is written, I will destroy the wisdom of the wise, and will bring to nothing the understanding of the prudent. Where is the wise? Where is the scribe? Where is the disputer of this world? . . . For ye see your calling, brethren, how that not many wise men after the flesh, not many mighty, not many noble are called; but God hath chosen the foolish things of the world to confound the wise; and God hath chosen the weak things of the world to confound the things which are mighty." [36] It was the charge of Celsus that the Christians did not wish to give or to receive a reason for their belief; that their battle-cries and slogans were: "Do not examine, but believe!" "Your faith will save you!" "The wisdom of this life is bad and foolishness is a good thing." [37] The Christians keep reiterating: "Do not investigate." [38] The Christians "repel every wise man from the doctrine of their faith, and invite only the ignorant and the vulgar." [39] The Christian invitation is: "Let no one come to us who has been instructed, or who is wise or prudent—for such qualifications are deemed evil by us—but if there be any ignorant or unintelligent or uninstructed, or foolish persons, let them come with confidence." "They desire and are able to gain over only the silly and the mean, and the stupid, with women and children." [40] The Christians consist only of "the uninstructed, the servile and the ignorant." [41] There is a sense in which Origen admits that that is true. It is quite true that the simple and the ignorant outnumber the intelligent in the Christian Church, as in fact they will in any society, in the nature of things.[42] If it were possible for everyone to leave his business and to become a philosopher, that indeed might be made a universal demand with justice; but since men are weak, and since only a very few can devote themselves, and will devote themselves earnestly to study, surely the Christian way is the best? [43] Origen

[36] *I Corinthians* 1. 19, 20, 26, 27.
[37] Origen: *Against Celsus* 1. 9.
[38] Origen: *Against Celsus* 1. 12.
[39] Origen: *Against Celsus* 3. 18.
[40] Origen: *Against Celsus* 3. 44.
[41] Origen: *Against Celsus* 6. 14.
[42] Origen: *Against Celsus* 1. 27.
[43] Origen: *Against Celsus* 1. 9.

in the end does not really deny the charge of Celsus; rather he accepts it, and turns it to the glory of God.

It was in fact always the simplicity of the Christians which impressed the heathen writers who turned their eyes to them. When Lucian tells the story of that rascally adventurer and pseudo-philosopher Peregrinus, he tells how he imposed upon the Christians. When he was put in prison old women, widows and young orphans hovered around. Whenever any cunning impostor comes upon the Christians he finds it an easy matter to lead these simple people by the nose.[44] Aristides, the orator, says that Christians never occupy seats in the civic council.[45] The impression that the Christians did in fact give was that of unlettered simplicity.

Nor did the Christians rebut the charge; they accepted it. Justin Martyr proudly claims that the deepest things can be heard and learned among the Christians from persons who do not even know the forms of the letters, who are uneducated and barbarous in speech, though wise and believing in mind. Some, indeed, are even maimed and deprived of their eyesight, so that all may understand that these things are not the effect of human wisdom, but are uttered by the power of God.[46] Theophilus of Antioch proves from the prophets how much wiser they were than the philosophers; and then says of the prophets that they themselves were illiterate and shepherds and uneducated.[47] Tatian, the great hater of all Greek culture, insists that the Christians have rejected everything that rests on human opinion. God's gift is free and certainly old women and striplings are welcome to the Christian fellowship.[48] Athenagoras does not question the intellectual wisdom of the philosophers; he had been one himself; but he does indict them for moral helplessness; on the other hand among the Christians you will find simple folk, artisans, and old women, who cannot tell you in words what Christian doctrine means, but who can show the effects of it in their lives.[49]

Irenæus remembers that it was not the chief priests and rulers who turned to Jesus when he was upon this earth, but those who

[44] Lucian: *Peregrinus* 12. 13. [45] Aristides: *Oration* 46.

[46] Justin Martyr: *Apology* 1. 60. 11.

[47] Theophilus: *Ad Autolycum* 2. 35. [48] Tatian: *To the Greeks* 32. 1.

[49] Athenagoras: *The Embassy for the Christians* 11.

sat begging by the highway and the deaf and the blind, to which he adds the inevitable Corinthian quotation.[50] Tertullian says that Plato may say that the maker of the universe is not easily found, and, when found, is with difficulty explained to the multitude, " but any Christian labourer both finds and sets forth God." [51] Minucius Felix well understands how the intellectuals are annoyed when those who are " untrained in study, uninitiated in letters, ignorant even of the meaner arts " should come to fixed conclusions about things which have been a matter of debate for centuries in the schools of the philosophers.[52] He knows well that the Christians are accused of being " fellows who gather together illiterates from the dregs of the populace, and credulous women with the instability natural to their sex." [53] He says that the intellectuals declare that it is enough for the " ignorant and uncultured and the rude and the boorish, to look at what is under their noses," without dabbling in the problems of eternity.[54] Clement of Alexandria, himself no mean philosopher, refuses to regard philosophy in the intellectual sense as a *sine qua non*. " Almost all of us," he says, " without training in arts and sciences and the Hellenic philosophy, and some even without learning at all, through the influence of a philosophy divine and barbarous, and by power, have through faith received the word concerning God, trained by self-operating wisdom." [55]

The fact that the Christians were humble and unlettered people in the main was, at least for a time, true; but what was meant for a jibe by their heathen opponents, the Christian apologists turned into a boast.

But there is another element which enters into this situation. We have seen that the apologists glory in the fact that Christianity opened the eternal mysteries to the simplest people; and that was a fact in which they might well glory. But we must also have noticed that there is a sense in which Origen was almost apologetic about all this. He accepted the non-intellectual character of Christian teaching as being part and parcel of the human situation, but he did not altogether like it. Had it been possible for all men to

[50] Irenæus: *Against Heresies* 2. 19. 7. [51] Tertullian: *Apology* 46.

[52] Minucius Felix: *Octavius* 5. 4.

[53] Minucius Felix: *Octavius* 8. 4. [54] Minucius Felix: *Octavius* 12. 7.

[55] Clement of Alexandria: *Stromateis* 1. 20. 99.

become philosophers in the true sense of the term he would have been happier yet. But there emerges in this situation a complete contempt, and almost a bitter hatred for all kinds of learning. There emerges a direct opposition to all culture and all learning, a kind of pride in ignorance and in uncouthness.

There were two obvious lines of attack. There was the attack on the poets. That was nothing new; that was an attack that Plato had made long ago. No one had ever more unsparingly condemned the poets for telling stories unworthy of the gods than Plato had. And this was an attack that the Christian apologists consistently and continuously made. It is Justin's consistent charge that the works of the poets were inspired by the demons. "Those who believe these things, we pity," he says, "and those who invented them we know to be devils." [56] He says of the myths of the poets: "We proceed to demonstrate that they have been uttered by the influence of the wicked demons, to deceive and lead astray the human race." [57] If anything in the myths bears any resemblance to any of the biblical stories, it is because the stories were imitated by the devils.[58] They are counterfeits which he who is called the devil is said to have performed among the Greeks.[59] The beauty of the poets was a devilish, a deceiving and a seductive beauty.

Mostly the sections in which the apologists deal with the poets are long; in them lengthy quotations are made, and the stories are discussed and criticised in detail.[60] The apologists certainly succeed in demonstrating that they themselves had had a more than adequate education in the classics which they condemned. We may quote only one, as being perhaps less accessible, and more inclusive, than most, that of Aristides:

> The Greeks then because they are wiser than the barbarians, have erred even more than the barbarians, in that they have introduced many gods that are made; and some of them they have represented as male, and some of them as female; and in

[56] Justin Martyr I. 25. 3. [57] Justin Martyr I. 54. I.

[58] Justin Martyr I. 64. I. [59] Justin Martyr: *Dialogue with Trypho* 69. I.

[60] Athenagoras: *Embassy for the Christians* 21 ff.; Theophilus: *Ad Autolycum* 2. 5 ff.; Arnobius: *The Case Against the Pagans* 2. 9 ff.

> such a way that some of their gods were found to be adulterers and murderers and jealous and envious, and angry and passionate, and murderers of fathers, and thieves and plunderers. And they say that some of them were lame and maimed, and some of them wizards, and some of them utterly mad; and some of them played on harps; and some of them wandered on mountains; and some of them died outright; and some were struck by lightning, and some were made subject to men, and some went off in flight, and some were stolen by men; and lo! some of them were wept and bewailed by men; and some, they say, went down to Hades.
>
> . . . .
>
> And of some of their goddesses they say that they contended about beauty, and came for judgment before men. The Greeks then, O King, have brought forward what is wicked, ridiculous and foolish concerning their gods and themselves; in that they have called suchlike persons gods, who are no gods; and hence men have taken occasion to commit adultery and fornication, and to plunder and do everything that is wicked and hateful and abominable. For if those who are called gods have done all these things that are written above, how much more shall men do them who believe in those who have done these things![61]

It has been said that in the case of the Greeks, it was not that men became so depraved that they abandoned their gods, but that the gods became so depraved that they were abandoned by men. The Christians had no difficulty in mounting a devastating attack upon the pagan gods.

The second line of attack was upon the philosophers—" senseless wise men " Aristides called them.[62] As Tertullian said in a notorious passage, one of the joys of heaven for the Christian will be the sight of the philosophers and poets, amongst others, burning in Hell:

> How vast the spectacle that day, how wide! What sight shall wake my wonder, what my laughter, my joy, my exultation?

[61] Aristides: *Apology* 8. The translation is from *The Newly Recovered Apology of Aristides*, by Helen B. Harris.

[62] Aristides: *Apology* 17.

as I see . . . those sages the philosophers blushing before their disciples as they blaze together, the disciples whom they taught that God was concerned with nothing, that men have no souls at all, or that what souls they have shall never return to their former bodies! And then the poets, trembling before the judgment seat, not of Rhadamanthus, not of Minos, but of Christ whom they never looked to see! [63]

The most violent of all the apologists against the philosophers is Tatian, who dealt in invective far more than he did in argument. The two main charges against the philosophers were that their lives belied their teaching; and that they had reached no kind of agreement amongst each other, but were for ever quarrelling. We may illustrate both points from Tatian:

What noble thing have you produced by your pursuit of philosophy? Who of your most eminent men has been free from vain boasting? Diogenes, who made such a parade of his independence with his tub, was seized with a bowel complaint through eating a raw polypus, and so lost his life by gluttony. Aristippus, walking about in a purple robe, led a profligate life, in accordance with his professed opinions. Plato, a philosopher, was dismissed by Dionysius for his gourmandising tendencies. And Aristotle, who absurdly placed a limit to Providence, and made happiness to consist in things which give pleasure, quite contrary to his duty as a preceptor, flattered Alexander, forgetful that he was but a youth; and, he, showing how well he had learned the lessons of his master, because his friend would not worship him, shut him up and carried him about like a bear or a leopard.[64]

And again:

Be not led away by the solemn assemblies of the philosophers who are no philosophers, who dogmatize one against another, though each one vents the crude fancies of the moment. They have moreover many collisions among themselves; each one

[63] Tertullian: *De Spectaculis* 30. [64] Tatian: *To the Greeks* 2.

> hates the other; they indulge in conflicting opinions, and their arrogance makes them eager for the highest places.[65]

In another passage he combines invective against the unphilosophic, luxury-loving life of the philosophers, and their internecine strife of words and ideas:

> They leave uncovered one of their shoulders; they let their hair grow long; they cultivate their beards; their nails are like the claws of wild beasts. Though they say they need nothing, . . . yet they need a currier for their wallet, and a weaver for their mantle, and a wood-cutter for their staff, and the rich and a cook for their gluttony. . . . You cry out in public with an assumption of authority, and take upon you to avenge your own self; and, if you receive nothing, you indulge in abuse, and philosophy with you is the art of getting money. You follow the doctrines of Plato and a disciple of Epicurus lifts up his voice to oppose you. You wish to be a follower of Aristotle and a follower of Democritus rails at you. Pythagoras says that he was Euphorbus, and the heir of the teaching of Pherecydes, and Aristotle impugns the immortality of the soul.[66]

It can hardly be considered likely that Tatian's invective ever won anyone over to Christianity; he was one of these writers who write always at the top of their voice.

Tertullian pours out the same spate of charges:

> I know the harlot Phryne ministers to the lustful embraces of Diogenes. I am informed too that a certain Speusippus of Plato's school died in the act of adultery. . . . Democritus, by blinding himself because he could not look on women without lust and was pained if he did not possess them, declares his incontinency in his attempted cure.[67]

Hippolytus talks of the "artificial sophisms of error."[68]

[65] Tatian: *To the Greeks* 4. [66] Tatian: *To the Greeks* 25.

[67] Tertullian: *Apology* 46.

[68] Hippolytus: *Refutation of all Heresies* 10. 1.

It looks as if there was a complete, and a disastrous, cleavage between the Christians and all the thinking that had gone before. Tertullian states this cleavage with all the brilliance of his oratory:

> What likeness is there between the philosopher and the Christian, the disciple of Greece and the disciple of heaven, the trader in reputation and the trader in salvation, the doer of words and the worker of deeds, the builder up and the destroyer of things, the friend and the enemy of error, the corrupter and the restorer and exponent of truth, its thief and its guardian?[69]

True wisdom is to be gauged not by the writings of the philosophers but by the words of the prophets.[70] Philosophy merely inflates the intelligence; the philosophers are distinguished more by diversity than by agreement; the truth has been excluded by the philosophers through the poison with which they have infected it.[71] We may conclude with the famous passage from the *De Præscriptione*:

> What indeed has Athens to do with Jerusalem? What concord is there between the Academy and the Church? What between heretics and Christians? . . . Away with all the attempts to produce a mottled Christianity of Stoic, Platonic, and dialectic composition! We want no curious disputation after possessing Jesus Christ, no inquisition after enjoying the gospel! With our faith we desire no further belief.[72]

It seems on the face of it that the cleavage between Christianity and all pagan culture and learning is complete. But that is exactly what it was not. Again and again the apologists call in the poets and the philosophers to their aid, when the teachings of the poets and the philosophers agree with those of Christianity. Justin Martyr could say that each man, Plato, the Stoics, the poets, spoke well in proportion to "the share he had of the spermatic word."[73] Justin Martyr cites his witnesses from the ranks of the poets and the philosophers themselves:

[69] Tertullian: *Apology* 46.
[70] Tertullian: *Against Hermogenes* 18. [71] Tertullian: *De Anima* 2.
[72] Tertullian: *De Præscriptione* 7. [73] Justin Martyr: *Apology* 2. 13. 2–6.

> While we say that all things have been produced and arranged into a world by God, we shall seem to utter the doctrine of Plato. While we say that there will be a burning up of all, we shall seem to utter the doctrine of the Stoics. While we affirm that the souls of the wicked, being endowed with sensation even after death are punished, and that those of the good are delivered from punishment and spend a blessed existence, we shall seem to say the same things as the poets and philosophers. While we maintain that men ought not to worship the works of their hands, we say the very things which have been said by the comic poet Menander, and other similar writers, for they have declared that the workman is greater than the work.[74]

So then Justin Martyr finds in the poets and the philosophers support for the Christian doctrine of creation, of life after death, with its rewards and its punishments, of Christian eschatology, and of the prohibition of the worship of idols. Aristides says that the poets and the philosophers declare that the nature of all their gods is one.[75] Athenagoras says that Plato believed in "an unbegotten God, the Maker of all things"; he reminds his hearers that the Stoics believed in what they called the "Breath" of God, and says of the great Greek thinkers that, although they never found the complete truth, "each was stirred by his own soul through some sympathy with the 'Breath' of God to go upon the quest, if haply he might find and understand the truth." The Stoics too believe in the burning up of the universe. Not only the Christians but many philosophers also claim that the body will rise again. Both Pythagoras and Plato believed it possible "that when bodies dissolve into the elements out of which they were originally made, they can come together again out of the same elements."[76]

Lactantius makes the usual charges against the philosophers. Philosophy is divided into sects, and dissolved into conflicting judgments; it is at the mercy of mutual antagonisms. "The philosophers, possessing no sort of defence, destroy one another with wounds on all sides, and philosophy ends by destroying itself

[74] Justin Martyr I. 20. 4. [75] Aristides: *Apology* 13.

[76] Athenagoras: *Embassy for the Christians* 5, 7, 19, 23, 36.

with its own weapons."[77] He has none the less no difficulty in showing that there are many testimonies in philosophy which teach "that there is one sovereignty over the world, one power, the origin of which cannot be discovered by thought, nor its might explained."[78] Lactantius can speak of "our Seneca."[79] "Both poets and philosophers," he says, "testify to one God. Orpheus speaks of a principal God, creator of heaven and earth, of sun and stars, of land and sea. Moreover our poet Virgil calls the supreme God now spirit, now mind, declaring that mind, as though poured into limbs, sets in movement the body of the whole world; that God passes over seas and lands and through the depths of heaven, and that from Him all creatures derive their life. Even Ovid knew that the world was made by God, whom he calls now the framer, now the architect of all things."[80] "Hermes," he writes, "justly called Trismegistus, by reason of his virtue and knowledge of many arts, who in the antiquity of his teaching preceded the philosophers, and is worshipped as a god in Egypt, extols with infinite praise the majesty of the one God, calling Him Lord and Father and declaring that He is nameless, because He needs no personal name, being alone and without parentage, because He exists of Himself and by Himself. Here are the opening words of his address to his son: 'To understand God is indeed hard; but to declare Him in speech is impossible, even for one who is able to understand, for the perfect cannot be comprehended by the imperfect, nor the invisible by the visible.'"[81] Sympathy is going far when Seneca is *our Seneca*, when Virgil is *our poet*, and when Hermes is justly *Trismegistus*, the Thrice-greatest One.

So then there are voices which utterly condemn all that heathen thought and culture had to bring; but on the other hand there are voices which find in it much that came to it by the Breath of God, and much that is an additional witness to Christian truth. One thing is clear, that even those who were most radically opposed to all heathen culture could not wholly free themselves from it, because they were saturated in it. One of the most significant passages, because it is quite unconscious, is the beginning of the

[77] Lactantius: *Epitome* 32.

[78] Lactantius: *Epitome* 6.

[79] Lactantius: *Epitome* 4.

[80] Lactantius: *Epitome* 3.

[81] Lactantius: *Epitome* 4.

seventh book of Hippolytus's *Refutation of all Heresies.* In it Hippolytus is warning the reader of the danger of being seduced into heresy. The passage is long, but it is worth quoting in full:

> The pupils of these men, when they perceive the doctrines of the heretics to be like unto the ocean when tossed into waves by the violence of the winds, ought to sail past in quest of the tranquil haven. For a sea of this sort is both infested with wild monsters and difficult of navigation, like, as we may say, the Sicilian Sea, in which the legend reports were Cyclops, and Charybdis, and Scylla, and the rock of the Sirens. Now the poets of the Greeks allege that Ulysses sailed through this channel, skilfully using for his own purpose the terribleness of these strange monsters. For the savage cruelty of those to these who were sailing through was remarkable. The Sirens, singing sweetly and harmoniously, beguiled the voyagers, luring by their melodious voice those who heard it towards the rocks. So, the story goes, that Ulysses, when he knew that this was so, smeared with wax the ears of his companions, and, lashing himself to the mast, sailed, free of danger, past the Sirens, although he heard their song. And my advice to my readers is to adopt a similar expedient, either on account of their infirmity to smear their ears with wax, and sail straight on through the tenets of the heretics, not even listening to teaching that is easily capable of seducing them into pleasure, like the luscious lay of the Sirens, or by binding oneself to the Cross of Christ, and faithfully obeying His word, not to be distracted, inasmuch as he has placed his trust in Him to whom long ago he has been firmly knit, and so to continue steadfastly in the faith.[82]

The interesting and the significant thing about that passage is that Hippolytus, when he wishes an illustration of the danger of heresy, goes to the *Odyssey* for it, and sees no incongruity in comparing the wood of the Cross to the wood of the ship's mast to which Ulysses for safety bound himself. There were many of the greatest Christian teachers who could not help thinking in pictures of pagan literature, for these pictures had become part of their very selves.

[82] Hippolytus: *Refutation of all Heresies* 7. 1.

Harnack speaks of " the marvellous attempt to present Christianity to the world as the religion which is the true philosophy, and as the philosophy which is the true religion."[83] There were two facts in the situation which in any event made a complete breach with pagan culture an impossibility.

The first fact was that many of the Christian apologists were themselves skilled and trained in all Greek knowledge and lore before they became Christians. Even Tatian, who speaks with the greatest violence and virulence about pagan culture was himself trained in it.[84] Aristides was an Athenian philosopher before he became a Christian.[85] Melito was also a most cultured philosopher.[86] There is an account of the life of Athenagoras attached to one of the manuscripts of his works. It was apparently extracted from the writings of Nicephorus Callistus by Philip of Side, and it reads:

> Philip of Side says in his twenty-fourth book: Athenagoras was the first director of the School of Alexandria; his *floruit* was about the time of Hadrian and Antoninus, to whom he dedicated his *Embassy* on behalf of the Christians. He was a man who professed Christianity while still wearing the philosopher's garb and was the leading man in the Academic School. Before Celsus he had planned to write against the Christians, but, reading the Holy Scriptures to make his attack the more telling, he was so won over by the Holy Spirit as to become, like the great Paul, a teacher and not a persecutor of the faith he was attacking. Philip says that Clement, author of the *Stromateis*, was his disciple.[87]

It is by no means impossible that Athenagoras is the Athenagoras to whom, according to Photius, Bœthius dedicated a book on *Difficult Sentences in Plato*.[88] Athenagoras was a scholar among scholars,

[83] A. Harnack: *History of Dogma* 2. 177. [84] Tatian: *To the Greeks* 29, 35.

[85] Helen B. Harris: *The Newly Discovered Apology of Aristides*, p. 5. See Eusebius: *Ecclesiastical History* 4. 3. 3, with the full note of A. C. McGiffert in the translation of Eusebius in *The Select Library of the Nicene and Post-Nicene Fathers*.

[86] Eusebius: *Ecclesiastical History* 4, 26. See again A. C. McGiffert's full note on the passage.

[87] This passage is quoted and its reliability discussed in Joseph Hugh Crehan's translation of Athenagoras in the *Ancient Christian Writers* series, p. 4.

[88] Joseph Hugh Crehan: *Athenagoras*, p. 7

and it was not possible that he should forget all that he had learned.

Justin Martyr was a philosopher and never ceased to wear the philosopher's robe. In the *Dialogue with Trypho* he himself outlines his own spiritual biography, and leaves us in no doubt of the equipment which he brought to Christianity.[89] To him philosophy was the greatest of possessions; and those who studied it were the truly holy men. First of all he surrendered himself to a Stoic; but he got no nearer the knowledge of God, instruction in which the Stoic said was unnecessary. Thereafter he attached himself to a Peripatetic, a man who fancied himself a shrewd man. Justin Martyr soon abandoned him as being no philosopher at all, for the shrewd Peripatetic allowed only a few days to pass before asking Justin to settle the matter of fees " that our intercourse might not be unprofitable." Then he met a Pythagorean, a very celebrated man, and a man who thought much of his own wisdom. But the Pythagorean told Justin that a man could not even begin on the road to the happy life, until he knew music and astronomy and geometry; and when Justin confessed his ignorance he was dismissed. Then he found a Platonist, a sagacious man. There he thought he was getting nearer things. " The perception of immaterial things quite overpowered me, and the contemplation of ideas furnished my mind with wings, so that in a little time I supposed that I had become wise; and such was my stupidity, I expected forthwith to look upon God, for this is the end of Plato's philosophy." But it was not till he met the old man, " by no means contemptible in appearance, meek and venerable in manner," that he found the truth. Justin had come to Christianity only after he had gone through the whole gamut of philosophy; and he could not leave all that equipment behind him.

It is well to remind ourselves of the at first sight astonishing fact that there was no better educated group of men in the Roman Empire than the Christian apologists. There is scarcely one of them who could not have had a scintillating career in secular life, and there were many of them who had actually had such a career. Let us briefly pass them in review from this point of view. H. M. Gwatkin writes: " The Latin apologists from Tertullian to Augustine form

[89] Justin Martyr: *Dialogue with Trypho* 2 ff.

a striking series. They were all Africans, all rhetoricians or lawyers, all converts at a mature age."[90] As a writer of Latin prose Tertullian would have been great in any company. According to Eusebius, he was " a man well-versed in the laws of the Romans, and in other respects of high repute, and one of those specially distinguished in Rome."[91] There was a Tertullian who was sufficiently famous as a Roman lawyer for his judgments to be quoted in the Roman Digests, and Harnack writes: " There is nothing, in my judgment, to upset the hypothesis that he is the lawyer whose words are quoted in the Digests."[92] We may well believe that Tertullian was one of the most distinguished lawyers in the Roman Empire. Lactantius says of him that " he was skilled in literature of every kind," although he finds his style obscure.[93] In the same passage Lactantius says of Minucius Felix that " he was of no ignoble rank among pleaders," and goes on to say how great a fame he might have achieved if he had given himself wholly to that profession. Lactantius himself had a glittering career. Trained in rhetoric, he was invited by Diocletian the Emperor to practise in Asia Minor; later he worked in Gaul; and he was appointed by Constantine as teacher of his son Crispus. Men called him " the Christian Cicero."[94] Jerome tells us that Lactantius was the pupil of Arnobius in oratory, and that Arnobius taught rhetoric with great success at Sicca in Africa. He says that he enjoyed great repute as a rhetorician in Africa, and advises that he should be read for his learning.[95] Cyprian was born of wealthy and distinguished heathen parents; he himself was a man of the highest culture; he may even have been a Roman senator.[96] He was not converted until he was about forty-six, and was steeped in pagan culture.

[90] H. M. Gwatkin: *Early Church History to A.D.* 313, 1. 176.

[91] Eusebius: *Ecclesiastical History* 2. 2. 4.

[92] A. Harnack: *Expansion of Christianity* 2. 187, footnote. (The Harnack reference to Eusebius should be corrected.)

[93] Lactantius: *Instit.* 5. 1. 21.

[94] E. H. Blakeney: *Lactantius' Epitome of the Divine Institutes*, p. ix.

[95] Jerome's remarks on Arnobius are given in full and evaluated in George E. McCracken: *Arnobius, the Case Against the Pagans, Ancient Christian Writers Series*, pp. 2 ff. The main Jerome references are *Concerning Famous Men* 79, *The Chronicon*, *Epistle* 62.

[96] Augustine: *Serm* 31. 7.

There can have been few men more learned in secular literature than Jerome. "I too," he says, "have had a liberal education. As Juvenal says: 'I too have often withdrawn my hand from the ferule.'"[97] He tells us of his famous dream:

> Many years ago, when for the Kingdom of Heaven's sake I had cut myself off from home, parents, sister, relations, and—harder still—from the dainty food to which I had been accustomed; and when I was on my way to Jerusalem to wage my warfare, I still could not bring myself to forego the library which I had formed for myself at Rome with great care and toil. And so, miserable man that I was, I would fast only that I might afterwards read Cicero. After many nights spent in vigil, after floods of tears called from my inmost heart, after the recollection of my past sins, I would once more take up Plautus. And when at times I returned to my right mind and began to read the prophets, their style seemed rude and repellent. I failed to see the light with my blinded eyes; but I attributed the fault not to them but to the sun. While the old serpent was thus making me his plaything, about the middle of Lent a deep-seated fever fell upon my weakened body, and while it destroyed my rest completely—the story seems hardly credible—it so wasted my unhappy frame that scarcely anything was left on me but skin and bone. Meantime preparations for my funeral went on; my body grew gradually colder, and the warmth of it still lingered only in my throbbing breast. Suddenly I was caught up in the spirit and dragged before the judgment seat of the Judge; and the light was so bright here, and those who stood around were so radiant, that I cast myself upon the ground and did not dare to look up. Asked who and what I was I replied: "I am a Christian." But he who presided said: "You lie; you are a Ciceronian and not a Christian."

Thereupon in the dream Jerome was scourged until he was ready to promise anything, and until he could only cry out: "Have mercy upon me, O Lord; have mercy upon me." He was told that he would be tortured till he agreed not to read the works of the

[97] Jerome: *Epistle* 50. 5.

Gentiles. "Lord," he said, "if ever again I possess worldly books, or if ever again I read such I have denied Thee."[98] So real was his dream that when he woke he was literally and physically black and blue.

But the abstention cannot have lasted, for we find Rufinus charging Jerome with breaking his vow because he taught the classics to the boys in his school at Bethlehem. We find him in correspondence with a certain Roman orator called Magnus who asked him why he quoted the classics so much. Jerome's answer is that Paul quoted Aratus, Callimachus, Epimenides and Menander, and to draw up a list of thirty-seven Christian writers who are all great quoters. In writers like that you cannot tell whether to admire "their erudition or their knowledge of the scriptures." In the end he hazards the opinion that Magnus has been encouraged to ask the question by his personal enemies who have not his skill and knowledge. "Beg him not to envy eaters their teeth because he is toothless himself, and not to make light of the eyes of a gazelle because he himself is a mole."[99] In one single letter to Heliodorus Jerome quotes Themistocles, Plato, Isocrates, Pythagoras, Democritus, Xenocrates, Cleanthes, Homer, Hesiod, Simonides, Stesichorus, Sophocles and Cato.[100] Aristotle, Demosthenes, Herodotus and Plato he knew well. He had most of Virgil by heart; and he was intimately acquainted with the works of Pliny, Sallust, Suetonius, Tacitus, Varro, and Juvenal. No man can ever have had a more encyclopædic knowledge of classical literature than Jerome had.

Finally of the Latins, we may note Augustine, the greatest of them all. He was schooled in Tagaste; he attended the university of Carthage; he taught rhetoric in Rome; and was finally appointed to the chair of rhetoric in Milan. He too, apart altogether from his Christianity, was one of the great scholars of his day. So then, when we look at the Latin defenders of the faith in the early days of the Church, we find that, so far from being ignorant and unlettered men, they were amongst the most widely read, the most carefully trained, the most highly intellectually equipped of their day and generation. Even if such men foreswore pagan learning, which they by no means always did, they could never divest them-

[98] Jerome: *Epistle* 22. 30.

[99] Jerome: *Epistle* 70. [100] Jerome: *Epistle* 60.

selves entirely of the weight of that learning which they had already acquired.

When we turn to the Greek writers, the story is the same or even more so. Let us look first at the great school of Alexandria. The first head of that school known to us is Pantænus.[101] He was a converted philosopher of the Stoic school, a man of great prudence and erudition, both in sacred and in secular literature. He is said to have become a Christian of such zeal that he was despatched on a mission to India, where he found a Hebrew copy of the Gospel according to St. Matthew which had been left there by Bartholomew. Our knowledge of Pantænus is shadowy, but he was clearly a philosopher of distinction, before he became head of the school of Alexandria, where, as Eusebius says, he " expounded the treasures of divine doctrine, both orally and in writing."

Pantænus was succeeded by Clement, who had been his pupil.[102] It may be, as H. M. Gwatkin says, that Clement's philosophy was eclectic, and therefore " fragmentary and heterogeneous," but it is also true that few men have ever carried such a weight of erudition as Clement did. Eusebius says that he was well fitted to face the challenge of paganism because he had passed through it, and had escaped its contagion.[103] It seems that Clement was so thoroughly initiated into paganism that he had even been initiated into some mystery religion. He writes: " I ate out of the tympanum; I drank out of the cymbalum; I carried the *kernos*; I entered the chamber." [104] His knowledge of pagan literature was immense. In the *Bibliographia Græca* of Fabricius the names of the pagan authors from whom Clement quotes take up no fewer than fourteen pages.[105] We may indicate Clement's quotational copiousness and facility by reference to two chapters in the *Stromateis*. In one of

[101] Jerome: *Lives of Illustrious Men* 36: Eusebius: *Ecclesiastical History* 5. 10; cp. C. Bigg: *The Christian Platonists of Alexandria*, p. 72; F. W. Farrar: *Lives of the Fathers* 1. 356 ff.

[102] For Clement see Jerome: *Lives of Illustrious Men* 38; Eusebius: *Ecclesiastical History* 5. 11; C. Bigg: *The Christian Platonists of Alexandria*, pp. 72 ff.; F. W. Farrar: *Lives of the Fathers* 1. 350 ff.; H. M. Gwatkin: *Early Church History* 2. 161 ff.

[103] Eusebius: *The Preparation for the Gospel* 2. 2.

[104] Clement: *Protreptikos* 2. 15.

[105] F. W. Farrar: *Lives of the Fathers*, 1. 360.

them [106] he deals with ideas which he says the Greeks have stolen from the Hebrew writers. In that chapter he makes 132 quotations—29 of them from Plato—from 43 different writers. Of the Platonic dialogues he cites by name the *Phædrus*, *Laws*, *Lysis*, *Timæus*, *Theætetus*, *Protagoras*, *Parmenides*, and the *Epistles*. In the other chapter [107] he sets out to prove that the Greeks are in fact inveterate plagiarisers by nature by showing how they plagiarise from one another. At a rough count there are in this chapter 137 quotations from 71 different writers. So catholic a quoter is Clement that it is in fact true that there are a number of writers whose only extant remains consist of quotations in the works of Clement. It is literally true to say that no contemporary of Clement, either pagan or Christian, can have surpassed him in width of knowledge of pagan literature and pagan philosophy. Clement was in fact a walking encyclopædia of Greek literature.

It is further to be noted that Clement did not always quote to destroy. He genuinely loved Greek literature and Greek philosophy and saw in them a very real preparation for Christ. He well knew their limitations and their fragmentary character, but they had their truth and they had their use. The most excellent among the Greeks worshipped the same God as the Christians do, although they had not the perfect knowledge which was delivered by the Son. Christians and Greeks knew the same God, though not in the same way. The one true God was known to the Greeks in a Greek way, to the Jews in a Jewish way, and to the Christians in a new and spiritual way. He who gave the covenants to the Jews, was He who gave philosophy to the Greeks, and in it He is glorified. In a sense God gave his prophets both to Jews and Greeks.[108] Even worship of the sun and the moon and the stars was given to the heathen that they might not become utterly atheistical and so perish; even that was a preparation.[109] Philosophy was necessary to the Greeks for righteousness. Philosophy was given to the Greeks, until the Lord should call the Greeks. Philosophy was a schoolmaster to lead the Hellenic mind to Christ, as the Law was to lead the mind of the Jews. The

[106] Clement: *Stromateis* 5. 14, and see Appendix F.

[107] Clement: *Stromateis* 6. 2, and see Appendix F.

[108] This is a catena of quotations from Clement: *Stromateis* 6. 5.

[109] Clement: *Stromateis* 6. 14.

way of truth is one, but it is like a river into which there flow many streams and many tributaries. Those who contemplate sacred things are called in manifold ways to their calling. Although we must not linger too long in secular culture, we must use it as a preliminary training for the word of the Lord. Philosophy is the study of wisdom, and wisdom is the knowledge of things divine and human and of their causes. Philosophy is investigation into the truth and into the nature of things.[110] Philosophy, being the search for truth, necessarily helps in the comprehension of the truth. The same thing can have many names; for instance, if a drachma is given to a shipmaster, it is the *fare*; if to a tax-collector, it is the *tax*; if to the landlord; it is *rent*; if to the teacher, it is a *fee*; if to the shopkeeper, it is an *earnest*, or *instalment*. Truth can be given many names but it is the same truth. But it must always be remembered that Christian truth differs from any other truth in respect of extent of knowledge, certainty of demonstration, and divine power.[111] For Clement pagan learning could never be a substitute for divine truth, but it had its place, and it was certainly not to be hated or despised. Clement had a sympathy which welcomed truth, where even a glimmer of it was to be found, for he believed that every glimmer of it, however faint, came from God.

Clement of Alexandria was succeeded as head of the school at Alexandria by one who was even greater than himself, by Origen.[112] Jerome calls him *vir magnus ab infantia*, a man great from his infancy.[113] Eusebius says of him that he was worthy of mention "even, so to speak, from his swathing-clothes."[114] He was apparently Coptic in origin, and was the son of Christian parents. His father Leonides was a schoolmaster, and gave the young Origen a thorough grounding in the Greek liberal sciences. But also he taught him the sacred scriptures, some of which each day he had the

[110] This is a catena of quotations from Clement: *Stromateis* 1. 5.

[111] These sentences are quotations from Clement: *Stromateis* 1. 20.

[112] Jerome: *The Lives of Illustrious Men* 54; Eusebius: *Ecclesiastical History* 6. 2–4; C. Bigg: *The Christian Platonists of Alexandria*, 151 ff.; F. W. Farrar: *Lives of the Fathers*, 391 ff.; H. M. Gwatkin: *Early Church History* 2. 179 ff.; B. F. Westcott's article on Origen in *Dictionary of Christian Biography*.

[113] Jerome: *Epistles* 84. 8. [114] Eusebius: *Ecclesiastical History* 6. 2. 2.

task of memorising. So searching and acute was the boy's mind that his father rebuked him and bade him be content, but, as Eusebius tells, "by himself he rejoiced greatly and thanked God, the author of all good, that he had deemed him worthy to be father of such a child. And they say that often, standing by the boy while he was asleep, he uncovered his breast as if the divine Spirit was enshrined within it, and kissed it reverently, considering himself blessed in his goodly offspring." (6. 2. 10, 11.) When Origen was only sixteen years of age his father was arrested and martyred, a fate which the lad would have insisted in sharing unless his mother had actually hidden his clothes to prevent him leaving the house (6. 2. 5, 6). He had thereupon to assume responsibility for his mother and his six younger brothers. He became a teacher. His erudition was famous. Jerome says of him that "he understood dialectic, as well as geometry, arithmetic, music, grammar and rhetoric, and taught all the schools of the philosophers, in such wise that he had also diligent students in secular literature, and lectured to them daily, and the crowds which flocked to him were marvellous." Jerome speaks of his immortal genius. Such was his fame that, when he was only eighteen years of age, he was chosen as head of the school of Alexandria, upon which he gave up his secular teaching and concentrated on the sacred writings. It was not that he despised secular knowledge, but he wished to concentrate on his primary task.

We shall best see Origen's width of learning and his attitude to wider culture in the *Panegyric* upon him which his pupil Gregory Thaumaturgus left. To Gregory the day on which Origen received him was the first of days. Gregory was captivated by the charm of Origen, for he was possessed of a rare combination of a certain sweet grace and persuasiveness, along with a strange power of constraint. Their relationship became like that of David and Jonathan. Origen was the first man to persuade Gregory to study the philosophy of the Greeks. He praised the philosophers, for they sought to know themselves, to know the things that are good, and which a man must pursue, and the things that are evil, and which a man must flee. He condemned deliberate ignorance, for the ignorant are like cattle, blind and without understanding. Reason must be the true master. There can be no genuine piety in any man who despises

God's gift of philosophy, for it is that very gift which distinguishes him from the beasts, and which makes him a man. No one can be truly pious who does not philosophise.[115]

Origen's preparation of students for the study of the sacred learning was wide. They must learn that capacity of the mind which deals critically with words and reasonings in an educated and rational manner. They must know natural science and the secrets of nature that they may be filled with wonder at the sacred economy of the universe; they must know mathematics, geometry, astronomy; each of these preparatory sciences must become ladders to reach the sky.[116] "No subject was forbidden to us, nothing hidden or inaccessible. We were allowed to become acquainted with every doctrine, barbarian or Greek, with things spiritual and secular, divine and human, traversing with all confidence and investigating the whole circuit of knowledge, and satisfying ourselves with full enjoyment of all pleasures of the soul."[117] Such was Origen's own output of work that he was only able to deal with it by the use of a team of shorthand writers and clerks with whom his wealthy friend Ambrosius provided him; and when he was writing his commentary on John he complains that he is held up because his customary shorthand writers are not with him to take down his dictation.[118] It can easily be seen that Origen was a man of the widest and most-embracing culture and wished his disciples to be like himself.

We shall mention only one more of these amazing Alexandrians, Didymus the Blind. Blind as he was, he was one of the greatest scholars of his age. Jerome writes of him: "Didymus of Alexandria, becoming blind while very young, and therefore ignorant of the rudiments of learning, displayed such a miracle of intelligence as to learn perfectly dialectics and even geometry, sciences which especially require sight."[119] Rufinus finely says of him that "he

[115] These sentences are collected from Gregory Thaumaturgus: *Panegyric* 6.

[116] Gregory Thaumaturgus: *Panegyric* 8.

[117] Gregory Thaumaturgus: *Panegyric* 13, cp. M. L. W. Laistner: *Christianity and Pagan Culture*, p. 61.

[118] F. W. Farrar: *Lives of the Fathers* 1. 408; C. Bigg: *The Christian Platonists of Alexandria* 156, 157.

[119] Jerome: *Lives of Illustrious Men* 109.

added studies to his prayers."[120] Theodoret says of him: "Although Didymus had lost his sight in youth, he had applied himself to the study of poetry, rhetoric, arithmetic, geometry and astronomy; he had acquired, by means of the organ of hearing alone, a thorough acquaintance with the logic of Aristotle, and with the eloquence of Plato. These branches of knowledge are not to be regarded as teaching truth, but as furnishing weapons which can be used against falsehood in the defence of truth. He also committed the sacred scripture to memory, and acquired the knowledge not only of words but of their significance."[121] It is Sozomen who gives us most detail about him. He tells us that he learned the letters of the alphabet by means of engraved tablets, which he felt with his fingers; and made himself acquainted with syllables by the force of attention and memory. He goes on to tell how Anthony, the famous hermit, met him on a visit to Alexandria and said to him: "Do not be distressed for the loss of a faculty enjoyed by gnats and flies, when you have that inward eyesight which is enjoyed by none but the saints."[122] Jerome was proud to call him master, and said of him: "In many points I give him thanks. I learned from him things which I had not known; and what I did know, his teaching has helped me to retain."[123] It can be seen that the blind Didymus was not the least of the intellectual stars of the Alexandrian firmament.

Before we leave this survey of the great Christian writers and defenders of the faith, and of the background which they brought to Christianity, there remains one group of great Christian writers and leaders at which we must look. These are the three great Cappadocian fathers, Basil, Gregory of Nazianzen, and Gregory of Nyssa. Not only were they all Cappadocians, but they were most intimately related. Basil and Gregory of Nyssa were brothers; and Basil and Gregory of Nazianzen were the closest friends. To all intents and purposes the educational background which Basil and Gregory of Nazianzen brought to their task was the same, while that of Gregory of Nyssa was very different.

Let us then first look at Basil and Gregory of Nazianzen in

[120] Rufinus: *Ecclesiastical History* 2. 15.

[121] Theodoret: *Ecclesiastical History* 4. 29.

[122] Sozomen: *Ecclesiastical History* 3. 15.

[123] Jerome: *Epistles* 84.

company. As we have said, they came from Cappadocia and that was no great start. Cappadocia was chiefly famous for its slaves.[124] The ancient world spoke proverbially of the three bad K's—Crete, Cappadocia and Caria; and such was the reputation of the Cappadocians that there is an epigram in the *Greek Anthology* which says that a viper bit a Cappadocian—and the viper died.

Basil was the son of Basil the Elder, who was one of the most famous teachers of rhetoric of his day, and of Emmelia, one of the greatest beauties of her day. It was a Christian home, and the boy was given every chance. When he was very young he was brought up under the care of his grandmother Macrina; when he was a boy his father took over his education. Since he was the most famous teacher in Pontus, he gave the boy an excellent classical education. From there he went on to study in Cæsarea, the capital of Cappadocia; from there he went on to Constantinople, where he became the friend of Libanius, the famous rhetorician; and finally he proceeded to Athens, where his stay must have amounted to years. Gregory of Nyssa, his younger brother by seven years, got no such chance. He had the bare minimum of education, and taught himself, because the instinct for scholarship was in him; but he could write to Libanius that he never had a teacher.[125] Gregory of Nazianzen was the son of a father also called Gregory and of a mother who was called Nonna, and who was almost as famous as Monica, the mother of Augustine. They were comfortably well-to-do. The elder Gregory had been a member of an unorthodox sect, but had been brought back to the fold of orthodoxy, and had become a bishop. Gregory received all the education that the little town of Nazianzen could give him; he then went on to Cæsarea, the capital of Cappadocia; then on to the other Cæsarea in Palestine, at that time a famous school; and finally on to Athens where he remained until he was thirty years of age. It was probably at Cæsarea in Cappadocia that he and Basil first met. Gregory arrived in Athens a little before Basil; and in Athens the two were inseparable and devoted friends.

Basil was the first of the two friends to die, and when he died

[124] Horace: *Epistles* 1. 6; Persius: *Satires* 6. 77. Cp. F. W. Farrar: *Lives of the Fathers* 1. 660, 661.

[125] Gregory of Nyssa: *Letters* 10.

Gregory wrote a long and famous panegyric on him, and in that panegyric there is a description of the studies which the two friends undertook at Athens, and in which both of them were so distinguished.[126] Even at Cæsarea Basil was clearly marked out for greatness, for there he equalled his masters and surpassed his fellow-students in every form of culture (13). With the quickness and the force of his powers, he soon assimilated all that Byzantium had to teach him (14). So finally he came to Athens. In Athens there was no branch of learning that he did not traverse. He was skilled in rhetoric which " breathes the might of fire." He was skilled in grammar, which perfects our tongues in Greek, and compiles history, and presides over metres, and legislates for poems. He was skilled in philosophy, the lofty and high-reaching science; and in dialectic it was next to impossible to escape his subtle arguments. He had such a grip of astronomy, geometry and numerical proportion that no expert in these sciences could baffle him. He was a master of the art of medicine—all the more because he was physically delicate—and knew it not only on its practical and empirical side, but also in its theory and its principles. And to all that there must be added the moral discipline of the man (23). Such is the curriculum which Basil went through in Athens, and Gregory accompanied him through it, for in academic and intellectual achievement Gregory was only second, if he was second, to Basil. It is clear that in Basil and in Gregory we meet two of the most outstanding scholars of their day.

As it happens both Gregory of Nazianzen and Basil have left us their view of education. In this very panegyric Gregory of Nazianzen writes:

> I take it as admitted by men of sense, that the first of our advantages is education; and not only this our more noble form of it, which disregards rhetorical ornaments and glory, and holds to salvation and beauty in the objects of our contemplation; but even that pagan culture which many Christians spit upon, as treacherous and dangerous, and keeping us afar from God. For, as we ought not to neglect the heavens, and earth, and air, and all such things, because some have wrongly seized upon

[126] Gregory of Nazianzen: *The Panegyric on Basil*: *Or*. 43.

them, and honour God's works instead of God, but to reap what advantage we can from them for our life and enjoyment, while we avoid their dangers, not raising creation, as foolish men do, in revolt against the Creator, but from the works of nature apprehending the worker, and as the divine apostle says, bringing into captivity every thought to Christ: and again, as we know that neither fire, nor food, nor iron, nor any other of the elements, is of itself most useful or most harmful, except according to the will of those who use it; and as we have compounded healthful drugs from certain of the reptiles; so from secular literature we have received principles of inquiry and speculation, while we have rejected their idolatry, terror and pit of destruction. Nay, even those have aided us in our religion, by our perception of the contrast between what is worse and what is better, and by gaining strength for our doctrine from the weakness of theirs. We must not then dishonour education, because some men are pleased to do so, but rather suppose such men to be boorish and uneducated, desiring all men to be as they themselves are, in order to hide what is appropriate to them among the common mass, and so escape the detection of their want of culture.[127]

In one of his poetical letters to Seleucus, Gregory writes:

Perfect yourself in studies, in the works of the historians, in the books of the poets, in the smooth-flowing eloquence of orators. Be versed too in the subtle disquisitions of philosophers. Have a prudent familiarity with all these, wisely culling from them all that is useful, carefully avoiding what is injurious in each, imitating the practice of the wise bee which alights on every flower, but with infinite wisdom sucks only what is useful from each. She has nature itself for preceptor. Do you then, acting with reason, take largely from what is beneficial; but if anything

[127] Gregory of Nazianzen: *Panegyric on Basil* 11. A translation of the *Panegyric* by E. H. Gifford is to be found in volume 7 of *Select Library of Nicene and Post-Nicene Fathers*. This passage itself is quoted in full in L. Millar: *Christian Education in the First Four Centuries*, p. 104; and in M. L. W. Laistner: *Christianity and Pagan Culture*, p. 55, which last translation we have here used.

be injurious, the moment you realize that, take wing in flight. The human mind is swift of flight. Whatever they have to say in praise of virtue, or again in censure of vice, do you earnestly study it, assimilate the thought and the charm of style. But their nonsensical writings about the gods, the obscene myths, the teaching of demons, laughable merely, or fit to move one to tears, avoid these as you would a trap or snare. Meeting in your reading both their theology and their eloquence, the former ridiculous, the latter charming, despise their pleasure-loving deities, but respect their eloquence. Pluck the rose but shun the thorns, the same tree bears both. These are the best principles with regard to profane learning.[128]

It is clear that Gregory of Nazianzen knew pagan literature, and that he loved it, and used it, and would have others use it.

Let us now turn to Basil. Before we turn to Basil's direct expressions of opinion on this subject, let us briefly look at him in another connection. There is a series of letters (335–49) purporting to be between Basil and Libanius, the great rhetorician. There is no doubt that the two were acquainted, and there is no doubt of their mutual respect; but, although the majority of the letters may be accepted as genuine there is a certain amount of doubt in regard to some of them. From them we learn that Basil was in the habit of sending to Libanius promising lads from Cappadocia.[129] In his replies Libanius makes much of the beauty of Basil's Greek style. Libanius writes to tell of the arrival of the letter of Basil: "Now when the bearers delivered the letter, after going through it all in silence, I said, smiling the while and rejoicing: 'We have been vanquished!' 'And in what have you been vanquished,' they (Libanius's friends) asked, 'and why do you not grieve at having been vanquished?' I said: 'I have been worsted in beauty of epistolary style. And it is Basil who has gained the upper hand. But the man is dear to me, and on this account I am delighted.'" The letter was read to the company, and they agreed on the supreme

[128] Gregory of Nazianzen: *Carmen* 8, *To Seleucus*, translation by L. Millar: *Christian Education in the First Four Centuries*, pp. 105, 106.

[129] Basil: *Letters* 337: "Behold, still another Cappadocian has come for you; he too is a son of mine."

beauty of Basil's style. The reader went out to show the letter to others, and was reluctant even to hand it back.[130] All this is in the answer of Libanius to Basil's letter. Basil writes disclaiming any ability to conquer the great Libanius in style. And when this letter reached Libanius, Libanius says that when it was read aloud to the company they could not refrain from leaping to their feet in admiration.[131]

It is certainly true that Libanius had the greatest admiration for Basil's Greek style. Libanius was not a Christian, but he was an admirer, for he writes: "What is our Basil doing now, and to what mode of life has he turned? Is he frequenting the courts and emulating the orators of old? . . . But when there came persons bearing the tidings that you were traversing ways of life far better than these, and that you were considering how you might become more pleasing to God rather than how you could amass wealth, I congratulated both you and the Cappadocians, you for wishing to be a man of that kind, them for being able to produce such a citizen."[132] Maybe there was a wistfulness behind the glittering career of the famous Greek rhetorician, which made him feel that Basil had chosen the better part. If this series of letters is genuine, and it may well be, it means that Basil and Libanius, the Christian teacher and the great Greek rhetorician, were on terms of intimate and affectionate friendship.

But in the case of Basil we are not left to deduce his attitude to pagan literature and culture. We possess a homily of his *To Young Men, on How they might profit from Pagan Literature*.[133] Basil begins by saying that experience has given him a certain wisdom; he has come a long way himself, and perhaps he can help others along the way (1). He has no doubt as to the value of pagan literature, but he has also no doubt that wise discrimination must be used. The good must be chosen and the harmful rejected (8. 1). He too uses the simile of the ability of the bee to pick out the flowers it can use and to avoid the flowers which are useless to it (4. 7). Pagan literature is specially useful as a preparation for the study of sacred

[130] Basil: *Letters* 338. [131] Basil: *Letters* 339, 340.

[132] Basil: *Letters* 336.

[133] Text and Translation by R. J. Deferrari and M. R. P. McGuire in *St. Basil, the Letters*, vol. 4, pp. 378–435, *Loeb Classical Library*.

literature. Moses was trained in the wisdom of the Egyptians, and Daniel in the lore of the Chaldæans (3. 3, 4). There is always preliminary exercise for any important activity, for music, or for athletics, or for warfare (2. 6; 8. 4). When craftsmen are going to dye cloth, they do not dye it straight away; first by certain processes they prepare the cloth to receive the dye (2. 8). So pagan literature can be a preliminary exercise for the study of the sacred writings. But, as we have said, there must be care and there must be choice. The poets tell many stories which are obscene and immoral, and the beauty of their poetry makes it worse, for then the poison is wrapped in honey, which hides its taste (4. 3, 5; 8. 1). The worst type of orator teaches nothing other than "the art of lying" (4. 6).

But there is much about virtue in the poets, and still more in the philosophers, and to that kind of literature we ought to devote ourselves (5. 1). When Hesiod says that the road to virtue is hard to travel, full of sweat and toil, and steep withal, we must listen to him (5. 3). All Homer's poetry, says Basil, is an encomium of virtue (5. 6). Plutarch tells of Pericles that once a man kept mercilessly abusing him and railing at him all day long. Then when the night came, and the dark came down, Pericles lit the man home with his own lantern, to show how philosophy ought to make a man behave. A certain man in anger took an oath that he would kill Eucleides of Megara, as Plutarch tells, but Eucleides took an oath that he would make the man forget his anger. A certain drunken man fell on Socrates and belaboured him with blows—again the story is Plutarch's—and Socrates in nowise retaliated. All that Socrates did, when the man ceased, was to write the man's name, on his own bruised forehead, as a man might write his name on a statue to say that: "So and so has made this." These things teach us that we should turn the other cheek and pray for those who despitefully use us and persecute us. Alexander the Great captured the daughters of Darius, but he would not even look at them, for he was told that they were surpassingly beautiful, and he held that no man who had captured men should be vanquished by women. Here we have an illustration that no one must look on a woman to lust after her (7. 2–10). There are excellent things in these pagan writers and we ought to use them (7. 1). Philosophy helps a man to master his fleshly passions, and therefore sets him free as from a prison (9. 2). Gymnastic has its place. It is well to remember how Pythagoras said to a man who was getting fatter and fatter and flabbier and flabbier: "Pray cease making your prison-house more wretched for you to live in!" (9. 14). The test must always be whether or not the literature promotes virtue; if it does not, it must be rigidly avoided; if it does, then it is always of use, no matter where it comes from (4. 10). Basil saw in pagan literature things of value that no man could afford to despise or to neglect.

Gregory of Nyssa, Basil's brother, never got the educational opportunities that Basil received, and sometimes he writes very differently. There is a letter of his addressed *To a Student of the Classics*.[134] It begins by saying: "Your eager pursuit of profane literature proved incontestably to us that you did not care about sacred." But the letter goes on to speak with gentleness, and with classical allusions in itself, and it is not a case of forbidding classical literature, but of insisting that the balance should be kept right.

But the thing which best indicates Gregory of Nyssa's attitude to this matter is a letter to Libanius who was also his friend. He has heard a rumour that Libanius is proposing to teach rhetoric no more, and he beseeches him not to retire and not to forsake the oratory which needs him so much.[135] It is a suggestive thing to find a great Christian teacher urging a great pagan rhetorician to stand to his post as a divine duty.

Beyond this we need not go. It is proved abundantly that those who were defending the Christian case, and those who were writing the Christian literature, of the early Church, were men of a knowledge and an academic background unsurpassed in the Roman Empire. Here were no rude, ignorant and unlettered men. Here were men able to address even Emperors, to associate with the great pagan teachers, and to be equals with those who might appear in any company. Most of them were very willing to use the riches that pagan culture gave them, as a gift from God. The writers of the Early Church were not deliberately ignorant obscurantists. They could meet the world, from the point of view of learning and of skill on more than level terms. It is the glory of the Christian

[134] Gregory of Nyssa: *Letters* 8. [135] Gregory of Nyssa: *Letters* 11.

faith that it attracted the scholars of the world, as well as the simple of the world.

There was another factor in the situation of the early Church, which must have gradually but profoundly affected the whole attitude of the Church to culture and to education at large. When Paul wrote *I Corinthians* it was no doubt true that not many noble and not many mighty were called.[136] But that was a situation which was literally changing every day. The longer the Church continued to exist, the more people of wealth and rank and substance were attracted into her fellowship, and the very fact that the Church was undergoing a social change must have affected her whole outlook on the cultural side of paganism.[137]

There are the first signs of the changing social grading of the Church even within the New Testament itself. Sergius Paulus, the proconsul of Cyprus, is touched by Paul.[138] Dionysius the Areopagite, member of the most ancient Athenian court, is converted at Athens.[139] At Thessalonica and Berea women of the upper classes are being won for the Christian way.[140] In the *Letter of James* social distinctions within the Church are already bringing their own problems, and the man with the gold ring is receiving more than his due amount of attention.[141]

As early as A.D. 57 Pomponia Græcina, the wife of no less a person than Plautius, the conqueror of Britain, is most probably being arraigned as being a Christian. H. B. Workman suggests with some confidence that she is probably the first Roman of whose sufferings for Christ we have any record.[142] By the time of Domitian Christianity has cost the life and the liberty of Acilius Glabrio, an ex-consul, and of Flavius Clemens and his wife Domatilla, whose two sons had actually been designated as the heirs of Domitian.[143] That is to say, Christianity had reached the royal household.

[136] *I Corinthians* 1. 26.

[137] See A. Harnack: *The Expansion of Christianity* 2. 183 ff. In this chapter Harnack deals with what he calls *The Inward Spread of Christianity*, and for what follows I have drawn freely on his abundant material.

[138] *Acts* 13. 7–12. [139] *Acts* 17. 34. [140] *Acts* 17. 4, 12. [141] *James* 2. 1–6.

[142] H. B. Workman: *Persecution in the Early Church*, p. 60.

[143] Dion Cassius 67. 14; Suetonius, *Domitian* 15. See H. B. Workman: *Persecution in the Early Church*, pp. 204, 205.

Very soon pagans and Christians alike are agreed that there are no ranks of society in which Christians are not to be found. It is the problem of the puzzled Pliny that if he seeks to deal generally with Christianity, " Persons of all ranks and ages, and of both sexes, are, and will be involved." [144] And in his doubt he writes to Trajan to ask what to do. As Tertullian tells us, it is the desperate complaint of the heathen that the state is besieged, that in the towns, the country, the villages and the islands Christians are to be found; that all, without discrimination of sex, age, circumstance or even rank, are deserting to this name.[145] He begins the *Ad Nationes* by saying: " Your constant cry is that the state is beset by us; that Christians are in your fields, in your camps, in your islands. You grieve over it as a calamity, that each sex, every age—in short, every rank—is passing over from you to us." [146] In the *Ad Scapulam* Tertullian points out that the Emperor Severus himself gave the Christian Torpacion free quarters in his palace because he had cured him by anointing him; that Antoninus, " brought up on Christian milk," also knew this man well; that men and women of the highest rank were freely permitted to be Christian.[147]

Long before this Hermas had lamented the fact that there were Christians who were immersed in business. There were those who were mixed up with business and riches and heathen friendships and the occupations of this world,[148] and there were those who had put on haughtiness because they were rich and in honour among the heathen.[149]

Clement was to point out that the word of Jesus did not remain in Judæa as philosophy did in Greece; " but was diffused over the whole world, over every nation and village and town, bringing already over to the truth whole houses, . . . and not a few of the philosophers themselves." [150]

The second rescript of Valerian in A.D. 258 is the proof of how far Christianity had penetrated into the Roman civil service: " Senators and prominent men and Roman knights are to lose their position, and moreover be stripped of their property, if they still

[144] Pliny: *Letters* 10. 96.

[145] Tertullian: *Apology* 1.

[146] Tertullian: *Ad Nationes* 1.

[147] Tertullian: *Ad Scapulam* 4.

[148] Hermas: *Mandates* 10. 1. 4.

[149] Hermas: *Similitudes* 8. 9. 1.

[150] Clement: *Stromateis* 6. 18.

persist in being Christians. After their goods have been taken from them, they are to be beheaded. Matrons are to be deprived of their property and banished into exile. But members of Cæsar's household are to have their goods confiscated and be sent in chains by appointment to the estates of Cæsar."[151] Origen becomes the consultant of Mammæa, the mother of the Emperor Alexander, and the correspondent of the Emperor Philip himself.[152] Eusebius tells us that just before the persecution of Diocletian "they committed to the Christians the government of provinces."[153] And he goes on to tell us that, when persecution did break out, in the Thebais those who were distinguished for wealth, noble birth, and honour, for learning and philosophy were most wonderful of all for they counted all things secondary to true religion and to faith in Jesus Christ.[154]

There is an amazing story here. The faith which began with the humble and the undistinguished and the poor and those of no account, had become the faith whose members penetrated into every grade of society, grew rich in the world of business, filled the Roman civil service, governed even provinces, and were found within the circle of the royal house. A situation like that would be bound to react on the Church's attitude to pagan culture. Such converts would want the best for their children. Arnobius has it that in his day, "orators, grammarians, rhetoricians, lawyers, and physicians, even those who explore the profundities of philosophy" seek instruction in Christianity and abandon the things to which they were once devoted.[155] In circumstances like these an uneducated Church, or even a Church which despised education was an impossibility.

There was inevitably a time at the beginning of things when the Christians considered all pagan knowledge and culture as an irrelevance certainly and a danger probably. That time did not wholly pass.

[151] Quoted in A. Harnack: *The Expansion of Christianity* 5. 189, 190.
[152] Jerome: *Lives of Illustrious Men* 54.
[153] Eusebius: *Ecclesiastical History* 8. 1. 2.
[154] Eusebius: *Ecclesiastical History* 8. 9. 6.
[155] Arnobius: *The Case against the Pagans* 2. 5.

There were always voices raised in protest. In the *Didascalia Apostolorum* it is set down:

> Avoid all books of the heathen. For what hast thou to do with strange sayings or laws or lying prophecies which also turn away from the faith them that are young? What is lacking to thee in the word of God, that thou shouldest cast thyself on these fables of the heathen? If thou wouldst read historical narratives thou hast the *Book of Kings;* if philosophers and wise men, thou hast the prophets, wherein thou shalt find wisdom and understanding more than that of the wise men and the philosophers. And, if thou wish for songs, thou hast the *Psalms* of David; if thou wouldst read of the beginning of the world, thou hast the *Genesis* of the great Moses; and, if laws and commandments, thou hast the glorious Law of the Lord God. All strange writings therefore which are contrary to these wholly eschew.[156]

But that total rejection is a note which grows less and less. It is not that the Christians ever wholly accepted pagan culture; and it is not that they were blind to its dangers. John Chrysostom, that master orator, can still write:

> Well then! Some say: Shall we raze the schools to the ground? That is not what I am saying, but that we must not destroy utterly the dwelling place of virtue or bury the living soul. If the soul is prudent, lack of the power to speak will not result in any loss; but if it is destroyed, the harm done is most serious, even though the tongue happens to be sharp and polished, and the greater the power of speaking, the greater the harm done. ... The study of eloquence requires good morals, but good morals do not require eloquence.[157]

Lucifer of Calaris could write against the heretics whom he was condemning: " We, to whom nature is sufficient for speaking, we who are strangers from all Gentile literature, are strong enough to

[156] *Didascalia Apostolorum* 12.

[157] Quoted M. L. W. Laistner: *Christianity and Pagan Culture*, p. 53.

destroy any heresy, because the thing itself and the truth are speaking. You and your helpers have multiplied the whole art of Gentile literature; we know sacred literature only. Our speech is the common speech; yours on the other hand is polished, ornate, carefully chosen. Nevertheless your artfully sweet and carefully wrought speech cannot persuade any Christian, unless he is no Christian, in which case it might result that, although you are a wolf, you might be reckoned to be one of the sheep, by those who have no knowledge."[158] Epiphanius can write with venomous bitterness that Origen is like a viper, that he is inflated with Greek education, that he vomits out the poison of his mind, which becomes the food of destruction to those who accept his views.[159] But, as Laistner caustically remarks, "A cynic might, however, find significance in the fact that an Epiphanius or a Lucifer of Calaris, whose opinions are most violent, were both, stylistically considered, very indifferent writers, and as thinkers not even in the second rank."[160]

It is true that there were few of the Christian writers who would openly have admitted that they loved pagan literature for its own sake, and for its own beauty. For the most part their official attitude was that a man must know it, because it provided him with an arsenal of weapons and methods of attack against the pagans themselves. Augustine writes:

> If those who are called philosophers, and especially the Platonists, have said anything that is true and in harmony with our faith, we are not only not to shrink from it, but to claim it for our use from those who have no lawful possession of it. . . . In the same way all branches of heathen learning, have not only false and superstitious fancies and heavy burdens of unnecessary toil, which every one of us, when we go out under the leadership of Christ from the fellowship of the heathen, ought to avoid; but they contain also liberal instruction which is better adapted to the use of truth, and some most excellent precepts of morality; and some truths even in regard to the worship of the one God are found among them. Now these are, so to speak, their gold

[158] Lucifer: *Moriendum esse pro Dei Filio.*

[159] Epiphanius: *Panarion Haer.* 72. 9.

[160] M. L. W. Laistner: *Christianity and Pagan Culture*, p. 51.

> and silver, which they did not create themselves, but dug out of the mines of God's providence, which are everywhere scattered abroad, and are perversely and unlawfully prostituted to the worship of devils. These, therefore, the Christian, when he separates himself in spirit from the miserable fellowship of these men, ought to take away with him, and devote to their proper use in the preaching of the gospel.

This process was called "spoiling the Egyptians." As the Jews spoiled the Egyptians when they went forth from Egypt so the Christian spoils the pagan writers when he goes out from paganism. So Augustine goes on to note how nobly Clement of Alexandria, Origen and Jerome did in fact spoil the Egyptians:

> And what have many good and faithful men among our brethren done? Do we not see with what a quantity of gold and silver and garments Cyprian, that most persuasive teacher and blessed martyr, was loaded when he came out of Egypt? How much Lactantius brought with him, and Victorinus, and Optatus, and Hilary, not to speak of living men? [161]

The best defence of the use of pagan literature comes from the historian Socrates. He was writing after the time when Julian had tried to debar all Christians from all learning, by debarring all Christian teachers from schools. Fortunately that prohibition did not last long, for the death of Julian caused it to be rescinded almost as soon as it was enacted. Socrates regards the speedy restoration of the way to learning as providential, and he goes on to justify himself for this point of view. He uses three arguments. He begins by laying it down that Greek literature certainly was never recognized either by Christ or his apostles as divinely inspired, but, on the other hand, neither was it rejected as wholly spurious. And this happened of deliberate intent that the use of it should not be banned. First, there were many wise men of the Greeks who were not far from the knowledge of God. That was only to be expected, for, since ever there was a world, the invisible things could be seen through the things which are visible (*Romans* I. 18–21). Second,

[161] Augustine: *De Doctrina Christiana* 40.

beyond doubt the sacred scriptures inculcate admirable and heavenly doctrines, and produce piety and integrity in those who study them, but they do not instruct in the art of reasoning, by which those who oppose the truth may be successfully resisted. Third, adversaries are most easily foiled, when we can use their own weapons against them.[162] As Socrates wisely saw it, pagan literature had its uses, uses which no prudent man could afford to neglect. The Christian Church had come to see that all wisdom and all beauty come somehow from God; but at the same time the Christian Church never forgot—and some to the end of the day felt it more acutely than others—that more than knowledge is necessary, for a devil is bad, but a clever and an educated devil is still worse.

[162] Socrates: *Ecclesiastical History* 3. 16.

VI. The Child in the Early Church

There is no gospel picture dearer to most people than the picture of Jesus setting the child in the midst, or taking him in His arms. There are comparatively few references to children in the pages of the gospels, but the few there are are of first-rate importance; and in them there is set out in a way that cannot be forgotten the importance of the child.

It is clear that Jesus was never too busy or too preoccupied to receive and to welcome a child. When His disciples would have kept them back, He bade them to be allowed to come to Him.[1] The disciples are not to be thought of in that passage as hard and unsympathetic men. If we place any reliance at all upon the chronology of the gospels, that incident of the children happened when Jesus was on His last journey to Jerusalem. His tension was apparent to the disciples, even if they did not fully realise its cause; and they sought to keep the children away, because they did not wish their Master to be worried by them at such a time as that. Even on the way to Jerusalem Jesus had time for the child.

There is one saying of Jesus, as it is reported to us, which means that Jesus believed that God too is never too preoccupied with greatness to receive the child. His warning is that men must have a care lest they offend the children, for, " In heaven their angels do always behold the face of my Father who is in heaven." [2] That can only refer to guardian angels. At a king's court it was only the most favoured courtiers and officials who had at any time access to the king's presence, and who at any time saw the king's face. So that must mean that Jesus taught that at any time God was willing to give complete attention to the care of the child.

It is the assumption of Jesus that every father will automatically and instinctively care for the child. Even men, who are evil, know

[1] *Mark* 10. 13; *Matthew* 19. 13; *Luke* 18. 15. [2] *Matthew* 18. 10.

how to give good gifts to their children.[3] The care of the child is a primary human duty.

It is the teaching of Jesus that the Christian duty to the child is absolutely binding. To receive a child is to receive none other than Jesus Himself.[4]

The responsibility of the Christian for the child is a terrible responsibility. The fate of the man who puts a stumbling-block in the way of the child is a more bitter fate than awaits any other human sin. It would be better for a man to have a great millstone hanged around his neck and to be drowned in the depths of the sea than to cause a child to stumble.[5]

The child is the very pattern of the citizen of the Kingdom, and unless a man becomes as a child he will not enter into the Kingdom at all.[6]

With a background like that in the teaching of Jesus, one would have expected that the rest of the New Testament would have had much to say about the teaching and the training of the child; but the amazing thing is the meagreness of the New Testament material dealing with the child. The children of believing parents are within the Christian fellowship, for the promise is to the Christian and to his children.[7] There is one brief glimpse of the Church at Tyre, when the children and the wives appear to speed Paul upon his way to Rome.[8]

The New Testament has practically nothing to say about the training of the child. Children must obey their parents.[9] Those who are to rule within the Church must first be the rulers of their own households. The bishop must be one who has his own children in subjection, and the deacon must be one who rules his own household well. The elder must be one who has faithful children in his own house.[10] Parents have the basic human duty of providing for their children, for the children ought not to lay up for the parents, but the parents for the children.[11] Fathers must not provoke their

[3] *Matthew* 7. 11; *Luke* 11. 13. [4] *Mark* 9. 36; *Luke* 9. 48.

[5] *Matthew* 18. 6–14; *Mark* 9. 42; *Luke* 17. 2.

[6] *Matthew* 18. 2–4; *Mark* 9. 33–6; *Luke* 9. 46–8.

[7] *Acts* 2. 39; *I Corinthians* 7. 14. [8] *Acts* 21. 5.

[9] *Ephesians* 6. 1; *Colossians* 3. 20.

[10] *I Timothy* 3. 4, 12; *Titus* 1. 6. [11] *II Corinthians* 12. 14.

children to wrath, as the letter to the Colossians adds, lest they be discouraged.[12] Bengel commenting on that passage says that fathers must never be too hard on their children, so that they may avoid that plague of youth, the broken spirit.

And there our material ends. The New Testament lays down no kind of curriculum of training for the child; the New Testament knows nothing about religious education and nothing about schools; for the New Testament is certain that the only training which really matters is given within the home, and that there are no teachers so effective for good or evil as parents are.

When we turn to the Apostolic Fathers the material is equally meagre; and the tone of it is precisely the same. That the Church was concerned with the children is shown by the repeated injunction that neither abortion nor child exposure must be practised.[13] That the children were very definitely within the fellowship of the Church is shown by the fact that they are included with the husbands and the wives and the widows in the closing greetings of Ignatius's letter to the Church at Smyrna.[14] The other references are to the duty and obligation of the parent to bring up the child in the knowledge and the love and the fear of God. Clement writes to the Church at Corinth:

> Let us reverence them that have rule over us, let us honour our elders, let us train our young in the fear of God, let us direct our women in the good way. . . . Let our children partake of the training that is in Christ. Let them learn how humility avails with God, what pure love can do with Him, how the fear of Him is good and great and saves those who live therein in holiness and a pure mind.[15]

Polycarp writes to the Church at Philippi:

> Let us teach, first of all, ourselves to walk in the commandments of the Lord. Next, teach your wives to walk in the faith given

[12] *Ephesians* 6. 4; *Colossians* 3. 21.
[13] *Epistle of Barnabas* 19. 5; 20. 2; *Didache* 2. 2; 5. 2.
[14] Ignatius: *To the Smyrnæans* 13. 1.
[15] Clement: *To the Corinthians* 21. 6–8.

> to them, and in love and in purity tenderly to love their own husbands in all truth, and to love all others equally in all chastity; and to train up their children in the knowledge and fear of God.[16]

It is the instruction of Hermas: "Make these things known to all your children and to your wife."[17] In the same work the angel gives instruction in the necessity of family training and family discipline:

> It is not for this that God is angry with you, but in order that you should convert your family, which has sinned against the Lord, and against you, their parents. But you are indulgent and do not correct your family, but have allowed them to become corrupt. . . . But the great mercy of the Lord has had pity on you and your family, and will make you strong and will establish you in his glory; only do not be slothful, but have courage and strengthen your family. For, as the smith, by hammering his work, overcomes the task which he desires, so also the daily righteous word overcomes all wickedness. Do not cease, then, correcting your children, for I know that if they repent with all their hearts, they will be inscribed in the book of life with the saints.[18]

In the same work Hermas is told of his duty to his erring family:

> But, Hermas, no longer bear a grudge against your children, nor neglect your sister, that they may be cleansed from their former sins. For they will be corrected with righteous correction, if you bear no grudge against them. The bearing of grudges works death. But you, Hermas, had great troubles of your own because of the transgressions of your family, because you did not pay attention to them; but you neglected them and became entangled in their evil deeds.[19]

[16] Polycarp: *To the Philippians* 4. 2.

[17] *The Shepherd of Hermas:* Vision 2. 2. 3.

[18] *The Shepherd of Hermas:* Vision 1. 3. 1, 2.

[19] *The Shepherd of Hermas:* Vision 2. 3. 1.

That is all the material we have from the Apostolic Fathers, but the general impact and direction of it is completely clear. The training of the child is a parental duty; and to fail in it is to bring sorrow to the child and sorrow to oneself. The whole task of education is laid squarely on the shoulders of the father as the head of the household and the home.

The surprising truth is that never at any time either in New Testament times or in the days of the Early Church did the Church ever provide any kind of general education for her children. This was a task that the Church never at any time undertook. She provided careful and detailed instruction for her catechumens, and for her ministry, but for her children she provided none at all. There were certain reasons why that was so.

There was one reason which explains not only this, but many surprising things in the history of the Early Church. The Early Church had an intense and passionate belief in the imminence of the Second Coming. And there was no point in setting up a system of secular education in a world where the time was short and where the Lord was at hand. If the world as men knew it was hastening to an end, there was no point in preparing for life in the world. In a rapidly dissolving world secular education was an irrelevance, which did not enter into men's calculations at all.

Further, in the early days the Church was poor. To have set up her own system of schools would have been completely beyond her means. She could have provided neither the buildings nor the staff necessary for any such undertaking.

Still further, it was not so very long before Christianity became illegal. When the time came when a man could be regarded as a criminal simply for the name of Christian, and not because of any crimes attaching to the name, Christian schools would be an obvious impossibility. No body of people who were automatically outside the law could possibly set up their own schools.

If the Church did not and could not set up schools for its own children, where then did the children of Christians receive their education? The answer is simple and extremely surprising—they were educated in the ordinary and normal secular schools. Let us recall the curriculum of any Greek or Roman school. Its curriculum was the poets, and especially Homer. These poets, and especially Homer, told of the gods, of their loves and wars and hates and exploits—a strange curriculum indeed for a Christian child. The whole school organisation was tied to heathen religion. The school holidays were religious festivals; the master received his poor payment on the Feasts of Minerva and Saturn. The school spent most of its time learning about the gods, and adjusting its time-table by the festivals of the gods; and yet it was to these schools that Christian children went.

In his work *On Idolatry* Tertullian deals with this very problem, and he comes to a conclusion which is very surprising. Tertullian was the last man in the world to compromise with heathenism, and the last man in the world to shrink from making the absolute demand, and from laying down the absolute standard. Tertullian is quite clear that no Christian could be a schoolmaster, or a professor of literature. The schoolmaster is in continuous contact with idolatry. He must tell of the gods and their doings; he must tell of their pedigrees and their honours; his whole educational course involves talking continuously about the gods, who fill the works of the poets. If he is a schoolmaster, he is bound to observe all the heathen festivals, and he is bound to bedeck his school with flowers and garlands on the days of the gods. That is something which no Christian can do; and for Tertullian the profession of schoolmaster is one of the forbidden professions.

It is when he takes the next step that Tertullian does the surprising thing. He admits that the obvious position is that, if teaching literature is unlawful for a Christian, then learning it must be equally unlawful. But that is precisely the position that Tertullian will not face. He pleads that secular education is a complete necessity. No man can live without it; he cannot even study sacred literature without the basic equipment that secular education gives him. Then Tertullian goes on to draw a distinction between *teaching* and *learning*. To teach a subject, he declares, is necessarily to commend it and to affirm its truth, and to bear testimony to it. But to learn is quite different. The teacher has to teach the whole material; but the Christian learner knows what idolatry is, and knows what to accept and what to reject. He is as safe as a man who knows that a thing is poison, and who accepts it in his hand, but has no intention of drinking it. Necessity, says Tertullian, is the excuse of the learner, because he has no other way to learn.[20] It is, then, the curious argument of the usually bluntly uncompromising Tertullian that it is unlawful for a Christian to be a schoolmaster in a heathen school, but it is quite lawful for a Christian child to attend a heathen school, for there is no other possible way for him to gain the basic elements of education at all.

Tertullian more than once insists that the Christian will have nothing to do with secular literature. "We will have nothing to do with pagan literature and teaching, which is perverted in its best results."[21] "We despise the teaching of secular literature," he says, "as being foolishness in God's eyes."[22] And yet in practice he refuses to go the whole way with this point of view; and he comes to the oddly irrational point of view that, while a Christian scholar may learn in a pagan school, a Christian teacher may not teach.

But, while that was Tertullian's point of view, it does not seem to have been the point of view of the Church as a whole. There exist two documents which deal with Church Order, called *The Canons of Hippolytus* and *The Egyptian Church-Order*. Their date is uncertain, as is their relationship; but it is not completely impossible that they may in substance go back to Hippolytus himself, and they are certainly evidence for the practice of the Church prior to A.D. 300.[23] They lay down what must have been the official attitude to the profession of school-teaching. *The Canons of Hippolytus* lay it down that a school-teacher may go on teaching, if he has no other way of making a living; but, if he does go on teaching, he must make it plain that he believes the gods of the heathen to be demons, and he must say daily in the presence of his class: There is no God except the Father, the Son and the Holy Spirit; and he must use his position as an opportunity to convert his scholars to the Christian faith. *The Egyptian Church-Order* says simply that if a man is engaged in teaching children, it is good that he should cease to do so; but, if he has no other profession or craft, he may be pardoned

[20] The whole argument is in Tertullian: *On Idolatry* 10.

[21] Tertullian: *On the Testimony of the Soul* 1.

[22] Tertullian: *De Spectaculis* 17.

[23] See C. J. Cadoux: *The Early Church and the World*, pp. 288–90.

for continuing to teach.[24] And in point of fact that was the general principle which was laid down.

We have now, therefore, reached a stage at which the Christian child receives his general education in a pagan school without any question, and as a regular custom; and at which the Christian teacher is bidden by the more rigorous to abandon his profession as impossible, because of its material, for a Christian, but is allowed by the general practice of the Church to continue as a teacher, provided that he makes his own Christian position clear, and that he uses his profession as a way of introducing his scholars to the Christian faith; and it is clear that the profession of school-teacher in a pagan school must have opened an almost unlimited missionary door of opportunity to the Christian teacher who was brave enough to take it.

Rather more than a hundred years later something was to happen which showed how deeply embedded the Christians had become in the educational system of the Roman Empire, and how great store they set by the education which these schools gave. On 3rd November, 361, Constantius died of a fever at Mopsucrene in Cilicia, and on 11th December Julian entered Constantinople as Roman Emperor. Julian was a man who wished to put the clock back, and to return to the ancient gods. On 4th February, 362, he proclaimed religious toleration throughout the Empire, and began to take steps to bring back the ancient ways. It is true that in the year which ensued there were outbreaks of violence against the Christians, and that for some the days of martyrdom came back, but Julian was not a persecutor in the sense in which the older persecutors were. He deliberately disclaimed any desire to injure the Christians.[25] Sozomen, the historian saw through this policy of toleration quite clearly. "It was not," he writes, "from any feeling of compassion towards the Christians that he treated them at first with greater humanity than had been evinced by the former persecutors, but because he had discovered that paganism had derived no

[24] *Canons of Hippolytus:* Canon 12. 69, 70: *Egyptian Church-Order* 11. 5. Both passages are quoted in Latin in C. J. Cadoux: *The Early Church and the World*, p. 323, footnote.

[25] Julian: *Letters* 37. We use throughout the numbering and the translation of the letters in the edition of W. C. Wright in the *Loeb Classical Library*.

advantage from their tortures, while Christianity had been specially increased, and had become more honoured by the fortitude of those who died in defence of the faith." [26] As Gregory Nazianzen put it: "He grudged the glory of martyrdom." [27] As Jerome put it, he initiated a mild (*blanda*) persecution "enticing rather than compelling people to sacrifice." [28] We must look at the steps which lead up to the famous edict which sought to drive Christians altogether from Roman schools.

His first step very naturally was to reopen the heathen temples. Many of these temples had been deliberately destroyed, and many of them had been used as quarries, from which stone had been taken for the building of other buildings; and Julian enacted that all such stone should be brought back, wherever possible, and used in the reconstruction of the temples from which they had been taken. He writes to his uncle Julian: "First of all, set up the pillars of the Temple of Daphne; take those that are in any palace anywhere, and convey them thence; then set up in their place others taken from the recently occupied houses." [29] He despoiled the Christian Churches of their treasures.[30] Those who had destroyed temples were ordered to rebuild them at their own cost.[31]

Julian took one very subtle step; he recalled all the bishops who had been banished for heresy.[32] He writes to Ætios, the notorious Arian: "I have remitted their sentence of exile for all in common who were banished in whatever fashion by Constantius of blessed memory, on account of the folly of the Galilæans. But in your case, I not only remit your exile, but also, since I am mindful of our old acquaintance and intercourse, I invite you to come to me." [33] Photinus was such an arch-heretic that he was disowned both by the Arians and the orthodox parties, but Julian writes to him as one who at any rate seems to maintain what is probably true, and who comes nearest to being saved.[34] He orders Eleusius, Bishop of

[26] Sozomen: *Ecclesiastical History* 5. 4.

[27] Gregory Nazianzen: *Orations* 21. 32. [28] Jerome: *Chronicle* 503. 4.

[29] Julian: *Letters* 29; Sozomen: *Ecclesiastical History* 5. 3.

[30] Sozomen: *Ecclesiastical History* 5. 5; Theodoret: *Ecclesiastical History* 3. 8.

[31] Sozomen: *Ecclesiastical History* 5. 5.

[32] Theodoret 3. 2; Sozomen 5. 5; Socrates 3. 11.

[33] Julian: *Letters* 15. [34] Julian: *Letters* 55.

Cyzicus, to rebuild the Church of the Novatians at his own expense, and imposes a heavy penalty if the work is not completed within two months.[35] The Donatists can actually speak of Julian as " the one man who had allowed justice to triumph." [36] The idea behind this was to sow dissension in the Christian Church, and to divide it once again into warring sects and factions, and so ultimately to destroy it. It is true that Julian's subtle plan did not prove in any way generally effective, but the subtlety of the move was typical of his method of attacking Christianity.

He did everything he could to humiliate the Christians without actually attacking them. He to all intents and purposes closed the law-courts to them by demanding that every pleader should burn a few pinches of incense before beginning his oration.[37] He ordained that they should no longer be known as Christians, but that they should be called by the contemptuous title of Galilæans.[38] Those who would not sacrifice to the gods, however blameless they might be, were deprived of their citizenship, and of the privilege of participating in the assemblies and in the forum. Magistrates and governors were dismissed from their posts on the ground that the Christian law forbade them to use the sword against those who were worthy of capital punishment.[39] In his own letter to Atarbius he writes: " I affirm by the gods that I do not wish the Galilæans either to be put to death or unjustly beaten, or to suffer any other injury; but nevertheless I do assert absolutely that the god-fearing must be preferred to them. For through the folly of the Galilæans almost everything has been overturned, whereas through the grace of the gods are we all well preserved. Wherefore we ought to honour the gods and the god-fearing, both men and cities." [40] In all cases preference was to be given to the man who was not a Christian.

Julian withdrew all the privileges which had been given to the Christian Church and the Christian clergy.[41] He withdrew the right of travel by the public post; he withdrew exemption from

[35] Socrates 3. 11. [36] Optatus: *De Schism. Don.* 2. 16.

[37] Gregory Nazianzen *Orations* 4. 96.

[38] Gregory Nazianzen: *Orations* 4. 76.

[39] Socrates 3. 13; Sozomen 5. 18. [40] Julian: *Letters* 37.

[41] Sozomen 5. 5; Theodoret 3. 3. These privileges are detailed in Eusebius: *Life of Constantine* 2. 30–42.

municipal service. He writes to the citizens of Byzantium: "I have restored to you all your senators and councillors whether they have abandoned themselves to the superstition of the Galilæans, or have devised some other method of escaping from the senate."[42] He even compelled Christian widows and orphans to refund the money which they had in their poverty received from public sources.[43]

It is quite clear that Julian did not unleash anything like the bloodthirsty persecutions of the earlier days; but he did mount against the Christians what might be called an administrative persecution, so that to be a Christian was to lose all the rights to citizenship, and to have to bid farewell to all hope of a public career, or even a public competence.

It is against this background that we must see Julian's final attack on Christianity, and it was an attack upon the front of education. It was an attack which was launched in three stages. On 12th May, 362, Julian issued a decree confirming their privileges to school-teachers. This was a quite colourless decree, giving little warning of what was to follow. On 17th June of the same year it was followed by a much more ominous decree, which read:

> Seeing that it is expedient that all masters and teachers should be patterns not less of morality than of eloquence, and seeing that I cannot be present in person in each individual township, be it enacted that whoever desires the work of a teacher do not intrude into the office suddenly or rashly, but that, after orderly examination held, his appointment be sanctioned by decree of the *curiales*, with the consent and confirmation of the *optimi*. Such decree shall be transmitted to me for endorsement, that, under our sanction, teachers may with more exalted honour conduct the studies of townships.[44]

It was still not clear what Julian was getting at, and he appeared only to be setting the local authorities an awkward problem in selection. But one thing was clear, that Julian was about to use the educational system of Rome as a propaganda weapon, and as an instrument for the deliberate formation of public opinion. But this decree was

[42] Julian: *Letters* 39. [43] Sozomen 5. 5.
[44] *Codex Theodosius* 13. 3. 5.

almost immediately followed by a rescript which made the whole matter clear. The rescript is long, but it must be quoted in full, because it is an extraordinary document:

> I hold that a proper education results, not in laboriously acquired symmetry of phrases and language, but in a healthy condition of mind, I mean a mind that has understanding and true opinions about things good and evil, honourable and base. Therefore, when a man thinks one thing and teaches his pupils another, in my opinion he fails to educate exactly in proportion as he fails to be an honest man. And if the divergence between a man's convictions and his utterances is merely in trivial matters, that can be tolerated somehow, though it is wrong. But if in matters of the greatest importance a man has certain opinions and teaches the contrary, what is that but the conduct of hucksters, and not honest but thoroughly dissolute men in that they praise most highly the things that they believe to be most worthless, thus cheating and enticing by their praises those to whom they desire to transfer their worthless wares. Now all who profess to teach anything whatever ought to be men of upright character, and ought not to harbour in their souls opinions irreconcilable with what they publicly profess; and, above all, I believe it is necessary that those who associate with the young and teach them rhetoric should be of upright character; for they expound the writings of the ancients, whether they be rhetoricians or grammarians, and still more if they are sophists. For these claim to teach, in addition to other things, not only the use of words, but morals, also, and they assert that political philosophy is their peculiar field. Let us leave aside, for the moment, the question whether this is true or not. But while I applaud them for aspiring to such high pretensions, I should applaud them still more, if they did not utter falsehoods and convict themselves of thinking one thing and teaching their pupils another. What! Was it not the gods who revealed all their learning to Homer, Hesiod, Demosthenes, Herodotus, Thucydides, Isocrates and Lysias? Did not these men think that they were consecrated, some to Hermes, some to the Muses? I think it absurd that men who expound the works of these writers should dishonour the gods whom they

used to honour. Yet though I think this absurd, I do not say that they ought to change their opinions and then instruct the young. But I give them this choice: either not to teach what they do not think admirable, or, if they wish to teach, let them first really persuade their pupils that neither Homer nor Hesiod, nor any of these writers whom they expound, and have declared to be guilty of impiety, folly and error in regard to the gods, is such as they declare. For since they make a livelihood and receive pay from these writers, they thereby confess that they are most shamefully greedy of gain, and that, for the sake of a few drachmæ, they would put up with anything. It is true that, until now, there were many excuses for not attending the temples, and the terror that threatened on all sides absolved men for concealing the truest belief about the gods. But since the gods have granted us liberty, it seems to me absurd that men should teach what they do not believe to be sound. But if they believe that those whose interpreters they are and for whom they sit, so to speak, in the seat of the prophets, were wise men, let them be the first to emulate their piety towards the gods. If, however, they think that these writers were in error with respect to the most honoured gods, then let them betake themselves to the Churches of the Galilæans to expound Matthew and Luke, since you Galilæans are obeying them when you ordain that men shall refrain from temple-worship. For my part I wish that your ears and tongues might be "born anew," as you would say, as regards these things in which may I ever have part, and all who think and act as is pleasing to me.

For religious and secular teachers let there be a general ordinance to this effect: Any youth who wishes to attend the schools is not excluded; nor indeed would it be reasonable to shut out from the best way boys who are still too ignorant to know which way to turn, and to overawe them against their will into being led to the beliefs of their ancestors. Though indeed it might be proper to cure these even against their will, as one cures the insane, except that we concede indulgence to all for this sort of disease. For we ought, I think, to teach, but not punish, the demented.[45]

[45] Julian: *Letters* 36.

And now the aim of Julian was quite clear, it was to close the secular schools against all Christian teachers. They must either abandon their belief in Christianity, and return to belief in the old pagan gods, or cease to teach.

Here indeed was a subtle method of persecution. It banned culture to the Church, and in effect shut the door on education. It is true that it was Christian teachers and not Christian scholars who were banned from the schools. It is true that for Christian scholars the door was left wide open. But it was quite clear that the whole design of Julian was to turn the schools into centres of pagan religion rather than of general culture; and the result would have been that it would have become impossible for Christian parents to send their children to them. Gibbon accurately assesses Julian's aim, and the certain outcome if this policy had become a permanency: "Julian had reason to expect that in the space of a few years the Church would relapse into its primæval simplicity, and that the theologians, who possessed an inadequate share of the learning and eloquence of the age, would be succeeded by a generation of blind and ignorant fanatics, incapable of defending the truth of their own principles, or of exposing the various follies of polytheism." This enactment of Julian might well have been a great step towards rendering ineffective the whole work of the Church in the long run.

It was not only elementary school teachers who were hit by this edict. Great professors of rhetoric had to lay down their offices. Victorinus in Rome chose to abandon teaching, as did Musonius and Prohæresius in Athens. Hecebolius apostatised in order to keep his chair. The case of Prohæresius is curious. He had been no less than the tutor of Julian himself. It is quite certain that Julian would have given Prohæresius special exemption and special consideration. Some time before, he had written to Prohæresius offering him access to state documents if he proposed to write a history of the times.[46] But Prohæresius chose to go. But before he went he consulted the oracle at Delphi to see whether or not Julian's enactment would last for long; the oracle assured him that it would last only a short time. "Prohæresius learned in this way what the future would bring, and took courage." [47] There is something characteristic of the age in a philosopher, who was credulous

[46] Julian: *Letters* 14. [47] Eunapius: *Lives of the Philosophers* 493.

enough to consult Delphi for guidance, and a Christian who was close enough to paganism to decide his future by the verdict of a pagan oracle. It is a curiously revealing incident; it shows that in many cases, and sometimes where one would least expect it, the ancient gods were not so very far away; and it shows that, if Julian had lived to enforce his decree for long enough, it might have had a very serious effect on the Christian Church.

Even the pagans themselves were shocked by this act of Julian. Ammianus Marcellinus praises Julian for simplifying legal procedure, and for making the laws more intelligible; then he goes on to say: "But his forbidding masters of rhetoric and grammar to instruct Christians was a cruel action, and was deserving to be buried in everlasting silence."[48] The very way in which Ammianus states this matter shows that he clearly saw its aim and its effect; for he does not say that Julian forbade Christian teachers to instruct, he says that it was forbidden that Christians should be instructed. Gregory of Nazianzen says that Julian declared: "Literature and the Greek language are naturally ours, who are worshippers of the gods; illiterate ignorance and rusticity are yours, whose wisdom goes no further than to say 'believe.'"[49]

It is interesting to note that in every case the Christian historians interpret this act of Julian in the same way as Marcellinus did. They do not mention the fact that Christian teachers were forbidden to teach; they all put it in the form that the schools were barred to Christian scholars. Fundamentally they all see in this prohibition an act of fear. Theodoret writes:

> First of all, he prohibited the sons of the Galilæans, for so he tried to name the worshippers of the Saviour, from taking part in the study of poetry, rhetoric, and philosophy, for, said he, "we are shot with shafts feathered from our own wing," for from our own books they take arms and wage war against us.[50]

Sozomen writes:

> He forbade the children of Christians from frequenting the

[48] Ammianus Marcellinus 22. 10. 7.

[49] Gregory Nazianzen: *Orations* 4. [50] Theodoret 3. 4.

> public schools, and from being instructed in the writings of the Greek poets and authors. . . . His sole motive for excluding the children of Christian parents from instruction in the learning of the Greeks was because he considered such studies conducive to the acquisition of argumentative and persuasive power.[51]

Socrates writes:

> He enacted a law by which Christians were excluded from the cultivation of literature, "lest," said he, "when they have sharpened their tongue, they should be able the more readily to meet the arguments of the heathen." . . . He knew very well that the fables it contains would expose the whole pagan system, of which he had become the champion, to ridicule and contempt. . . . It is well known that in ancient times the doctors of the Church by unhindered usage were accustomed to exercise themselves in the learning of the Greeks, until they had reached an advanced age; this they did with a view to improving themselves in eloquence, and to strengthening and polishing their minds, and at the same time to refute the errors of the heathen.[52]

The subtlety of this measure of Julian can easily be seen, and the Christians were well aware of the effect it would have been bound to have, if it had become a permanency. Later Augustine was to write about the persecutions which were to precede the coming of Antichrist: "Why are not Julian's villainies reckoned amongst the ten? Was he not a persecutor that forbade the Christians to be taught the liberal arts?"[53]

But death was to take a hand to frustrate all Julian's endeavours, for on 26th June, 363, only a year later, he was mortally wounded in his campaign against the Persians in Phrygia, and died. Ammianus Marcellinus tells us that he died discussing the sublime nature of the soul with the philosophers Maximus and Priscus "while the wound of his pierced side was gaping wide."[54] Philostorgius said that he died reproaching the Sun, whom he had worshipped and who had

[51] Sozomen 5. 18. [52] Socrates 3. 12 and 16.

[53] Augustine: *De Civ. Dei* 18. 52.

[54] Ammianus Marcellinus 25. 3. 23.

failed him.[55] Sozomen quotes a report that it was by the hand of a Christian that Julian was slain, and of a story that, when Julian was wounded, he took some of the blood which flowed from the wound, and threw it into the air, as if he had seen Jesus Christ appearing, and intended to throw it at him, in order to reproach Him with his slaughter.[56] It is Theodoret who gives us the famous tradition that, as he died, Julian filled his hand with his own blood, and flung it into the air, with the cry: "Thou hast conquered, O Galilæan."[57] It was from that tradition that Swinburne took his famous line:

> Thou hast conquered, O pale Galilæan; the world has
> grown grey from Thy breath.[58]

The edict of Julian was rescinded by his successor Valentinian; and so the death of Julian saved Christianity from what might well have been a very dangerous situation, for the withholding of all educational rights would have been bound to have had a most serious effect on the Church. The only solution would have been for the Church to supply her own education, an undertaking which might have taken generations to achieve, and which would have had the dangerous consequence of producing two kinds of education in every land.

Before we leave the events connected with Julian, we must notice an educational oddity which they produced. The effect of Julian's legislation was to make the classical writers unobtainable for Christians as instruments of education. In Laodicæa there were a father and son, both called Apollinaris. The father was a grammarian; the son was a rhetorician. Faced with this situation they took steps to meet it. The father produced a grammar "consistent," as Socrates put it, "with the Christian faith." To replace Homer, he turned the antiquities of Israel down to the age of Saul into an epic in twenty-four books. He made poetical paraphrases of all the books of Moses, and of all the historical books of the Old Testament, in which he used all the different kinds of metres, so that a student might learn them all. He took the biblical material and from it

[55] Philostorgius 7. 15. [56] Sozomen 6. 2. [57] Theodoret 3. 20.

[58] A. C. Swinburne: *Hymn to Proserpine.*

produced comedies to replace Menander, tragedies to replace Euripides, and odes to replace Pindar. That apparently was the work of the father, the old Apollinaris. The son took the " Gospels and the apostolic doctrines " and turned them into a series of Platonic dialogues in order to replace Plato. Thus a whole Christian literature was produced, apparently in a matter of months, which reproduced all the classical forms, and which was designed to replace them.[59] Sozomen speaks as if all this was the work of one Apollinaris, and not of two, and when he has described it he says: " In short, taking themes of the entire circle of knowledge from Scripture, he produced within a very brief space of time, a set of works which in manner, expression, character, and arrangement are well approved as similar to the Greek literatures, and which were equal in number and force. Were it not for the extreme partiality with which the productions of antiquity are regarded, I doubt not but that the writings of Apollinaris would be held in as much estimation as those of the ancients." [60] Lietzmann's comment on the work of the industrious father and son is not so enthusiastic. " These productions," he writes, " were admired at the time, though soon laid aside. Happily most have been lost, but a Psalter in hexameters has come down to our own day." [61]

Such then was the basic history of the education of the child within Christianity. The Church never wrought out any primary education system of its own. It simply used the existing system of primary education. There was a time, shown in the attitude of Tertullian, which regarded that as an unfortunate necessity, and which, at its strictest, denied that a Christian could act as a schoolmaster at all. But the events connected with the actions of Julian show that in fact the Church had annexed the Roman educational system, and had made it her own. She had in fact baptised pagan education into the service of the Church.

It remains for us to examine the characteristically Christian education in action. We shall begin by looking at a great saint's recollection of his own school days in a pagan elementary school.

[59] This reconstruction combines the information in Socrates 3. 16 and Sozomen 5. 18.

[60] Sozomen 5. 18.

[61] H. Lietzmann: *From Constantine to Julian*, p. 275.

Augustine leaves us what cannot be other than a highly-dramatised account of his school days in the first book of the *Confessions*.[62]

From his boyhood Augustine had heard of eternal life, even from his mother's womb, for he had been sealed with the mark of the Cross, and salted with His salt (17). And yet when he looks back on his school days, not so much as a human being as a theologian, he sees himself so small a boy, so great a sinner (18). Original sin had him in its grip in his cradle. "I flung about at random limbs and voice, making the few signs I could, and such as I could, like, though in truth very little like, what I wished. And when I was not presently obeyed (my wishes being hurtful or unintelligible) then I was indignant with my elders for not submitting to me, with those owing me no service, for not serving me; and avenged myself on them with tears" (8). True, Augustine does not claim to remember this personally, but, "Such have I learnt infants to be from observing them." Original sin had him in its grip when he cried for his mother's milk. Was it good to cry, to lash out with tiny fists, when wishes were denied which it would have been harmful to satisfy? Augustine claims to have seen an infant turn pale with envy when the breast was given to its foster brother and withheld from it (11). So to school he went, and, if he was idle, he was beaten. And even then, though small, he prayed with no small earnestness that he might not be beaten, and his elders only mocked his stripes (14). Play was his only interest (16). He loved the pride of victory (17). He would cheat to win, and, if found out, fly into a passion, and if he discovered anyone else cheating, he would violently upbraid another for what he did himself; he would steal from the table and the larder, not so much to eat himself as to give to his companions (30). He hated study, and specially he hated Greek. Reading, writing and arithmetic were weariness to him (19). One and one are two, two and two are four was a weary chant to him (22). The instruction that he received was utterly immoral. There he was taught of the love of Dido for Æneas (21); of Zeus descending on Danæ in a golden shower (26); he was made to compose a declamation to be given by Juno, as she raged and mourned that she could not

[62] The translation used is that by E. B. Pusey in the *Everyman's Library* edition and the chapter references in the text are from its enumeration.

This Trojan prince from Latium turn (27).

A noble deed was condemned, if it was recited in a faulty style, and an immoral deed praised, if its style was faultless (28). A man was taught to be more afraid to murder a word by dropping an aspirate than to murder a fellow man (29). And yet it was not all loss: "I learned to delight in truth, I hated to be deceived, had a vigorous memory, was gifted with speech, was soothed by friendship, avoided pain, baseness, ignorance."

When we strip away Augustine's self-dramatisations, we find that he had a normal boy's distaste for work, a normal boy's love of play, and was guilty of the normal pranks and fits of temper which are characteristic of a normal boy. Augustine's account of his school days is not so much emotion recollected in tranquillity, as it is boyhood recollected in theology.

There are two most interesting letters of Jerome on the bringing up of children.[63] The one is to Læta, who has written to ask how she shall bring up her little daughter Paula, who has been dedicated to God before ever she was conceived. The other is in answer to Gaudentius, who had written asking for advice as to how to bring up his daughter Pacatula, "Little Peaceful," who has also been dedicated to God. It is to be remembered that neither of these letters describes a normal education, at least after its very initial stages; they describe the education which Jerome thought necessary for a little girl who was dedicated to perpetual virginity, and to the life of the convent apart from the world. In our account of the educational curriculum which Jerome advises we shall weave together the material of both these letters, for in both the scheme is the same. The letter to Læta is *Letter* 107 and the Letter to Gaudentius is *Letter* 128. But before we relate their substance, we may note that the beginning of the letter to Gaudentius is one of the most charming things in early Christian literature. Jerome pretends to be writing to the little baby; it is "an old man's letter to a little child" (128. 4). It is difficult to write to a little girl whom you do not know. How can you talk of self-control to a little girl

[63] Jerome: *Letters* 107 and 128. The translation we have used is that of W. H. Freemantle in *The Principal Works of St. Jerome* in *A Select Library of Nicene and Post-Nicene Fathers of the Christian Church*, pp. 189–95 and 258–60.

longing for cakes, chattering on her mother's knee, and who would rather have a spoonful of honey than a bookful of words? How can you preach sermons to a little girl who would much rather hear a nursery tale? How can she listen to the warnings of the prophets, when her nurse can scare her with a frowning face? How can you tell her to obey her parents when she is slapping her mother with her chubby fist? (128. 1). If later on in these letters Jerome sounds mercilessly rigorous, the initial tenderness must not be forgotten. Nor must we forget the end of the letter to Paula. Jerome thinks that the kind of education which the little Paula requires is not to be had in Rome; it will be better to send her to the monastery at Bethlehem where her aunt Eustochium and her grandmother Paula are already shining lights of piety. He will look after her. "Old as I am I will carry her on my shoulders and train her stammering lips." It will be the noblest of all tasks. Aristotle only trained the Alexander who was to be the king of Macedon; Jerome will train the little girl who is to be the bride of Christ. Let us then to the actual advice of these letters.

The little girl must learn her alphabet, her grammar, her spelling and her syntax (128. 1). Let her be given a set of little letters made of boxwood or of ivory. Let her arrange them; then with a sweep of your hand disarrange them, and let her begin all over again. When she can hold a stylus and make a mark on the wax, guide her soft fingers by laying your hand on hers; or get simple copies cut on a tablet that they may guide her faltering hand (107. 4). Offer prizes for work well done, cakes, mead, sweetmeats. She will work much better, if she hopes to get some bright bunch of flowers, some glittering bauble, or some enchanting doll. Teach her to spin, shaping the yarn with her tender thumb; she may break the threads now; but the day will come when she will not break them (128. 1). It will be good to let her have her lessons with some little companions; the competition will incite her to do better, and she will try all the harder when she hears them praised.

Never scold her if she is slow to learn. Urge her on by always encouraging her. She must never acquire a distaste for lessons which will continue into her maturer years. When she gets the length of putting words together, and memorising things, do not leave it to chance. Set her to memorising the lists of the prophets or the apostles or the patriarchs from Adam downwards as the list is given in Matthew and in Luke. Get her the best teacher that you can. Aristotle taught Alexander letters, great scholar though he was. Do not let her be at the mercy of a silly nurse who will teach her to shorten long words in baby talk or to deck herself with gold and purple; she must never learn when a child that which she will have to unlearn afterwards. Early impressions are hard to eradicate from the mind. You cannot take the dye from wool that has been dyed; an unused jar will long retain the smell of the liquid with which it was first filled (107. 4). The child must sometimes relax. Little Pacatula may sometimes hang round her mother's neck or steal kisses from her relations. While the little Paula must leap at her grandfather—who was a pagan—and fling her arms round his neck, and, whether he likes it or not, sing Alleluia in his ear. She must be taught so to behave that the whole family will rejoice to possess such a rosebud. She must learn as soon as possible in what army she is enrolled as a recruit, and what captain it is under whose banner she has been called to serve. And let her long to be with those who have passed on; and sometimes let her make playful threats that she will leave you (107. 4).

Sometimes we wish that Jerome had stopped here; but both Paula and Pacatula have been vowed to the Lord (107. 3), and a Christian is made, not born (107. 1). Such a one must be educated to be the temple of the living God (107. 4). And so there follows the education of the little girl who is dedicated for ever away from the world and to Christ.

Boys the little girl must never see, nor young men when she is a maiden. Boys with their wanton thoughts must be kept from Paula (107. 4). A girl should only associate with girls; she should know nothing of boys and should dread even to play with them (128. 3). As she grows older let no young man greet her with smiles, no dandy with curled hair pay compliments to her (107. 9). She must never look at a young man, or turn her eyes on curled fops (128. 3). She must never be alone with a man, not even a Christian teacher with whom she wishes to discuss some problem in religion (128. 2).

Her nurse and her companion must be carefully chosen. Let her choose for a companion not a handsome well-dressed girl, able to warble a song with liquid notes, but one pale and serious, sombrely attired and with the hue of melancholy (107. 9). A young nurse or companion is a grave danger, for spruce and gay young men often seek access to the girl by paying court to or even bribing the nurse (128. 3). Choose a misshapen old woman whose continence is approved in the Lord. Why should you find pleasure in a young girl, pretty and voluptuous?

The little girl should never hear an unclean word, and, even if she does hear one, she should not be able to understand it (128. 3). Her obedience should be absolute. Her mother's nod should be to her as much a command as a spoken injunction (128. 3).

Her dress should be of the plainest, and she should be without adornment. Do not pierce her ears, or paint the face consecrated to Christ with white lead or rouge. Do not hang gold or pearls about her neck. Do not redden her hair until it becomes like the flames of Gehenna. She must do her own spinning, but she must despise silken fabrics, Chinese fleeces, and gold brocades. Her clothing must be such as to keep out the cold, and never to expose the body which it is meant to cover (107. 5, 10). Baths are absolutely forbidden. A girl should blush to see herself undressed. She must cultivate a deliberate squalor to spoil her natural good looks. Why should Paula add fuel to a sleeping fire by taking a bath? (107. 11).

Her food must be of the simplest. She is not to have food with her parents lest she see something that she longs for (107. 8). Let her food be herbs and wheaten bread, with now and then a small fish or two. She must always leave the table hungry and able at the moment to begin reading and chanting psalms. It is rather continuous abstinence than occasional rigorous fasting that Jerome advocates (107. 10).

As she grows older she must go to Church, but she must never walk upon the streets (107. 7). She must have a care when the Church is crowded; her pleasure must rather be in her own room (128. 3). She must never even go to Church or visit a martyr's grave unless her mother is with her (107. 9). If the mother goes even on a short journey into the country she must take her daughter with her. Leave her no power or capacity of living without you, and let her feel frightened when she is left to herself (107. 11).

As for music, she must have no knowledge of the world's songs, for her tongue must be steeped while still tender in the sweetness of the psalms (107. 4). Let her be deaf to the sound of the organ, and not even know the uses of the pipe, the lyre and the cithern (107. 8).

Her devotions must be constant. She must rise in the night to recite prayers and psalms; she must sing hymns in the morning; at the third, the sixth and the ninth hour she must take her place in the line to do battle for Christ; she must at evening kindle her lamp and offer her prayers. Reading must follow prayer and prayer succeed to reading (107. 9).

Her treasures must not be silk or gems, but manuscripts of the holy scriptures; and in them she must not be concerned with Babylonian parchment or artistic arabesques, but rather with correctness and accurate punctuation (107. 12). It is in this same passage that Jerome lays down the order in which the child must study the scriptures, and it is of the greatest interest. She must begin with the *Psalter*. Then she must gather the rules of life from *Proverbs*. Then she must gain the habit of despising the world by reading *Ecclesiastes*. Then from *Job* she must learn the virtue of patience. Then she must turn to the *Gospels* never to be laid aside once they have been taken in hand. Then she must drink in the *Acts* and the *Epistles*. Then she must commit to memory the *Prophets* and the *Heptateuch* (*Genesis* to *Judges*). Then she must study *Kings* and *Chronicles*, *Ezra* and *Esther*. When she has done that—but not before—she may read *The Song of Songs*, for then she will see the spiritual meaning behind the fleshly pictures. She must avoid the apocryphal writings. Cyprian's writings she must have always in her hands; the letters of Athanasius and the treatises of Hilary she may read without stumbling.

Such is the curriculum which Jerome sketches for Paula and for Pacatula. There is little wonder that he doubts if this can be done in Rome at all. Let Paula be sent to Bethlehem to the convent there. It is better to regret her absence than to be for ever trembling for her (107. 13). There is nobility here, and there is discipline; but there is here already that tragic fear of beauty which has so often cast its shadow on the Christian faith and the Christian Church.

Last of our material, we must look at John Chrysostom's homily *On Vain-Glory and the Right Way for Parents to Bring up Their*

Children.[64] As Chrysostom saw it in the glitter and the glare of Constantinople, the greatest of all danger was vain-glory, the pride of life, the desire for earthly fame and for earthly possessions.

No sooner is the boy born than the father is planning how to clothe him with luxury and to adorn him with gold, and how to be excited by things of profit (16). These are not trifles. The girl who has been reared by her mother to be excited about female ornaments will grow up to be a sore vexation to her husband, and a greater burden to him than the tax-collector (21). A boy must be taught, and the tragedy of the situation is that every effort is made to train him in literature and the arts, but no effort is made to train him in virtue and in character (18). This is ruinously wrong, for the boy should be trained as the athlete of God, not to withdraw from the world, but to live for God in the world (19). The early years are all important. Make use of the beginning of life as you should. When the wax is soft it will take the imprint, but when the imprint is hardened it cannot be taken out. Chrysostom makes use of a strange belief about pearls. When pearls are first collected, he says, they are nothing but water. But he who receives them is skilled in his craft, and places the drop of water in his hand, and rotates it gently and shapes it into a pearl. But once it has received its form, nothing can mould it any more. The boy is like that (20, 21). The parent should be like an artist, for ever at work on a canvas to make it perfect. The parent should be like a sculptor, removing what is superfluous and adding what is lacking (22).

The father is like a governor ruling over a city, which is the soul of his child. In the city there will be all kinds of people, good citizens and bad citizens, obedient and rebellious. It is the father's duty to rule that city well, to draw up laws, and to enforce and to withhold them (23–7). In any city there are gates through which things and people enter and go out. It is so with the soul of the boy.

There is the gate of the tongue, which is busiest of all. The child must be taught to use grave and reverent words; and all words which are insolent and slanderous, foolish, shameful, common and worldly, must be expelled (28). He must be taught never to speak

[64] A translation of this homily, with introduction and notes, is given as an appendix in M. L. W. Laistner: *Christianity and Pagan Culture*, pp. 75–122 and 133–40.

insultingly, never to speak ill of any man, never to swear, never to be contentious. The lesson must be driven home by sternness and gentleness combined, but not by the rod, for the rod in the end only defeats itself (30). The lad's words must be fair and courteous. If he ever misuses and maltreats a slave, he must be called to account and punished at once. He will have to learn that he cannot misuse a slave, much less a free man (31). Mother and tutor and father must combine to see that no ill word comes out of the lad's mouth (32). It is Chrysostom's view that, if training is correctly given, it will take no more than two months to train the lad in correct speech, and to keep safe and secure the gate of the tongue.

The next gate is the gate of hearing. It is a most important gate, for if no bad thing goes in by hearing, no ill thing will come out by speaking (36). Servants, tutors and nurses must tell the child no foolish tales, none of these tales which begin: " The youth kissed the maiden " (37, 38). Tell the boy stories from the Bible. The first story which Chrysostom suggests is the story of Cain and Abel, the two brothers. Tell him the story one evening at supper; another day let his mother tell it to him; then say to him: " You tell it to me." Get it fixed into his memory. Take him to Church; one day he will hear the story read as the lesson, and he will jump with joy because he knows it already and recognises it (39–42). Go on to tell him a story about another two brothers, the story about Jacob and Esau (43–6). Here Chrysostom digresses to urge parents to give their boy the good start of a good name. Do not call the child after his relations; call him after one of the martyrs, bishops or apostles—the very name will be an incentive to him (47–9). When he is fifteen years of age, let him hear of hell. You may begin earlier, when he is eight or ten, with the stories of the Flood and of Sodom and Gomorrah, but keep hell until then. Then when he is a little older, take him to the New Testament, and let him hear deeds of grace, and deeds of hell (52). Never let any man speak lewdly in the boy's presence. As for women, let an old woman come near him; but from a young woman shield him as from the fire (53).

The next gate is the gate of smell. Chrysostom deals briefly with this gate. It must be barred. Nothing relaxes the right tension of the soul so much as pleasure in sweet odours. As soon as perfume penetrates to the brain, the whole body is relaxed. Bar this gate, its function is to breathe the air, not to receive sweet odours (54).

The next gate is the gate of the eyes. This is the most difficult of all to guard. Never let the boy go near the theatre, for in it he will suffer corruption through his eyes and ears. The boy's attendant must be careful what the boy sees as he passes through the streets. The boy's own appearance must be no temptation to him; therefore clip his hair close; take away his charm, and let the only charm left to him be the charm of simplicity (55–7). Show the boy fair sights—the sun, the flowers, the meadows, and good books; and let him not be sent into any company of women; and above all let him not bathe with them (59, 60). Tell him the story of Joseph, and instil into him a resolute spirit against womankind; let him have no converse with any woman, let him see no woman, except his mother. Give him no money; let nothing shameful come his way; and teach him to despise all luxury.

There is one last gate, the sense of touch. The boy must have no truck with soft raiment, or soft bodies, or soft couches. Austerity must be the aim, for it is an athlete of Christ whom we are training.

Not only the gates of the city of the soul must be guarded, the parts of the soul must also be guarded.

There is the spirited part, from which come sobriety and equability on the good side, and rashness and ill temper on the bad side. That part must be trained in patience and self-control. There must be constant practice. Instead of punishing a slave for a disobedience or misdeed, the boy must be compelled to examine his own faults. Within the family circle, let the family practise trying to provoke the boy and let the boy practise trying to resist provocation, like an athlete in the wrestling-school training for the real contest (65–8). If he strikes a slave, let him punish himself at once; he must be taught to be neither harsh nor indulgent, but always equable. He must be taught independence; no freeman will do his own cooking, but let him wash his own feet, attend upon himself in his bath, put on his own cloak (69, 70). Dispose him to gentleness, and make him treat servants like brothers (71, 72). Let him learn self-control by not becoming angry about the loss of a pencil or a pen or the strap of his writing tablets. If he learns to take such little troubles lightly when he is a boy, he will take great troubles equably, when he is a man (73).

There is the part of the soul in which desire dwells. How shall we tie down this wild beast? What bridle shall we put upon it? "I know none," says Chrysostom, "save only the restraint of hell-fire" (76). Never let him enter the theatre, where he will see things which will wake desire (77). Provide him with harmless pleasures, the society of saintly men, and clean recreation (78). Never allow any young servant-maid to serve him, but only a slave of advanced years. Let him learn to fast on Wednesdays and Fridays. Let him go to Church. Take him to the door of the theatre when the people are pouring out. Ask him what these people have gained, and answer: "Nothing but shame, reproach and damnation" (79). Let him learn to pray with fervour and contrition (80). If he is to enter the business of the world, let him marry young, and make him see that there is nothing lovelier than the love of two young people of virgin purity, the one for the other (82). Let him often see the head of the church, and let him hear words of praise and encouragement from the bishop's mouth.

There is the part of the soul in which reason dwells. Teach him the true philosophy that he may know God and all the treasure laid up in heaven, and hell and the kingdom of the other world (85). The summit of wisdom is refusal to be excited at worldly things. So let him be taught to think nothing of wealth or worldly reputation or power or death or the present life on earth. Then let him be taken to his own marriage, soberly conducted, a marriage to which Christ is invited, and at which the disciples of Christ are the guests. Thus we shall rear our children as the athletes of Christ, and they will be enabled to light on the blessings which He has promised to them that love Him (87-90).

Such then is the picture of Christian education in the Early Church. One thing becomes clear. The Church was far more concerned with the transmission of life than with the transmission of facts. The Church was not intensely concerned with schools as such; it was willing to use such schools as there were for the purposes of ordinary education. But the Church was intensely concerned with the home. The Church saw that in the last analysis the only true teachers of any child are the parents of that child. Jerome writes to Læta: "Never let Paula see either in you or in her father that which she cannot imitate without sin."[65] As the Church saw it, the school is at best only an adjunct to the home. It is the parent who is responsible for bringing the child into the world; and it is the parent who is responsible for bringing the child to God. The child is the gift of God to the parent, and the child must be the gift of the parent to God.

[65] Jerome: *Letters* 107. 9.

APPENDIX A

Child Exposure in the Ancient World

THIS custom raises the whole question of child-exposure in antiquity. However shocking it may seem to us, the fact is that the Spartan custom was only a regularising and a systematising of that which was a perfectly normal custom both in Rome and in Greece. In Athens it was said that the laws of Solon permitted the parent to put his child to death (Sextus Empiricus: *Hypotyp.* p. 3, 24; Hermogenes: *De. Invent.* I. I). In Rome the same right existed; but there was an ancient law, traditionally traced back to Romulus, which ordered a father to bring up all his male children and his eldest daughter. It was forbidden to destroy any child until it had completed its third year, in order that parental affection might have a chance to develop. But it was permitted to destroy any deformed or weakly child, with the consent of the five nearest relatives (Dionysius of Halicarnassus: *Roman Antiquities* 2. 15). The fact remains that in both Greek and Roman custom the exposure of infants was an accepted practice. The commonness of the custom can be seen in the way in which it is referred to. In the *Amphitryon* of Plautus (499–501), when Jupiter is saying good-bye to Alcmena, he says: "Good-bye and God bless you, my dear. Continue to look out for our common interests, and do be sure not to overdo things; you are near your time now, you know. I am obliged to leave you—but don't expose the child." In the famous Hilarion to Alis letter (1 B.C.), Hilarion writes to Alis, his wife: "If —good luck to you!—you bear a child, if it is a boy, let it live; if it is a girl, throw it out." (P. Oxy. 744; G. Milligan: *Selections from the Greek Papyri*, p. 33.) The whole tone is that of someone speaking of something which is by no means out-of-the-way, but which is a normal custom.

When a child was born, it was laid at the father's feet. If he lifted it, he acknowledged it, and thereby indicated his intention of retaining it, and of nourishing it; if he did not, then the child could be exposed and abandoned. Thus the verbs *suscipere* and *tollere* in Latin and *anaireisthai* in Greek, which normally mean "to lift," come to mean in relationship to the child "to acknowledge paternity." In Terence's *Lady of Andros* Davus tells how Pamphilus and the Andrian lady have decided to acknowledge any child whom she bears—"any child she bears, they have decided *to acknowledge as legitimate.*" The Latin is: "*Quidquid peperisset decreverunt tollere.*"

As we have seen, the custom, especially with daughters, was tragically common.

Stobæus (*Ecl.* 75) writes: "The poor man raises his sons, but the daughters, if one is poor, we expose." But not only was it practised by the ordinary people; it was also approved by the great thinkers. It is however true that in ordinary practice the sole aim was too often simply to be rid of the unwanted child, whereas in the philosophers the aim is to put an end to the life of the deformed and diseased child. Plato writes: "If we are to keep our flock at the highest pitch of excellence, there should be as many unions of the best of both sexes, and as few of the inferior, as possible, and only the offspring of the better unions should be kept. . . . Those of the inferior parents and any children of the rest that are born defective will be hidden away, in some appropriate manner that must be kept secret" (*Republic* 460 B). Aristotle writes: "As to exposing or rearing the children born, let there be a law that no deformed child shall be reared" (*Politics* 7. 14. 10). Even Seneca writes: "Mad dogs we knock on the head; the fierce and savage ox we slay; sickly sheep we put to the knife to keep them from infecting the flock; unnatural progeny we destroy; we drown even children who at birth are weakly and abnormal. Yet it is not anger but reason that separates the harmful from the sound" (*On Anger* 1. 15. 2). Epictetus was one lonely voice who protested against this. He held that not even sheep in all their foolishness or wolves in all their fierceness abandon their offspring. Then how can men? (*Discourses* 1. 23). There is an undoubted difference between the selfish and the reckless exposure of the unwanted child, and the unfeeling, but nonetheless intelligible, view of the philosophers. But the practice itself went through ancient society from top to bottom. Suetonius tells us that on the day when Germanicus died such was the sorrow of the people that "the temples were stoned, and the altars thrown down, while some flung their household gods into the street and cast out their newly born children" (*Caligula* 5). And he also tells us that even so fine a character as Augustus would not allow the child of his granddaughter Julia to be recognised or reared (*Augustus* 65. 4). Sometimes children were exposed because the family was already large enough and the inheritance of each would have been lessened by the existence of another child. Longus says: "Some fathers expose a child because they already have a sufficiency of older children" (*Pastor* 4. p. 126). But the commonest reasons for exposure were poverty, illegitimacy, and sheer reckless and selfish irresponsibility.

The ancient writers actually mark out as extraordinary the nations in which this custom of exposure is not practised. Ælian notes that it is not lawful for a Theban to expose his child, to cast it into a desert place, or to condemn it to death (*Var. Hist.* 2. 7). Tacitus says of the German tribes, whose purity and chastity he idealises, that "to limit the number of their children, to make away with any of the later children is held abominable, and good habits have more force with them than good laws elsewhere" (*Germania* 19). And he notes of the Jews that "it is a crime for them to kill any newly-born infant" (*Hist.* 5. 5).

So widespread was this custom of exposure that Polybius saw in it the ruin of Greece: "It is the unanimous opinion of all, that Greece now (in the first period of the Roman rule, after the taking of Corinth) enjoys the greatest prosperity; yet there is such a scarcity of population, and the cities are so desolate, that the soil begins to lose its fertility for lack of hands to cultivate it. The reason is that men, even when they live in the married state, will not bring up their children, and this because of their effeminacy, love of comfort and idleness; at best they will only rear one or two out of many, in order to leave them a good inheritance. Hence the evil has become gradually greater; for when war or sickness has snatched away the only child, the family, of course, dies out. This state of things is not to be remedied by recourse to gods or oracles; men are able to help themselves, and ameliorate it by adopting another practice, and where they will not, the law should define that all children who are born shall be brought up." (Quoted J. J. I. Döllinger: *The Gentile and the Jew*, ii, 246, 247.) As so often the moral problem had become an economic problem as well.

What then happened to the children who were exposed? Obviously many of them would simply perish. Quintilian draws a picture of the naked child at the mercy of the birds of prey and of the wild beasts (*Dec.* 306). But death was often a better fate than many of the others which awaited these abandoned children. In Rome children were often abandoned by the Lactarian pillar and in the Velabrum. And there were those, especially in Rome and elsewhere, who collected these abandoned children for their own purposes.

Many of them were reared up and then sold as slaves. Some of the boys were nurtured to be gladiators in the arena. A very common fate for girl babies was that they were nourished up to stock the brothels of Rome. In Terence's *Self-Tormentor* Chremes had ordered his wife to kill their daughter. She confesses that she has given it away; and he upbraids her by reminding her that for all she knows the child may well be turned into a prostitute or a slave (iv. 1. 640). Justin Martyr declares that the custom was so common that a man who frequents the brothels is liable at any time to be served by his own daughter (*First Apology* 1. 27. 3). The elder Seneca draws an even grimmer picture. There were professional beggars who collected these children, and who then deliberately maimed them, and then used them to solicit alms from compassionate passers-by. He describes the wretched children with their shortened limbs, broken joints and curved backs, exhibited by the beggars who had collected them and who had deliberately maimed them (*Controvers.* 10. 4; quoted by C. L. Brace: *Gesta Christi*, pp. 73, 74). And Pliny the Elder has an even more terrible picture of those who hunt for " the brains and the marrow " of infants for nefarious medical and magical purposes (*Natural History* 28. 2). The kindest fate was when an abandoned child was collected by some mother, who was either unable to have a child of her own, or unwilling to face the processes of child-birth. Chrysostom says that he knows that free women often substitute a child of another when they themselves cannot conceive (*Orations* 15, p. 447). And Juvenal draws a picture of the wealthy woman, who is herself unwilling to face bearing a child, collecting one of these abandoned infants (*Satire* 6. 602–9).

It was only to be expected that the early Christian writers would condemn these customs in the most unsparing terms. Justin Martyr writes: " As for us, we have been taught that to expose newly-born children is the action of wicked men. This we have been taught lest we should do anyone an injury, or be guilty of impious conduct. We refuse to do this, first, because we see that almost all so exposed—boys as well as girls—are brought up for prostitution. As the ancients are said to have reared herds of oxen, or goats, or sheep, or grazing horses, so now we see that you rear children for this shameful purpose. And because of this a multitude of females and hermaphrodites, and those who commit unmentionable iniquities, are found in every nation. . . . And anyone who uses such persons, is not only guilty of godless, infamous and impure intercourse, but may possibly be having intercourse with his own child or kinsman or brother " (*First Apology* 1. 27. 1–3). Athenagoras answers the slander that Christians kill infants in their sacrifices: " The same man cannot forbid the exposure of children, equating such exposure with child murder, and then slay a child that has found someone to bring it up " (*Embassy for the Christians* 35). Minucius Felix answers the same charge: " None can believe it, but one capable of the crime. Among you I do see newly-born sons at times exposed to wild beasts and birds, or violently strangled to a painful death " (*Octavius* 30. 1, 2). Tertullian also answers the same charge in his own passionate rhetoric: " How many, think you, of these persons standing round and panting for Christian blood,—how many of you, most just magistrates and most severe upon us, how many shall I touch in their consciences for killing their own children, born to them? Since there is a difference between one kind of death and another, surely your way is more cruel, to choke out the breath in water, or to expose to cold, starvation and the dogs? " (*Apology* 9. 6, 7). " The laws," he says, " forbid you taking the lives of your newly-born children, but never was law so little heeded, or set aside with such indifference " (*Ad Nationes* 15). Lactantius says: " Can they be considered innocent who expose their own offspring as a prey to dogs, and, as far as it depends on themselves, kill them in a more cruel manner than if they had strangled them? Who can doubt that he is impious who gives occasion for the pity of others? (Lactantius refers to those who expose their children in the hope that someone will pick them up.) For although that which he has wished should befall the child—namely, that it should be brought up—he has certainly consigned his offspring to slavery or to the brothel " (*Div. Instit.* 6. 20).

However shocking the Spartan law may sound, it was none the less only an open acknowledgment of that which was well-nigh universal in Greek and Roman civilisation, and which was to require many centuries of Christian influence to eradicate.

APPENDIX B

The Patria Potestas

SO UNIQUE and extraordinary was the *patria potestas* that it is worthwhile examining it at some length. Gaius, the Roman jurist writes: "The right of dominion which we have over our children is peculiar to the citizens of Rome, nor is there any race of men who have a dominion over their children similar to ours" (Gaius I. 55). Becker writes: "The great mistake consisted in the Roman father considering the power, which Nature imposes as a duty on the elders, of guiding and protecting a child during infancy, as extending over his freedom, involving his life and death, and continuing during his entire existence" (W. A. Becker: *Gallus:* English translation by Frederick Metcalfe, p. 178). Gwynn says that it was hardly less absolute than the dominion exercised over slaves. It involved the right to refuse to acknowledge the child, to expose the child, to sell the child into slavery, to condemn him to work in his own fields as a slave, and even to condemn his child to death, subject to the approval of the sentence by a family council. During his father's lifetime a son could not own one pennyworth of property. "The one legal difference between the son and the slave was the right to inherit" (A. Gwynn: *Roman Education*, pp. 12, 13). This went right back to The Twelve Tables, which were the Roman catechism and the basis of all law. The second provision on the fourth tablet related "to the control of the father over his children, the right existing during their whole life to imprison, scourge, keep to rustic labour in chains, to sell or slay, even though they may be in enjoyment of high state offices" (a very convenient summary of the Twelve Tables is given in Paul Monroe's *Source Book of the History of Education*, pp. 334–343). Dionysius of Halicarnassus gives a full description of the extent of the *patria potestas:* "The law-giver of the Romans gave virtually full power to the father over his son, whether he thought proper to imprison him, to scourge him, to put him in chains, and keep him at work in the fields, or to put him to death; and this even though the son were already engaged in public affairs, though he were numbered among the highest magistrates, and though he were celebrated for his zeal for the commonwealth. Indeed in virtue of this law men of distinction, while delivering speeches from the rostra, hostile to the senate and pleasing to the people, and enjoying great popularity on that account, have been dragged down from thence, and carried away by their fathers, to undergo such punishment as these thought fit; and, while they were being led away through the forum, none present, neither consul, tribune, nor the very populace which was flattering them, and thought all power inferior to its own, could rescue them " (*Roman Antiquities* 2. 26. 4).

The extent of this *patria potestas* is clearly laid down in the formulæ of adoption. Adoption was the transference from one *patria potestas* to another—if the father was alive—and was clearly a most serious step. Cicero, referring to the adoption of Clodius, demands " whether it was with your full consent that Publicus Fonteius received powers of life and death over you, as over a son " (*De Domo* 29. 77). Adoption could be carried out before the *comitia curiata*, and the request of the person wishing to adopt was: " Express your desire and ordain that Lucius Valerius be the son of Lucius Titius, as justly and lawfully as if he had been born of that father and the mother of his family, and that Titius have that power of life and death over Valerius, which a father has over his son " (Aulus Gellius: *Attic Nights* 5. 19. 9). Only if a son became *flamen dialis*, priest of Jupiter, and only if a daughter either married or became a Vestal Virgin, was this power broken (Gaius 3. 114; Tacitus: *Annals* 4. 16).

It must always remain doubtful how far this power was exercised, although there is no doubt at all of its legal existence; but it is clear that it was in no way repugnant to Roman sentiment from the number of times that it was said to have been exercised in the legendary stories of the early days of Rome. One of the most famous of all stories was the story of how the father of Virginia killed his daughter, rather than see her violated by the lust of Appius Claudius the decemvir (Livy 3. 44 ff.).

Livy tells how Horatius was returning home after the struggle with the Curiatii. At the Porta Casena he was met by his unwedded sister who had been betrothed to one of the Curiatii. She saw the cloak of her lover, a cloak which she had woven with her own hands, among the spoils and knew that he was dead. Immediately she collapsed in tears. Thereupon Horatius drew his sword and killed her for, what he considered, her traitorous tears. He was arrested, tried and released. Livy goes on: " What influenced men most of all in that trial was the assertion of Publius Horatius, the father, that his daughter had been justly slain; if he had not thought so, he would have used a father's authority, and would have punished his son himself" (Livy 1. 26).

The case of Spurius Cassius Viscellinus was widely reported. During his consulship he appeared to be wooing the people with gifts of land and money, with the intention of setting up a tyranny. As soon as his consulate was ended, he was executed. Dionysius of Halicarnassus says that his father was at once informer and accuser and took him home and put him to death. Livy is more cautious: " There are those who say that his father was responsible for his punishment, that he tried the case in his own house, and that, after causing his son to be scourged and put to death, he consecrated to Ceres his personal property, from the proceeds of which a statue was made inscribed, ' The gift of the Cassian family.' " The statue is referred to by Pliny the Elder in the *Natural History*. Livy himself prefers the account that Spurius was brought to trial by the quæstors, Cæso Fabius and Lucius Valerius, and so officially executed (Dionysius of Halicarnassus: *Roman Antiquities* 8. 7. 9; Livy 2. 41; Valerius Maximus 5. 8. 2; Pliny: *Natural History* 34. 4).

Valerius Maximus has a story of a certain Decius Silanus. He was accused of financial maladministration by the Macedonians, of whose province he was governor. His father claimed from the senate the right to investigate the complaints. After a two-day investigation he found the charges proved, and banished the son from his presence as being unworthy both of his family and his state, whereat the son committed suicide; and he also tells of a certain Lucius Gellius, who tried his son on a charge of intended parricide, and acquitted him (Valerius Maximus 5. 8. 3; 5. 9. 1).

Livy, retails, but personally rejects, a story that after the defeat of the Volscians, the victory was said to be darkened, because the son of Aulus Postumius, " who, tempted to an opportunity of fighting to his own advantage, had left his post unbidden, was in the hour of his victory beheaded by his father's orders " (Livy 4. 23).

One of Livy's most famous stories is the story of the fate of the son of Titus Manlius Torquatus in the war with the Tusculans. There was an express order that no Roman should engage in single combat with a Tusculan. Manlius's son had gone out on a reconnaissance. Taunted by a Tusculan, he had engaged in single combat, and had won a glorious victory. He returned home amidst the acclamations of his comrades, carrying his spoils, and rejoicing that he had proved himself his father's son. But his father, even in the moment of victory, executed him for disobedience to an express command (Livy 8. 7. 1). Livy also tells the dramatic story of how Junius Brutus expelled Tarquin, and then found his own sons amongst those who were plotting to bring kings back. " He put off the father and put on the consul . . . He preferred to live bereft than to fail in public justice . . . In a father's anguish he administered a nation's retribution." And so he executed his own sons (Livy 2. 5; Valerius Maximus 8. 1).

All these instances which we have quoted come from legendary stories; but this right of life and death over a son was still being exercised in historical times. During the time of the Catiline conspiracy Aulus Fulvius, the son of a senator, had attached himself to Catiline. He was arrested, and, on his own father's orders, executed. His father declared that he had begotten him, " not for Catiline against his country, but for his country against Catiline " (Sallust: *Catiline Conspiracy* 39; Valerius Maximus 5. 8). Seneca, in his *De Clementia*, quotes two instances which involved the *patria potestas*. He writes: " Within my own memory the people in the forum stabbed Tricho, a Roman knight, with their writing-styles because he had flogged his son to death; Augustus Cæsar's authority barely rescued him from the indignant hands of fathers no less than sons." On the other hand he quotes the instance of a certain Tarius, who detected his son in a plot against his life. He called a family council, at which no less a person than Augustus himself consented to be present. The son was proved guilty, but the punishment was limited to banishment to Marseilles, and the father still continued to give him the same generous allowance which he had given him, before his guilt had been proved (Seneca: *De Clementia* 1. 15; 1, 2).

It is clear that in any civilised community public opinion would limit the exercise of the *patria potestas*, even before the law had withdrawn it, but the very existence of such a right made the home of necessity the centre of everything, and clearly in the early days, when the right was still real, the home was bound to be the main centre of education for any family.

APPENDIX C

The Bulla

THE ROMANS had many theories as to the *bulla*. It was obviously a very ancient practice; Juvenal calls the *bulla* the *Etruscum aurum* (5. 164), and therefore its use must go back to Etruscan times. Pliny the Elder dates the custom back to a legendary act of Priscus Tarquinius who granted the right to wear the gold *bulla* to his son who had slain an enemy while still wearing the *toga prætexta* (*Natural History* 33. 10). Macrobius says that the *bulla* was worn by a general in the hour of an official Triumph; at such a time, in the hour of his success, he was specially liable to the evil eye, and the *bulla* was an amulet to protect him (*Satires* 1. 6. 9). It was after the Second Punic War that the right to wear it was conceded to the children of freedmen (Macrobius 1. 6. 14). It always remained the sign of the freeborn youth (Cicero: *Verr.* 1. 152; Suetonius: *Rhet.* 1).

Plutarch outlines the various theories about it: "Is this one of the many honours which they voted to the wives they captured, that their offspring should be so decorated? Or, in honour of the courage of Tarquin? It was said that while he was still but a boy, in the battle against the combined Latin and Etruscan forces, he charged the enemy, fell from his horse, withstood with vigour those who attacked him, and so encouraged the Romans. A brilliant victory was won over the enemy whose loss amounted to sixteen thousand men, and he received this prize of valour from his father the king. Or, because among the ancients it was not counted dishonourable or shameful to love handsome young slaves, as we can still learn from comedies, but they were careful to keep their hands off freeborn boys, and so to prevent mistakes, even if they were met with naked, the children used to wear this distinguishing mark? Or, is it a guard against licentiousness, a kind of bridle on their passions, making them ashamed to indulge in a man's vices before they lay aside the badge of childhood? The explanation of Varro and his school is certainly wrong; it is to the effect that the *bulla* is the Æolic word *bolla* (i.e. *boulē*, counsel) and that this ornament is worn by boys as a symbol of good counsel. But may this symbol not be another moon emblem? The moon at her full does not look like a sphere, but like a lentil-seed or a disk; nay Empedocles holds that this is her true form." (*Rom. Quest.* 101.)

APPENDIX D

The Spoilt Child

The age of Quintilian was the age of the spoilt child. Petronius writes: "It is the parents who should be attacked for refusing to allow their children to profit by stern discipline. To begin with, they consecrate their young hopefuls, like everything else, to ambition. Then if they are in a hurry for the fulfilment of their vows, they drive the unripe schoolboy into the law courts, and thrust eloquence, the noblest of all callings, upon children who are still struggling into the world. If they would allow work to go on step by step, so that bookish boys were steeped in diligent reading, their minds formed by wise sayings, their pens relentless in tracking down the right word, their ears giving a long hearing to pieces they wished to imitate, and, if they would convince themselves that what took a boy's fancy was never fine, then the grand old style of oratory would have its full force and splendour. As it is, the boy wastes his time at school, and the young man is a laughing stock in the courts. Worse than that, they will not admit when they are old the errors they have once imbibed in school." (*Satyricon* 4).

Seneca writes *On Harmful Prayers:* "Do you still desire what your nurse, your guardian or your mother has prayed for on your behalf? Do you not yet understand what evil they prayed for? Alas, how hostile to us are the wishes of our own folk! And they are all the more hostile in proportion as they are more completely fulfilled. It is no surprise to me at my age that nothing but evil attends us from our early youth; for we have grown up amid the curses invoked by our parents" (*Ep. Mor.* 60. 1). He writes: "The angry prayers of our enemies instil false fears in us; and the affection of our friends spoils us through their kindly wishes. . . . We are not allowed, I maintain, to travel a straight road. Our parents and our slaves draw us into wrong" (*Ep. Mor.* 94. 54). He writes: "We ask, not what a thing truly is, but what it costs. . . . Our parents have instilled into us a respect for gold and silver; in our early years the craving has been implanted, settling deep within us, and growing with our growth" (*Ep. Mor.* 115, 11).

Tacitus in the *Dialogue on Oratory* compares the present with the past. Eloquence has fallen from her high estate "because of the laziness of our young men, the carelessness of parents, the ignorance of teachers, and the decay of old-fashioned virtues." There was a day when the child was nurtured at his mother's breast and on her knee, a day when Cornelia trained the Gracchi; Aurelia, Cæsar; and Atia, Augustus; but now things are different: " Nowadays on the other hand, our children are handed over at their birth to some silly little Greek serving-maid, with a male slave, who may be anyone, to help her,—quite frequently the most worthless member of the whole establishment, incompetent for any serious service. It is from the foolish tittle-tattle of such persons that the children receive their earliest impressions, while their minds are still pliant and unformed; and there is not a soul in the house who cares a jot what he says or does in the presence of his baby master. Yes, and the parents themselves make no effort to train their little ones in goodness and in self-control; for they grow up in an atmosphere of laxity and pertness, in which they come gradually to lose all sense of shame, and all respect both for themselves and for other people. Again there are the peculiar and characteristic vices of this metropolis of ours, taken on, as it seems to me, almost in the mother's womb—the passion for play-actors, and the mania for gladiatorial shows and horse-racing; and when the mind is engrossed in such occupations, what room is left over for higher pursuits? How few are to be found whose home-talk runs to any other subjects than these? What else do we hear our younger men talking about whenever we enter their lecture-halls? And the teachers are just as bad. With them, too, such topics supply material for gossip with their classes more frequently than any others; for it is not by the strict administration of discipline, or by giving proof of their ability to teach that they get pupils together, but by pushing themselves into notice at morning calls and by the tricks of toadyism " (*Dialogue on Oratory* 28, 29).

Even when we make every allowance for the exaggerations of oratory, it is a dark picture of the home environment in which the child grew up.

APPENDIX E

The Roman Grammatica

IT IS A matter of interest to see how the actual *grammatici* measured up to Quintilian's high standards, as the thumb-nail sketches of Suetonius depict them in his *On Grammarians.*

Suetonius begins by saying that this kind of teaching began from the humblest of beginning; but reached a stage when even the most eminent men contributed to it, and when there were no fewer than twenty well-attended schools in Rome. A *grammaticus* who was a real scholar, and an outstanding teacher could command a very high price. Lutatius Daphnis was bought for 700,000 sesterces, and afterwards set free. Lucius Appuleius was hired by Eficius Calvinus to teach for 400 sesterces a year (3). Most of the *grammatici* were freedmen. Such were

Sævius Nicanor (5), Lucius Ateius (9), Cornelius Epicadus, who was the freedman of Sulla (12), Lenæus, who was the freedman of Pompey (15), Quintus Cæcilius Epirota, who was the freedman of Atticus (16), Gaius Julius Hyginus, who was the freedman of Augustus (20). Some of them had very humble origins. Marcus Gnipho, one of the most famous, who had an Alexandrian education, and who never stipulated any class fee, but depended entirely on the free gifts of the gratitude of his pupils, had been exposed when a child, and was educated by the man who picked him up. Gaius Melissus, who was helped by Mæcenas, and who arranged the library in the Colonnade of Octavia, was another who had been exposed when he was a child (6, 21). Staberius Eros, who numbered Brutus and Cassius among his pupils, had been a slave, and, when he was put up for auction, had purchased himself with his savings (13). Scribonius Aphrodisias is described as the slave and pupil of Orbilius (19).

Many of them came from the oddest backgrounds. Lucius Orbilius, notorious as the *plagosus Orbilius* of Horace, had had a varied career. He was left an orphan when a child; he became a magistrates' attendant, then a subaltern (*corniculus*) serving in Macedonia, and then a cavalry officer, before he became a *grammaticus* (9). Lucius Crassicius had been connected with the stage as an assistant to writers of farces (18). Marcus Pomponius Marcellus, the most pedantic critic of them all, seems to have begun life as a boxer (22). Quintus Remmius Palæmon began life as a woman's home-born slave; he became a weaver to trade; he succeeded in educating himself by listening to the lessons of the teacher when he was acting as *paidagogus* to his master's son (23). Marcus Valerius Probus, as Suetonius puts it, " for a long time sought an appointment as a centurion, finally grew tired of waiting, and devoted himself to study " (24).

Some few of the grammarians became very rich, but many either existed or died in poverty. Marcus Pompilius Andronicus was so poor that he had to sell for a pittance books written by himself, which afterwards became famous as works of literary criticism (8). Publius Valerius Cato lived to an old age, but died in extreme poverty, and almost destitution, buried in a little hovel (11). Gaius Julius Hyginus, though he was the freedman of Augustus and the librarian of the Palatine library died in poverty (20). Even Orbilius himself was so poor that, as he said, " he lived under the tiles " (9). Some of them made real contributions to their subject. Quintus Cæcilius Epirota was the first to lecture in Latin and on Latin authors; he it was who introduced Virgil into the curriculum (16). It may well be that Marcus Valerius Probus did useful work. Suetonius tells us of him that in the provincial school where he had studied he had read certain of the earlier authors who had lingered on in the provinces, but who were forgotten in Rome. He continued to teach these authors in Rome, and devoted his time to producing accurate texts of them. This may have been a not unuseful contribution to the scholarship of his day (24). Marcus Verrius Flaccus was the most successful of them all. His income amounted to 100,000 sesterces a year. Augustus chose him as the teacher of his grandsons. He has a special niche in the hall of fame for he seems to have been the inventor of the prize essay. The prize he provided was some old book, " either beautiful or rare " (17).

Some of these *grammatici* were voluminous writers. Lucius Ateius, who dignified himself with the self-chosen name of *Philologus*, writes to Hermas: " Remember to recommend my *hylē* (*hylē* in Greek is used as the Latins used *silva*; the meaning is ' timber '; books entitled *hylē* or *silva* provided in rough form the raw material for oratory; sermon outlines and illustrations would be a not unfair parallel) to others; as you know, it consists of material of every kind in eight hundred books " (10). Gaius Melissus produced no fewer than one hundred and fifty volumes of " Trifles " or " Jests " (21). Marcus Antonius Gnipho left two volumes on the Latin language (7).

Some few of these *grammatici* left very unsavoury reputations. Quintus Cæcilius Epirota, for all his other distinctions, seems to have been an unpleasant character. He was dismissed from his post, when he was teaching the daughter of Atticus, who was the wife of Marcus Agrippa, for improper conduct to her, and later was said to live on terms of more than decent intimacy with Cornelius Gallus (16). Quintus Remmius Palæmon, teacher of Quintilian and author of the first Latin grammar, was a notoriously and shamelessly licentious character. He was constantly in debt although his school brought him in 400,000 sesterces a year. He was a big business man as well as a *grammaticus*, owning a chain of tailors' shops and vineyards. Both Tiberius and Claudius declared that there was no man less fitted to be entrusted with the education of boys, for he was notorious for every kind of vice (23).

It is clear that the *grammatici* were a very mixed lot, and few could have reached the standard which Quintilian regarded as necessary.

APPENDIX F

The Quotations of Clement of Alexandria

As a matter of interest we list the authors quoted with the number of quotations, if more than one, in brackets: Epicurus, Aristotle, Plato (29), Zeno, Thales, Antipatros, Aristobulus, Pindar (6), Homer (13), Callimachus (2), Hesiod (5), Epicharmus (2), Aratus (5), Democritus, Empedocles (3), Heraclitus (7), Solon (2), Anthisthenes, Xenophon, The Sibyl (2), Xenophanes (3), Bacchylides (2), Cleanthes (3), Amphion (3), Hecatæus, Sophocles (4), Euripides (2), Pirithous, Æschylus (2), Timæus the Locrian, Orpheus (10), Xenocrates, Menander (3), Diphilus (2), The Orphic Hymns, Archilochus, Phocylides, Philemon, The Oracles, Thearidas, Parmenides, Metrodorus, Agathon.

It is of interest to note how Clement finds his parallels. He finds forecasts of the Sabbath in the following quotations: " The first, the fourth and the seventh day were held sacred (Hesiod) "; " And on the seventh day came the sacred day "; " The seventh was sacred "; " It was the seventh day and all things were accomplished "; " And on the seventh morn we leave the stream of Acheron " (all from Homer); " It was the seventh morn and they had all things done "; " Among good days is the seventh day, and the seventh race "; " The seventh is among the prime, and the seventh is perfect " (all from Callimachus). He finds a forecast of the Trinity in the following passage from Plato's *Timæus*: " Around the king of all, all things are, and because of him are all things; and he is the cause of all good things; and around the second are the things second in order: and around the third, the third." He finds a near-prediction of what he calls " the economy of salvation " in the following passage from Plato's *Republic*: " Thus he who is constituted just shall be scourged, shall be stretched on the rack, shall be bound, have his eyes put out; and at last, having suffered all evils, shall be crucified."

Once again for interest we list the writers quoted: Orpheus (4), Homer (15), Musæus (2), Archilochus (3), Cratinus (2), Euripides (22), Æschylus, Menander (2), Theognis (5), Epicharmus (2), Sophocles (9), Solon (2), Hesiod (2), Plato (6), Theodectes, Bacchylides, Moschion, Aristophanes (4), Anacreon, Thrasymachus, Xenophon (2), Alcmæon, Posidippus, Simonides, Augias, Antimachus of Teos, Callias, Panyasis, Eumelus, Pherecydes, Critias, Philistus, Thucydides (2), Philemon (2), Empedocles (2), Parmenides, Stasinus, Nicias, Æschines, Hyperides (2), Isocrates (2), Antipho, Philinus, Demosthenes (4), Theopompus, Heraclitus (2), Athamas the Pythagorean, Aristotle, The Mysteries, Acusilaus, Gorgias, Bion, Aristocles, Leandras, Hellanicus, Hecatæus, Androtion, Philochorus, Democritus.

BIBLIOGRAPHY

TRANSLATIONS

As a general rule the translations of classical authors are from the *Loeb Classical Library*.

Translations of the early Christian writers have been taken mainly from the following sources:

The Antt-Nicene Christian Library, edited by A. Roberts and J. Donaldson: Edinburgh, 1867–72.

The Select Library of the Nicene and Post-Nicene Fathers, edited by H. Wace and P. Schaff: Oxford and New York, 1890–1900.

The Ancient Christian Writers, the Works of the Fathers in Translation, edited by J. Quasten and J. C. Plumpe: Maryland and London, begun in 1947 and still in progress.

ENCYCLOPÆDIAS AND DICTIONARIES

Dictionary of the Bible, edited by J. Hastings: Edinburgh, 1905.

Dictionary of Christ and the Gospels, edited by J. Hastings: Edinburgh, 1906.

Dictionary of the Apostolic Church, edited by J. Hastings: Edinburgh, 1915.

Dictionnaire des antiquités grecques et romaines, edited by C. V. Daremberg and E. Saglio: Paris, 1877–1919.

Dictionnaire d'Archéologie chrétienne et de Liturgie, edited by Fernand Cabrol: Paris, 1907–39.

Dictionnaire Encyclopédique de la Bible, edited by A. Westphal: Paris, 1932.

Encyclopædia of Religion and Ethics, edited by J. Hastings: Edinburgh, 1912.

Encyclopædia Biblica, edited by T. K. Cheyne and J. Sutherland Black: London, 1899.

Encyclopædia and Dictionary of Education, edited by Watson Foster: London, 1921.

Dictionary of Christian Antiquities, edited by W. Smith and S. Cheetham: London, 1875.

Dictionary of Christian Biography, edited by W. Smith and H. Wace: London, 1877.

Dictionary of Classical Antiquities, edited by O. Seyffert, revised and edited, with additions, by H. Nettleship and J. E. Sandys: London, 1899.

A Manual of Roman Antiquities, by William Ramsay: London, 1851.

The Jewish Encyclopædia: New York and London, 1901.

The Oxford Classical Dictionary: Oxford, 1949.

Bibliography

GENERAL WORKS

Baeck, L.: *The Essence of Judaism:* London, 1936.

Bailey, C.: *The Mind of Rome:* Oxford, 1926.
ed. *The Legacy of Rome:* Oxford, 1928.

Bardy, G.: *Greek Literature in the Early Church,* English translation by Mother M. Reginald: London, 1929.

W. A. Becker: *Gallus, or, Roman Scenes of the Time of Augustus,* English translation by F. Metcalfe: London, 1866.
Charicles, or, Illustrations of the Private Life of the Ancient Greeks, English translation by F. Metcalfe: London, 1866.

Benammi: *The Letters of Benammi, Aspects of Jewish Life and Thought:* London, 1922.

Bewer, J. A.: *The Literature of the Old Testament:* New York, 1922.

Bigg, C.: *The Church's Task under the Roman Empire:* Oxford, 1905.
The Christian Platonists of Alexandria: Oxford, 1913.

Boissier, G.: *Fin du Paganisme:* Paris, 1913.

Bosanquet, B.: *The Education of the Young in the Republic of Plato:* Cambridge, 1900.

Bouquet, A. C.: *Everyday Life in New Testament Times:* London, 1953.

Boyd, W.: *History of Western Education:* London, 1921.

de Burgh, W. G.: *The Legacy of the Ancient World:* London and New York, 1924.

Burnet, J.: *Aristotle on Education:* Cambridge, 1913.

Butcher, S. H.: *Some Aspects of the Greek Genius:* London, 1891.

Cadoux, C. J.: *The Early Church and the World, A History of the Christian Attitude to Pagan Society and the State down to the time of Constantinus:* Edinburgh, 1925.

Carcopino, J.: *Daily Life in Ancient Rome, the People and the City at the Height of the Empire,* edited with bibliography and notes by H. T. Rowell, translated from the French by E. O. Lorimer: London, 1941.

Clarke, G.: *Education of Children at Rome:* London, 1896.

Cochrane, C. N.: *Christianity and Classical Culture, a Study of Thought and Action from Augustus to Augustine:* London, 1944.

Cohen, A.: *Everyman's Talmud:* London, 1932.

Cruttwell, C. T.: *A Literary History of Early Christianity:* London, 1893.

Danby, H.: *The Mishnah:* Oxford, 1933.

Davies, J. G.: *Daily Life in the Early Church, Studies in the Social History of the first Five Centuries:* London, 1952.
Social Life of the Early Christians: London, 1954.

Delitzsch, F.: *Jewish Artisan Life in the Time of our Lord,* English translation by P. Monkhouse: London, 1877.

Dill, S.: *Roman Society from Nero to Marcus Aurelius:* London, 1911.
Roman Society in the Last Century of the Western Empire: London, 1910.

Donaldson, J.: *Woman, her Position and Influence in Ancient Greece and Rome, and among the Early Christians:* London, 1907.
A Critical History of Christian Literature and Doctrine from the death of the Apostles to the Nicene Council: London, 1864.

Earp, F. R.: *The Way of the Greeks:* Oxford, 1929.
Edersheim, A.: *The Life and Times of Jesus the Messiah:* London, 1900.
The Temple, its Ministry and Services, as they were at the time of Jesus Christ: London, n.d.
Sketches of Jewish Social Life: London, n.d.
Epstein, I.: *The Jewish Way of Life:* London, 1946.
Farrar, F. W.: *Lives of the Fathers:* London, 1907.
Freeman, Kathleen: *God, Man, and State, Greek Concepts:* London, 1952.
Freeman, Kenneth J.: *Schools of Hellas:* London, 1907.
Friedländer, L.: *Roman Life and Manners under the Early Empire*, English translation by J. H. Freese, with a supplementary volume of notes translated by A. H. Gouch: London, 1913.
Fowler, W. Warde: *Social Life at Rome in the Age of Cicero:* London, 1922.
Girard, P.: *L'Education Athénienne au ve et ive siècle avant Jésus Christ:* Paris, 1889.
Glover, T. R.: *Life and Letters in the Fourth Century:* Cambridge, 1901.
The Conflict of Religions in the Early Roman Empire: London, 1909.
Democracy in the Ancient World: Cambridge, 1927.
The World of the New Testament: Cambridge, 1931.
Greek Byways: Cambridge, 1932.
Grasberger, L.: *Erziehung und Unterricht im Klassischen Alterthum:* Würzburg, 1864–81.
Guignebert, C.: *The Jewish People in the Time of Christ*, English translation by S. H. Hooke: London, 1939.
Gwatkin, H. M.: *Early Church History to A.D. 313:* London, 1909.
Gwynn, A.: *Roman Education from Cicero to Quintilian:* Oxford, 1926.
Haarhoff, T.: *Schools of Gaul:* Oxford, 1920.
Halliday, W. R.: *The Pagan Background of Early Christianity:* Liverpool, 1925.
Harnack, A.: *History of Dogma*, English translation by N. Buchanan: London, 1894.
The Expansion of Christianity in the First Three Centuries, English translation by J. Moffatt: London, 1905.
Hatch, E.: *The Influence of Greek Ideas and Usages upon the Christian Church:* London, 1901.
Hodgson, G.: *Primitive Christian Education:* Edinburgh, 1906.
Jaeger, W.: *Paideia, The Ideals of Greek Culture*, English translation by G. Highet: Oxford, 1945.
Keith, K. E.: *The Social Life of a Jew in the Time of Christ:* Liverpool, 1926.
Laistner, M. W. L.: *Christianity and Pagan Culture in the later Roman Empire, together with an English Translation of John Chrysostom's Address On Vain-glory and the Right Way for Parents to bring up Their Children:* New York, 1951.
Laurie, S. S.: *Historical Survey of Pre-Christian Education:* London, 1895.
Livingstone, R. W. ed.: *The Legacy of Greece:* Oxford, 1921.
The Pageant of Greece: Oxford, 1923.
Lodge, R. C.: *Plato's Theory of Education:* London, 1947.
Mahaffy, J. P.: *Old Greek Education:* London, 1883.
Marquardt, J.: *Das Privatleben der Römer:* Leipzig, 1886.

Bibliography

Marrou, H. I.: *A History of Education in Antiquity*, English translation by G. Lamb: London, 1956.

Millar, L.: *Christian Education in the First Four Centuries:* London, 1946.

Monroe, P.: *Source Book of the History of Education for the Greek and Roman Period:* New York, 1913.

Montefiore, C. G., and Loewe, H.: *A Rabbinic Anthology, selected and arranged with commentary and introduction:* London, 1938.

Moore, G. F.: *Judaism:* Cambridge, 1932.

Nettleship, R. L.: *The Theory of Education in Plato's Republic*, contained in *Hellenica:* London, 1898; and published as a separate volume: Oxford, 1935.

Lectures on the Republic of Plato: London, 1901.

Oesterley, W. O. E., and Box, G. H.: *The Religion and Worship of the Synagogue:* London, 1907.

Paterson, J.: *The Book that is Alive, Studies in Old Testament Life and Thought as set forth by the Hebrew Sages:* New York, 1954.

Schechter, S.: *Studies in Judaism, First Series:* London, 1896.

Schürer, E.: *A History of the Jewish People in the Time of Jesus Christ*, English translation by S. Taylor and P. Christie: Edinburgh, 1893.

Smail, W. M.: *Quintilian on Education:* Oxford, 1938.

Smith, D.: *Life and Letters of Saint Paul:* London, 1919.

Stapfer, E.: *Palestine in the Time of Christ:* London, 1886.

Taylor, C.: *Sayings of the Jewish Fathers:* Cambridge, 1897.

Thomas, E.: *Roman Life under the Cæsars:* London, 1899.

Tucker, T. G.: *Life in the Roman World of Nero and St. Paul:* London, 1910.

Life in Ancient Athens: London, 1922.

Whibley, L.: ed. *A Companion to Greek Studies:* Cambridge, 1916.

Whiston, A.: *The Works of Josephus:* London, 1873.

Wilkins, A. S.: *National Education in Greece:* London, 1873.

Roman Education: Cambridge, 1905.

Workman, H. B.: *Persecution in the Early Church, a Chapter in the History of Renunciation:* London, 1906.

ACKNOWLEDGMENTS

The author and publishers wish to express their indebtedness to the following for permission to include in this book passages from the books listed below:

THE JEWISH WAY OF LIFE by Dr. Isidore Epstein: Dr. Isidore Epstein.

CHRISTIAN EDUCATION IN THE FIRST FOUR CENTURIES by L. Millar: The Faith Press Ltd.

CHRISTIANITY AND PAGAN CULTURE IN THE LATER ROMAN EMPIRE by M. W. L. Laistner: Cornell University Press.

A HISTORY OF EDUCATION IN ANTIQUITY by H. I. Marrou: Sheed and Ward (Publishers) Ltd.

DAILY LIFE IN ANCIENT ROME by J. Carcopino: Routledge and Kegan Paul Ltd.

THE CLOUDS AND THE FROGS by Aristophanes (translated by B. B. Rogers): G. Bell and Sons (Publishers) Ltd.

THE LEGACY OF GREECE edited by R. W. Livingstone: Oxford University Press.

ROMAN EDUCATION FROM CICERO TO QUINTILIAN by A. Gwynn: Oxford University Press.

And to the editors of THE LOEB CLASSICAL LIBRARY for permission to include translations from the Library.

INDEX

Index